EQUINE EDUCATION

EQUINE EDUCATION

Marthe Kiley-Worthington

What can my horse learn? How does he learn?
How best to teach him?

Whittet Books

First published 2004

Copyright ©2004 by Marthe Kiley-Worthington

Whittet Books Ltd, Hill Farm, Stonham Rd, Cotton, Stowmarket, Suffolk IP14 4RQ
www.whittetbooks.com
e mail: Annabel@whittet.dircon.co.uk

Cataloguing in publication data
A catalogue record for this title is available from the British Library.

ISBN 1 873580 66 5

Dedication

For all those horses, ponies, donkeys and zebras whose 'behavioural problems' I have been asked to sort out over the last 35 years. This is an effort to try to avoid more of you being drawn into that category, by helping humans to try to understand you all better.
To Druimghigha Oberlix and Chris, my partners and great pals, and, of course, the princess, Druimghigha Shemal, with gratitude and love.

Throughout this book, to avoid confusion, the equines are referred to as 'him' and the humans as 'her', except where gender is particularly important.

Frontispiece illustration: Lilka following Sioban around the manege

Printed and bound in the UK by Cromwell Press

CONTENTS

INTRODUCTION

'Education is what survives when what has been learned has been forgotten'
Skinner, 1969

There have been many books written on training horses through the 2,500 years or so that humans have been associating with them, and writing down what they think or find; so why yet another book? Is there anything new to say, or any need for yet another book summarising how to teach equines? My apology for this rests with the use of the word 'educating'. This is not intended to be 'fey', a how to be sweet and kind, a 'natural' new approach. It is rather intended to suggest to all who have to do with equines or other mammals, those who look after them, teach them, are interested in them, study them or those studying their minds, that we have **not** (as many believe) reached the zenith of what equines are capable of: a great deal remains to be discovered about them. Progress is not only possible, but seriously necessary in our knowledge and understanding. This demands **thinking.** It is necessary to think about what you do, why, how, where, when, or even if it is a good idea. It is unhelpful and destructive of progress in this pursuit to unthinkingly accept conventional practices, tradition or preconceived ideas of your own or others. As Mary Midgeley, one of my respected mentors, constantly reminds us 'thinking is hard work'.

The approach that I have adopted overlaps with many existing practices, but its central theme is to discuss and argue about what and how and then marry the theory with the practice. This is what we have been doing at our research centre for the last 35 years. Many ideas have been gleaned from developmental and educational psychology of children. The interesting thing here is that in the last few decades there have been developments in our knowledge and understanding of how to educate humans which may be applicable to other mammals, including equines. To date, the training of other mammals has not made particular progress, although the fashionable 'natural horsemanship' movement has emphasised one or two important points.

But … are equines just like motorcars where pressing one button results in a certain response, where there are no 'feelings' involved (from the motorcar at least)? There may be some humans who consider equines are just like this, but they are few because the majority of human mammals that have to do with equines know that they are not like robots or motorcars, they can be unpredictable, they make choices, and above all they have feelings: they are like us. However much someone has been taught that other mammals are just robots, when they come face to face with them and exchange some form of emotion or feeling with them, they know (if they are a mammal and not robots themselves!) that this is untrue.

Some of us have to do with equines because they will buy us fame and fortune, others for other forms of social status within the human community, but the majority of us, however we justify it, have to do with equines because, as well as them being useful in one way or another, they are our companions, sometimes our friends, sometimes our enemies. Above all, they react to us and respond to us with emotions and feelings we can understand because we also feel them. Some may like us, some hate us, some are frightened of us, some are curious, others confused. They experience things, they also feel happiness and joy, and they can suffer, just like us.

If equines, even when humans are not around, demonstrate that they perform many mental tasks and acquire knowledge, then the job of the 'educator' is to encourage and develop these mental abilities, and perhaps to teach new ones. The job of the 'trainer' by contrast, is not concerned with this, it merely involves ensuring that the student can *do* certain tasks; it has no concern with other mental events. The trainer's central concern, though, is with the *doing*, not on *how it is done*.

My interest has for many years focused more on what equines (not only horses, but ponies, donkeys and zebras as well) do themselves, and why and how they are doing these things; that is, what mental events they are experiencing. So it is the educating rather than the training of equines that interests me most. In order to educate equines better, it is necessary to study all aspects of how they have evolved to live and therefore what mental life they have. The real challenge is to try to better understand their minds in order to help them develop them further. This may be along the lines that we humans 'think' or use our minds, but it must also take into account that there will be differences in our 'world views'. It will help us to glimpse the different, but not inferior, mental world that they may occupy. Thus, our own lives can be enriched by being with equines, observing them, pondering on what and why they do things, and particularly teaching them.

I do not pretend to have all the answers or to know what there is to know. But this is founded on a serious study of them over some 35 years now and represented by some empirical evidence and a scientific appraisal.

When considering equine education, it may be sensible to use some of the ideas developed for human education, and what we know of developmental psychology, and philosophy of mind. For example, it is well known now that learning is faster, easier, and more thorough if the student is motivated to learn by pleasurable experiences. It is also more effective if the teacher co-operates with the student, rather than just dominating him/her. Philosophy of mind considers what one might expect of the mind of an equine. Finally, allowing the student to be themselves, but helping them to solve problems in their own way may be effective.

Good education is not a bed of roses. It is often hard and frustrating for both the student and the teacher. It requires commitment, hard work, serious attention and, particularly for the teacher, an ability to be a good observer, and act on what is observed. There is no way of getting away from it, it is tough, but the rewards are immense resulting in the sheer delight in another's abilities and physical and mental prowess, amusement, companionship and mutual respect. But perhaps the greatest reward is the enrichment of one's own life as a result of having chinks of light through half blinded windows into another's world, and to begin to apply this naissant knowledge in one's own life. There are things for all of us to learn from equines. For me, one of the most important mental acquisitions from equines' expertise is to become much more aware of the world around at any moment, to be aware of the wholeness of it rather than just dispersed bits.

The book then addresses how to educate equines in order for each one of them to be able to do a whole variety of things that will benefit them, and us too. It is emphasised that there are no simple recipes, there are many roads to Rome, and, through the ages many different approaches have been successful, but there are some general rules on which equine education can be based. All we do here is suggest tips using these general rules which we have found useful. There is no dogma, it is for everyone of you to develop your own approach, and as long as you and your equine enjoy it, what could possibly be wrong with that?

For the scientists among you, dismissing some of the statements and discussions here is unwise. Science is concerned with acquiring knowledge, and one of the ways, but my no means the only one, of doing this is by empirical measurement. But good science must combine this with critical thinking, particularly when it comes to issues concerning minds, how they work and what they are. It is positively unscientific to believe that similarities in behaviour between equines and humans do not exist until it is proved empirically in some way. We are all mammals, and a more rational approach is to consider that we are similar until it is proved otherwise. If you believe that equines do not have a mind or mental events something like human ones, your challenge is to prove it. My challenge is merely to point out that the rational approach (since we are all mammals) is to shift the burden of proof to you. This does not mean that they are just like me, or you, it simply gives us a starting point to begin to find out what their life is all about and consequently how their education might be better structured.

1

EDUCATING EQUINES

The growth of understanding more often comes from opposition than from agreement. Our views, which seem to us so evidently true and complete, instead of meeting the acceptance we expected, encounter disagreement, rejection, caution, or simply indifference. If we take this opposition as something to be fought against, argued away, or just shrugged off, then the opportunity it represents for the growth of our understanding is lost. We become a fixed, dogmatic kind of person. But if we encounter this opposition as a resistance to be worked with, then it becomes our point of application. Taken in a more positive spirit, opposition to our views becomes the means of development whereby our understanding is enhanced, instead of, as it seems at first, threatened. We are taken further by this opportunity in the direction which we would not have found ourselves, instead of being overcome by it. Our previous understanding, which we took at first to be the end of the story, is now seen as only a beginning, a stage on the way which is to be incorporated as part of a further, more comprehensive viewpoint.

This book attempts to develop our understanding of educating horses. My views may be controversial; some may think I am labouring the obvious and others that I am dreaming. I don't pretend to know all the answers, but I do have some of the questions. I firmly believe that we must escape our traditions and preconceived notions and begin to think, which, as we all know, is hard work and something many of us try to avoid. But there is no substitute for it!

So, why 'educating' equines, not the normal 'breaking' or, a little better, 'training'? Does it really make a difference? Well, yes. The reason is to start the reader with a different mind set. It is clear the word 'breaking' for training a horse has unpleasant and violent connotations, the idea being presumably to 'break the animal's spirit'.

Training is widely used for both animals and humans. Dogs are trained to be obedient, to work sheep, to retrieve; humans are trained to be carpenters, plumbers, nurses and doctors. Horses are trained to be driven, work in a circus, be ridden, show jump, do dressage, race and so on. The central idea of training is to acquire a series of practical skills that will be useful to human society. For humans at any rate, a training may also have benefits for the individual, to allow her to earn money, or have a life of quality in one way or another. It is less clear that 'training' an animal benefits the animal. Training can be accompanied by peculiar, irrational traditional beliefs. For example it is often believed that a working sheep dog cannot live in the house with people, she must be tied up outside or kept in a kennel apart. The same applies to horses: for example, an advanced dressage

Shemal and Chris, Oberlix and Vicki enjoy a quiet country walk in the spring. The horses wear no bridles, head collars or saddles. There is no restraint. Both humans and horses are doing what they want to do.

horse must not be allowed to run around in paddocks with others, she must be kept isolated and almost immobile in a stable except for a couple of hours' 'work' a day. A trained equine (or other animal) *may* have a better quality of life as a result of her training (and will be of greater use to humans); but this is not necessarily so.

The aim of education is *to benefit the individual.* The individual is helped to develop her mind, body and skills so that she will benefit and it will allow her to have a happier quality of life – at least that is what is behind the idea of human education. Education encourages the development of mental skills and acquiring information, which may or may not be related to practical tasks. So, you may say, what relevance does this have for horses, which, if they have a mind at all, is not much of one; they do not behave rationally, mull over events or make decisions?

Recent developments in the behavioural sciences working with primates, birds, sea mammals, and now equines, indicate that these species may not have such a limited mental life and mental abilities as we thought. It is an exciting time. The traditional idea that humans' mental abilities are unique is now being questioned by scientists and philosophers. Instead of going into the details of the complex arguments which can and do fill whole books I will simply summarize some of the findings relevant to horses. (If you want to find out more, see my book *Equine Lore*, 2004.)

So, very briefly, what evidence do we have that equines can be educated and benefit as a result, rather than just being 'trained' or 'broken'? In the first place, equines, like humans and other mammals, do learn; some of this is a reflexive type of 'conditioning' requiring no decisions to be made, but other learning is not. Much of the time, particularly when learning to do things that we are teaching them, equines must make choices and decisions – they have to have mental activity, indeed in some sense, this must be a conscious mental process of learning with us (see chapter 2 for a detailed description of how equines learn). As a result of this learning they acquire knowledge about the world and things in it that they can remember and use later. Learning is involved with the central nervous system. It involves receiving messages, transferring them and *analysing* them in the central powerhouse: the brain. Learning, acquiring and retaining knowledge, therefore, requires a mind in order to do things like receiving messages, analysing them, remembering, predicting, and so forth. Thus, if equines can learn, they have a mind.

Although Aristotle believed that the mind and the body were inevitably integrated parts of the 'essence' or 'telos' of an individual (man or horse), in much of western European thinking, even today, Descartes' ideas have had a profound effect. This seventeenth-century philosopher put forward another hypothesis which gained an enormous following. This is that in humans the mind is somehow separated from the body, thus what affects the mind may not affect the body and *vice versa*. This belief, which is often part of the way modern scientists are taught to think, is called dualism. But, today, 'holistic' thinking, where even the whole biosphere may be thought of as interrelated, is gaining ground, and there are 'holistic scientists' who take the more Aristotelian position: that the mind and the body are interrelated parts of the whole being, and that the whole being is more than the sum of its parts.

The consequences of the belief in dualism have been to deny other mammals minds. They have bodies, which we can see, feel, hear and so on, but, the position taken by scientists is often that until we have undisputed evidence that they can think and perform other mental events, we cannot assume other mammals have minds. Today, many experimental psychologists, cognitive scientists and cognitive ethologists, including myself, believe that the way equines (for instance) learn, make decisions and choices, indicates that they do have a mind. A more interesting question than *if* they have a mind is what *sort* of mind does the equine have, and how similar or different from mine is it?

Horses do not come from Mars, we are all mammals together. At the same time we must not assume they are 'just like us'.

Let us not go too far the other way and ascribe to horses a complex mental life similar to ours. This is commonly done, unfortunately, by those who believe they can 'talk to horses (or dogs)' – the new breed of 'intuitive communicators'. They may have some very interesting and useful mental skills to teach, but they lose credence when they describe the horse's world as being just like ours, and they lose the excitement too. The fact is that trying to understand the equine's world, what it is to be an equine, is much more interesting; although we have much in common, enough to recognise and learn from each other, equines are *not* just like us. They do not have all the concepts and beliefs that we do, but they may have others new to us. They have feelings like ours much of the time – frustration, anger, joy, sex and distress – but they may have other emotions that we do not have; for example, what is the feeeling of a stallion who with a 'snake face' herds his mare away from another stallion? Is it *just* jealousy or a complex interplay of anxiety, jealousy, affection and loyalty?

They can learn many of our concepts of the world, and if we try, we may be able to learn about theirs. Like us, they have pre-programmed instinctive tendencies to do certain things, for example to get up and walk after being born, but when and how we do this is very different ... Equines get up within three hours of birth, babies within around a year, equines have a pre-programmed tendency to walk on four legs, babies on two. But when, where, how and whether they do these things is different for every individual and the result of its lifetime experiences, human or horse.

To summarise so far, we can extract four basic similarities between equines and human:-

(1) They have interrelated minds/brains/bodies.

(2) They are sentient, that is they feel, and 'mind' about things. They feel pain, pleasure and other emotions.

(3) These mammals learn and can do voluntary acts thus they have desires, beliefs, memories, work towards goals, and make decisions and choices. Both species have some form of mental life.

(4) They have instinctive tendencies to behave in various way, but how, what, when and why they do things is moulded by their lifetime experiences.

One of the most important aspects of human primates and equines is that they are both very **adaptable** species who live in an enormous range of ecosystems, and can adapt to changes remarkably. Perhaps the most dramatic testament to human and equine adaptability is their ability to survive and even breed when kept in conditions where their physical, emotional, social and intellectual needs are far from fulfilled.

Although humans and horses have fundamental anatomical similarities in their skeletons and muscles, there are also differences: primates, particularly humans, are manipulators of the world, and they do this with their hands. By contrast horses react to the world, the leg of a horse being a highly specialised appendage for running at speed with the muscles carefully distributed in the main body structure to allow more efficient movement of the limbs. The elaboration of the muscles in the horse are found particularly in the movement of the ears and the slightly prehensile nose which, in a sense, has a similar function to our hands – it manipulates the world, but at the same time, it smells and tastes the world. Perhaps you can begin to see how horses may have a similar world to ours, but at the same time they may have the ability to have different multi-sensory experiences as a result of their body structure. They have the same type of sensory receptors as we do, and they function in the same way, but there are also differences, for example they are much more able to smell and construct 'smell worlds' than we are; they are very sensitive to very slight movements and muscle changes in another which we do not pick up because we concentrate more on hearing and disentangling the meaning of language. But, we can learn something about their smell and visual worlds if we try, just as they learn something about our language world, whether we teach them or not, when they are with us.

Equines, in order to live the life they do when left alone in wild or feral state, have to acquire a great deal of knowledge, let us not underestimate this. They have to become good field ecologists, they have to learn what to eat, where to find it at what time of year, so they must become good field botanists, zoologists, geographers, meteorologists, or they will not survive. They do this by learning from each other, that is social learning, but also by experimenting (trial and error). They are social animals and must become sociologists in order to know who to approach, who to avoid, who to follow, who to learn from; to be allowed to stay around in the group, there are social norms or rules that must be learnt. To read the intention of others in the group and learn the intricacies of equine communication they must use smells, which opens up a whole different world with different assessments of such everyday things we take for granted such as finite space and measured time. They are sophisticated visual communicators and observe the whole world around them at any time, in contrast to our more linear attention and directed sight.

One of the interesting questions today concerning animals and their mental abilities and minds is whether or not different species are aware that others have minds. Are they conscious, can they think and reflect on things? We don't know the answers to these questions, but we need to think about them.

Because of the mental abilities equines do display, they can, like humans, be educated, that is, learn to develop mental and physical abilities which will benefit them, as well as us. But, in order to be good teachers, we need to discover the similarities and differences between us and equines. In this book, we shall be taking account of what we know about their mental abilities, and structuring ways in which the teacher may be able to learn more about these, as well as showing ways in which we can use this understanding to educate equines better.

I don't claim that all this is new, or that I educate equines better than all masters through history, that is of course nonsense. I will put forward some new and different ideas, and many old ones: what I hope I will do is to explain why certain things work, and others don't, to articulate what the great horsemen through history have been doing, and lace this with some of our recent understanding of minds and how they work, and our own critically assessed experiences. The idea is to get people to *think* when educating their horses; to critically assess others' efforts, and learn from the equines themselves in order to develop their own individual way, just like parenting!

REFERENCES
Adam, C. & M. Bekoff. 1997. *Species of Mind*. MIT. Cambs USA.
Bateson, P. P. G. 1966. 'The characteristics and context of imprinting', *Biol. Rev.* 41. 177-220. ch8,p2.
Bortof, H. 1996. *The wholeness of Nature. Goethe's way of science*. Floris books. Edinburgh.
Braddon-Mitchell, B. D. , & F. Jackson. 1996. *Philosophy of mind and cognition*. Blackwells. Oxford.
British Horse Society. 1982. *Horse Management*. BHS. Stoneleigh.
Burghardt, J. M. 1991. 'Cognitive ethology and critical anthropomorphism. A snake with two heads and hog-nosed snakes that plays dead', in: *Cognitive Ethology*. ed: C. A. Ristau. Erlbaum. Hillsdale.
DeGrazia, D. 1996. *Taking Animals Seriously*. CUP. Cambridge.
Imam, S. A. H. A. A. 1983. *Mis-en-Main without a bit*. Imam Hazaribagh.
Iwanowski, G. 1987. *You and Your Horse*. Shutter and Shooter. Jo'burg.
Johnson, B. 1995. *The skilful mind of the guide dog*. G. D. B. Herts.
Kennedy, J. 1992. *The New Anthropomorphism*. Cambridge University Press.
Kiley-Worthington, M. 1990. *Animals in Circuses and Zoos. Chiron's World?* Little Eco-Farm Publishing. Basildon.
Kiley-Worthington, M. 1998. 'Competition and Cooperation. A detailed study of communication and social organisation in a small group of horses (*Equus caballus*)'*Eco Research Centre*. ISBN 367-

2045, paper 024.

Kiley-Worthington, M. 2000. *Right in Front of Your Mind, Equine and Elephant Epistemology*. M. Phil thesis in Philosophy. University of Lancaster.

Midgley, M. 1978. *Beast and Man: The Roots of Human Nature*. Cornell Press. Ithaca. N. Y.

Nagel, T. 1974. 'What is it like to be a Bat?', *Philosophical Review* 83. 435-50

Svendsen, E. 1994. *Handbook of Donkeys*. Donkey Sanctuary. Sidmouth.

Swift, S. 1996. *Centred Riding*. J. A. Allen.

2

EQUINE NEEDS AND CO-OPERATIVE TEACHING

• Equine needs
• A life of quality
• Needs relating to both the way he is kept and the way he is taught.
• Guidelines and general rules are given, and exercises to help the reader understand an equine's point of view using the conditional anthropomorphic approach.

So how do we know what an equine's needs are? Are they just what the nutritionist tells us about what he needs to eat, the vet who tells us how to stop him being physically sick, the farrier who tells us how to take care of his feet, the animal behaviourist who may help us with his behavioural problems, the 'very good' trainer who has had horses who have won events of all sorts, and all the other professionals in the 'equine industry' as it has come to be called who know all the answers to this question?

Well, they may have some of the answers here and there, but, unlike a motor car or a computer, which can be fixed mechanically, an equine requires more than all of this put together. There is the whole problem of experiences and feelings which motor cars and computers do not have, and so far no one can build them in. Related to this there is learning ... equines and human can learn all sorts of things and profit from their past experiences, motor cars cannot, and computers can only learn the most simple of all things, and that only in the hands of specialists at present. It has been maintained by scientists particularly that since experiences are personal things, and equines are so different from us, we can never know what they experience, consequently it is a waste of time trying. The majority of scientists (including ethologists) involved in any way with equines still take this view. They will argue that all we can do is fulfil his physical needs and, because equines are social, also their social needs. The rest is left to mystery and magic, and explained by the magical word 'instinct' which, the majority maintain, controls the majority of behaviour of any non-human animal. What this is and how it works is never explained, but nevertheless it is used as a convenient explanation. 'It is instinctive': no further questions need to be asked. The problem with this approach has been that it has placed an effective break on investigating what the experiences of an equine are, and how and what he learns and how to teach him.

Interestingly, even though the majority will say this, we do not do it. For

EQUINE NEEDS

Physical needs

Food This is not just the right sort of food for the work done, but also involves psychological factors: time spent eating, the tastes and textures of food, nutritional wisdom and above all the importance of learning what to eat. Many recommended feeding regimes take into account the animal's physiological needs, but miss out his psychological ones, as a result frequently causing serious evidence of distress.

Water The importance of learning about water to drink increases the chance of the horse being able to make sensible discriminations and reduces risks.

Shelter He needs to learn how and where to shelter, not to be over-protected which will prevent him learning to make choices. If living in a small flat field without hedges or trees, some form of field shelter is necessary, but if there is changing topography, hedges, trees, etc, available, then this may be sufficient even for the thoroughbred or Arab.

Physical health/ lack of pain & disease are important. But there are issues here that need addressing. Is it entirely necessary for the horse to have his wounds stitched and consequently to have to be kept on box rest, isolated from others, unable to move about? Psychological pressures may reduce healing and the action of the immune system. Sometimes less treatment may benefit him in the long run.

Good feet and body Terrain to keep his feet in trim, or good blacksmithing is important, but shoeing may not always be necessary for the work he is doing. It is not necessary when equines are not working on hard surfaces.

Social needs

• Equines are social animals. Keeping one horse alone is not acceptable. They must have some companionship, preferably of other equines. If you cannot arrange or afford to have a pony or donkey companion for your horse, then you should not have one. Keeping horses in adjoining stables where they can see and smell each other but have no contact is also unacceptable. Some come to terms with it, but some do not, and the horse will be a more relaxed and pleasant companion as well as healthier and fitter if he has free access to others at least part of the day.

• Equines live in family groups, where their relationships are often life long. However, they are adaptable, and can learn to adapt to groups that change.

• Equines have very strong inter-generation bonds (that is, bonds between mother and young, who follow mother everywhere). Forcible weaning followed by isolation of the foal is almost guaranteed to cause severe trauma to mother and foal. Natural weaning is best, if not it should be performed slowly, and from early in life the foal be accustomed to staying for short periods with other mares and foals.

• Courtship is long and involved, and allows the mare to bond with the stallion. Normally, sex only takes place with well known stallions living with the group.

Consequently being raped by an unknown covering stallion is unacceptable and often does not result in pregnancy (68% only even with the help of steroids,etc). Select stallions which run with their mares, if you care about your mare. Complex relationships are set up among horses. Stallions, like men, can learn to control themselves sexually.

• It is crucial that the young equines are brought up with older horses, from whom they will learn about social relationships and the environment. Social learning is very important in these species. Thus different stables will have different horse cultures depending on the way they are kept and the relationship they have with the humans. It is very important equines are allowed to learn how to behave acceptably socially. They can only do this if allowed to be with others of different ages and sexes, particularly when young. Frequently horses raised in conventional horse establishments have not had this opportunity and as a result they have learnt to be frightened of others. If they have no social skills they resemble autistic humans.

• Social play is important for equines as well as humans. It seems its function is to develop an ability to read others' intentions.

EMOTIONAL NEEDS

• Equines form strong long-term bonds of affection with mother, offspring, social partners and other species.

• They must be allowed to express a range of emotions of joy, happiness, anger, sadness.

• They must not be kept in environments where they are unhappy, frustrated or in some form of conflict for long periods. That is, they must not be showing evidence of prolonged distress, although short periods of stress or even having to do things they may not particularly want to do may be necessary.

INTELLECTUAL NEEDS

• Allow them to use their brains to make decisions and choices. Do not over-protect them.

• Give them opportunities to acquire knowledge by having a life full of different experiences and occasions to adapt.

• They have an ability to acquire a considerable ecological knowledge. If it is not possible for them to acquire this, then other knowledge must be substituted.

• They must be allowed to acquire social knowledge.

• They must have mental stimulation in order to remain healthy and happy. Repeating the same thing all the time is not sufficient, however good at it they may be. They must have the opportunity, particularly when young or when they have had the habit of learning, to continue to learn new things.

example, the reason we have equines, and we want to teach them, is because we want to know more about them, and understand more about what it might be like to be one of them. How is their world similar to mine, or yours? In fact most of us start from believing that their world is very like ours. For example, we know that our equine feels tired, hungry, angry, sore, delighted, bored, frustrated. We know he can see things, smell, feel by touch, taste and hear things, that he can starve to death, die of exhaustion, that he needs company, looks after and suckles young and forms friendships. We also know that equines learn and will or will not do things as a result, they remember, forget and are aware of things and their own bodies, that is have some form of consciousness. In other words they are in many respects very like us. . . But on the other hand they are also different: they have four feet with hooves not hands, they are bigger, can run faster and further, live exclusively on vegetation (mainly grass). They do not manipulate and make things like we do, and they do not have a human type language but it does not necessarily follow as a result of these differences that they do not have many of the same mental events and experiences that we have.

Those who teach equines may not have thought about all this much, but they do intuitively recognise that there are similarities and differences between us. Equines are not robots or motor cars, nor are they 'just like us'. This is the fascination. We enrich our own lives by understanding better another similar but different interpretation of the world. We can sit back amazed from time to time when we come to better understand their world and learn new ways of looking at the world from their point of view.

An equine has eyes at the sides of his head, an enormous visual field, most of which is monocular. He is acutely aware of very slight movements or changes around him much of the time, even when he does not appear to be paying direct attention. As a result, when equines communicate they can be stating what, in human language terms, would be a whole paragraph at any instant. By contrast, we humans pay attention to one thing after another. Our language, which largely controls how we think, is based in this linear way, and we usually consider it is the *only* way to think. I, like many others who may however not articulate it, have learnt a great deal about being a better observer and cultivating different habits of mind from years with horses. Our interpretation may not be exactly the way they experience the world, but slightly more like it. At least we have learnt 'different ways of seeing' from them ... it has enriched our own worlds.

There is no reason to believe that these experiences are not mutual. Equines sometimes indicate by their behaviour that they have had their world enriched and may be thinking in different ways, and 'seeing the world differently' as a result of their association with us.

To be able in the first place to recognise similarities and differences in the way we experience the world and the way our horse does, we need to gather information from all the relevant sciences and from critical thinkers. We need to be sure that these experiences are first hand, they come direct from the horse; they are not just the result of what someone else said about the horse. Only in this way will the experiences be genuine and not just the result of someone else's interpretation of

A fashionable new stable block where all the horses are kept in individual prisons, unable to see out or experience the outside in any way. In these stables, levels of distress are very high, unless the animals are outdoors all day at least.

what the horse may be feeling, that is 'pre-conceived notions' or traditional unexamined beliefs. This effort to try and understand more about another species' mental life and experiences is called 'conditional anthropomorphism' and it is gaining ground today among the growing band of cognitive scientists who are becoming more and more interested in these questions. 'Anthropomorphism' (that is, assuming similarities with humans) is no longer considered unscientific in helping us to answer such questions, but it must be tempered with the 'conditional', this refers to what we know about our species differences.

What are the similarities? Firstly, we are both mammals, we all have similar, although not identical, physical, emotional, social and cognitive or intellectual needs (see page 17). So the first and most useful step when confronting a problem when educating a horse is to think how you would behave in that situation and why. Often this will help to solve the problem, and I will give many examples of this as we investigate how to improve education of equines.

But, we also have differences, this is where the 'conditional' part comes in. I have outlined what we know about these to date as a result of reviewing the literature and critically assessing personal and others' experiences in detail in *Equine Lore* (chapter 1-11, 2004).

Let me emphasise that there is little new in this approach. It is equines' and humans' physical and mental similarities laced by their known differences that have been used through the ages by *good* equine teachers in many parts of the world, and particularly in the European classical school of riding and horse teaching. The difference is that we can inject new knowledge which should result in changes as we learn more about equines from science and understanding other minds better.

We must sift out the grain from the straw in traditional beliefs and practices and ensure the voice of tradition does not hold a stranglehold on both the way horses are kept and on how they are taught and ridden. Throughout history there have been very poor teachers who have forcibly emphasised the importance of the use of restraints to 'dominate' the horse, or 'show who is leader'. The sad thing is that this erroneous view is widely held today by the establishment, and even some of the so called 'natural horsemen'.

(1) How horses are **kept.** It is traditional practice to keep competition horses in single stables, isolated from their own kind the majority of the time. If they are allowed out to move around, they are often not allowed to be with others in case they are kicked or hurt. The result is that the majority of horses kept in these conditions show evidence of behavioural distress, and are pathological social misfits. If normal equines evolved to naturally hurt each other when they were together, how on earth could horses have managed to breed and remain social animals for some 10 million years?

(2) How horses are **taught and ridden.** The British Dressage society sponsors teaching people (through their 'Pyramid teaching scheme') on how to use running or German reins in order to hold the horse's head down, rather than insisting that the rider improve his/her riding so that the horse voluntarily puts his head down in the right position. When I challenged them on this stance (April 2003), instead of even publishing the letter in order to generate discussion, the editor of their magazine wrote back saying that since people used running reins anyway, they must know the 'right way' of using them ... *but how can there be a 'right way' to a restraint that is quite contrary to the whole philosophy of European dressage?* (which is to have the horse going in such a way as to naturally and voluntarily hold himself with his head in the correct position, and not have it restrained)

When the top end of the professional riders and teachers think so little and are so reluctant to debate these issues, progress in teaching equines is unlikely to be made. The whole of 'dressage riding' becomes an exercise in history and 'tradition', a sort of museum piece! But, it remains baffling, since in the UK the establishment organisations such as the British Horse Society stipulate that their central concern is 'equine welfare'!

We all have a problem separating 'folk belief' or traditional practice (that is, what we believe because it is generally believed to be so, or because it is 'done that way') from 'folk knowledge' (that is, an understanding based on rationally thought-out convincing evidence). Folk knowledge is the result of critically examined personal experiences put together with scientifically measured information. It is teasing folk belief apart from folk knowledge that we need to address so that we really improve the education and care of our equines ... not sweeping the issues under the carpet.

The relatively recent approach to training horses, called 'natural horsemanship' or 'horse whispering' started by Williams, Rees, Wright, Parelli, Gentilli, Teddington-Jones and Roberts is sprouting like a triffid in almost every continent. Its very popularity indicates the public's wish to understand more and to change previous approaches. This approach began as a reaction to the brutal, dominating and restrictive training of horses used in rodeo riding in the US, outback riding in Australia, and the curious male orientated 'dangerous challenge' method for backing young thoroughbred race horses that evolved in racing stables in the UK, where the European classical school was little known.

The 'natural horsemanship' approach (note, it is not 'horse-personship', despite the fact that more than ³/₄ of the people who are interested are female!) is valuable in emphasising certain aspects of communication with equines, for example, the use of body language and encouraging people to observe their horses and try and understand them better. On the other hand, as with other methods (e.g. the classical school), when it becomes fashionable and popular, it can become another unquestioned dogma. The result is that one traditional dogma is replaced by another, which may be equally inadequate for improving how we teach or have to do with equines. In the last decade, I and many others, have become disillusioned with much of the natural horsemanship. This is not to say that there are not valuable bits and pieces that can be picked up from them, put with other information and experiences and built into your own approach to equine education. But the time is now ripe for 'thinking horse-people'! This book is to encourage the reader not to sell out to any one without very serious critical appraisal (including of this book!). Failing this, no progress will be made and in the end both you and your horse will be the losers.

My own approach lies in asking questions, assessing evidence, and then encouraging others to develop their own approaches. We all know that there are many ways to educate children or equines, even though each of us usually has strongly held opinions on the best one. My leanings are to try and extract the most rational general rules that fit best with what we know about equines, how they learn and their view of the world. At the same time it is crucial to keep thinking, reassessing and learning. This inevitably means that no dogma or tradition will do, rather it must be a continual process of learning what to do, and what not to do, from others. This is not what people want to hear, they want a quick 'how to' book, which, like the right drug, will solve their and their horse's learning problems.

As a result of having some idea 'what it is to be' an equine, we can outline some general rules for educating equines which may be helpful but, remember, there are many routes to put these 'rules' into effect (see page 67).

Let me suggest that first of all, go out there, learn and try things out, don't ask for advice or join some group, make your own group with your equines, and enjoy yourselves. Only afterwards discuss what you have tried and found out with other humans, and begin to select ideas from them too.

Before we embark on this search though, we need to answer some serious questions. First, do equines have to suffer in order to be taught by humans and

Behaviour restricted	1.environment wild/feral	2.extensive pastures	3.small pastures shelter	4.yards	5. loose boxes 24 hours	6.12 hours	7.stalls 24 hours	8.12 hours
unrestricted movement	0	0	0	3	4	2-3	5	4
all gaits possible	0	0	0	4	3	0-2	5	4
unrestricted grooming	0	0	0	0	2	3	5	4
unrestricted social contact	0	2-3	2-3	4	5	3	5	4-5
choose social contact	0	2-4	2-4	4	5	4-5	5	4-5
sex possible	0	0-5	0	5	5	5	5	5
maternal behaviour possible	0	0-2	0	2-4	2-5	2-5	5	4
unrestricted feeding	0	0	0	0-3	3-5	3-4	5	2-4
choose food	0	0	0	0-3	3-5	2-3	5	4
changing/ stimulating environment	0	0	2-5	3-5	4-5	2-3	5	4
can acquire ecological knowledge	0	0	1-3	5	5	3-5	5	4
TOTAL	0	±8	±9	±35	43±	30±	55	43±
always water and food	4	0	0	0	1	1	3	3
shelter available	4	3-4	0	0	0	0	0	0
veterinary treatment for illness/wounds etc	5	2	0	0	0	0	0	0
stimulation from humans	5	3-5	0	0	0	0	0	0
learning new things	3	3	0	0	0	0	0	0
TOTAL	21	±25	±8	35±	44±	31±	58	46±

← A → ← B →

POSSIBLE INDICATORS OF DISTRESS IN ANIMALS

• Evidence of **physical ill health**
• Evidence of frequent **occupational diseases**(e.g.lameness due to strain)
• Need for the **use of drugs and/or surgery**
• **Behavioural changes**
1. Performance of abnormal behaviours (not normally in the animal's repertoire, and which appear to be of little benefit, e.g. pacing, stable walking)
2. Stereotypies, i.e. performance of repeated behaviour fixed in all details and apparently purposeless (e.g. crib biting, wind-sucking, weaving, head-twisting)
3. Substantial increase in inter- or intra-specific aggression compared to the wild or feral state
4. Large differences in time budgets from the wild or feral animal
5. Substantial increases in behaviour related to frustration or conflict (often behaviour relating to locomotion and/or skin irritation)
substantial ontogenic behavioural changes (animals performing behaviour characteristics of a very different time in their development, e.g. one or two-year-olds being unable to maintain their balance on circles because they have not had an oportunity to learn how to move at speed)
• **Behavioural restrictions** - the inability to perform all the behaviour in the animal's natural repertoire which does not cause severe or prolonged suffering to others

The amount of behavioural restriction for horses in different environments
(opposite):
A=restrictions as a result of being domestic/in contact with humans
B=restrictions as a result of not having contact with humans
1. Wild or feral equines in areas of several hundred hectares
2. Groups of horses (without stallions) kept in extensive pastures (more than 6 hectare fields with varying terrain)
3. Horses kept in groups in small pastures with a stallion, shelter and varying terrain, with ad lib access to grass or hay/straw and silage in the winter. The experimental Druimghigha horses are kept like this most of the time
4. Horses kept in groups of varying ages in yards with barns or shelter that they can use when required. High fibre food ad lib. This reduces restrictions.
5,6. Horses kept in conventional loose box system (4m square). Either 24 or 12 hours a day
7,8. Horses tied in stalls either all time (excluding exercise) or 12 hour periods

compete or work for them? Do they have to be slaves working against their wills? If your answer to this is NO then you must be quite sure that your horse is not suffering, physically, emotionally, socially or intellectually/cognitively or the answer will be YES. It is not enough to say to yourself or others, 'I love my horses, I care for them and they are happy. ' You can and must, if you care, have evidence to

Oryx flehmen - savouring and investigating a smell or taste.

show that this is the case.

If your answer is YES, then I will try and convince you that this is not the case, by examples and logical argument.

So, the first thing to do is to find out if, from the equine's point of view, things are definitely wrong. This can be done by assessing whether your equine pupil is showing any signs of prolonged distress (see page 23) during his teaching, but also during the other part of the day and night.

Exercise 1. Honestly assess all the measures given in the table on page 23.

There are many causes for these behaviours. If you really do not have an idea why your equine is performing one or other of them, then ask one of the growing number of behavioural consultants that specialise in equines, but be sure they have had some serious training in science and ethology. Generally, however, you will probably have an idea why. But, just because he had a rough time before you had him is not sufficient to explain it all away. It is your responsibility, if you want to have an equine that learns easily and well, to change things so that distress is less often shown, at least.

One of the most common causes of behavioural distress, and one of the most obvious but least talked about, is the degree of behavioural restriction the equine is suffering. Here, with a little thought, changes can usually be made in any situation, including if you have your horse at livery with someone else.

Exercise 2. Assess the degree of behavioural restriction honestly and quantitatively by ticking the row in a table such as that given in the table on page 22. Compare the scores you obtain with those for your neighbour's horses or the local stable, and with other people. You may find you give different scores and score more different behaviours, than someone else, that is fine. The important thing is to do it honestly, and then sit down and think how in practical terms you might be able to decrease the scores for behavioural restriction for your horses by making simple inexpensive changes, perhaps. Also discuss it with your friends.

The next thing if the teacher is going to improve and the equine learn well, is to ensure, not only that the equine is not suffering but that he has a life of quality.

This means that his needs should be fulfilled. His needs are like humans' in some respects, but different in others. They are summarised on page 17, and divided into: physical, social, emotional and intellectual or cognitive needs.

Exercise 3. Assess whether or not your equine's physical, social, emotional and intellectual needs are fulfilled (see page 17). If you think they fall short (which if you are honest will always be the case), assess where, and think how in your situation, you might be able to improve this.

If the equines are behaviourally restricted with a score above, say above 10-12 for an unfulfilled need, or show evidence of distress in any way (such as being over-excited, aggressive, bored, refusing to do things, spooking or leaping about, as well as showing any stereotypie, needing drugs, sick or lame much of the time) then, before your start teaching your equine, work out why they are distressed, where their needs are not being fulfilled and how to reduce thir behavioural restrictions. Then change the husbandry and teaching to put this right, or at least reduce where there is something wrong.

Although the 'natural horse-personship' approach can help with the training of the horse, it usually ignores consideration of husbandry which may be the cause of the horse not learning as quickly and easily as he might.

All equines who have a life of quality are relaxed, well natured beings, who, provided they have not had bad previous experiences, will be curious and interested in humans. If they are frequently excited, jumpy, scared, aggressive, lethargic or unco-operative, then their environment and/or their teaching is not right somewhere. There are no exceptions to this rule. First change the environment, then progress to changing handling, teaching and the way he is ridden.

Even though an equine might have had a bad experience (such as a trauma at weaning, fright when loading into a vehicle, being beaten or being heavily restricted when being ridden), it is *not possible* to pass the buck. Of course it is necessary to take the individual's past experience into account, but just as important is to change his conditions of living. What is not acceptable is to ignore the husbandry conditions when treating any behavioural problem, as, alas, is too often done. If a child has trouble learning at school, it is taken for granted that it would be sensible to look at his home background and find out how he lives there, yet for some reason the way the equine has to live and his teaching have become quite separate, no wonder there are so many problems with horses! If your livery yard owner will not listen, take your horse to another yard where they will.

Over the years that I have been teaching students and teachers, it has become evident that a little effort to try and understand the individual's particular point of view is invaluable. This applies to members of our own species, but also to others. In order to be able to do this for an equine pupil, we must have some idea of the world they live in, not just some preconceived notions of this. This involves knowing something more about the equine's point of view, and his individual past experiences. Although many people are sympathetic to this idea in principle, when things do not go smoothly, they tend to consider the animal at fault, his past experience, his breed, his stupidity, and so on, rather than blaming themselves and trying to change the way they are approaching the problem!

To help the teacher have glimpses into a somewhat different world view, and different habits of mind, we have developed various exercises (see below). Some of these exercises will work better than others for different individuals, and there are many more that people will be able to invent. They have been selected as the most successful from many that we have tried out at workshops worldwide which have encouraged participants to think, have fun and teach better thereafter.

The first exercises are to help the teacher critically assess how the sensory information acquired by the various senses differs between humans and equines.

Exercise 4. **Smells and tastes**

1. Try giving different substances to your equines by squeezing some dilute juice into the mouth: lemon, garlic, salt, vinegar or whatever will not burn or cause him to have an unpleasant experience. The close relationship between smelling and tasting will become evident, his nose may start to run, and he may flehmen. He will also demonstrate his interest, his dislike, or even his delight. Repeat the same substance several times and record what you think his response is. After a while you may have to review how you interpreted it.

2. Try giving equines with different experiences or from different places, both old and young, different new things to eat and see how they try or don't, and how they smell and taste before they eat.

Exercise 5. **Smell only**

1. In order to try and awaken the perception of smells and their importance try this exercise. Have a friend collect a bunch of different smelling plants, not necessarily particularly strong smelling; then get yourself blindfolded, and have them presented to you to smell, one at a time, and without touching them. Try and think, *not* what it is and its name, but rather, what *experiences* that the smell conjures up to you. Describe the picture that it gives rise to. If there is not one, don't worry, just keep trying and gradually there will be for every smell, a situation, an experience, a moment. This may help you realise how important smells may be to equines. This exercise can be quite fun to do in a group, each taking turn in smelling and describing, but remember, try not to be affected by the picture that someone else paints of the smell, an equine will not have an account given to them, they will have to make up their own!

2. Observe how your equines smell you when you approach them. Wear someone else's dirty clothes, or rub some stallion faeces, or splash a little urine of another equine on you and see how this attracts attention. Do not use synthetic cosmetics for a day or so first or they may mask the smells and he may have learnt not to bother to smell you.

Exercise 6. **Sight**

1. The position of the eyes on the head gives a different view.

(a) Hold your arms up sideways and while looking straight forwards, draw them back until you can only just see your hands out of the corner of your eyes. This tells you how wide your peripheral visual field is.

(b) Get someone to hold an object in the peripheral visual field of one eye and, without moving your eyes, tell them what it is. This will demonstrate how relatively poor the peripheral vision is.

(c) Now cover up one of your eyes with one hand, and place the other hand vertically against your nose, with the little fingers forward. This gives one an idea about the separation of the monocular visual fields, with the barrier created by the hand in front of the eye giving an idea of the horse's face between his eyes.

(d) Next, place the fingers together in a praying type position, then, holding that position, place the base of the thumb against the nose with the praying fingers pointing forwards. Open both eyes, and see what a barrier this creates to the binocular visual field; you will find that there is a blind spot in front where your fingers are, and, if things are nearby, it is easier to see them by turning the head sideways.

These exercises will help you think and perhaps understand something about equine's visual field and head movements when watching things, particularly their teacher.

2. The equine's ability to pick up very small visual cues. Various games can be invented here between people to increase their powers of observation of visual cues.

(a) As a start for beginners, get one person to try and get some simple message across to another without making any movements, just using the eyes.

(b) The next one will be making only small movements of one part of the anatomy, the feet, for example, to put across messages concerning intention.

(c) A more difficult variation of this exercise is to have someone try and imagine feeling a particular emotion (acting it without making any particular movement), and the others try and tell which emotion they are feeling.

3. Try writing down what you see watching an equine in an enclosed space in order to be able to predict his next likely actions. Discuss this with others. Gradually you will get better at this, but not if you just listen to others, because they may be making mistakes, only if you do it yourself and correct yourself will you have the experience and learn from it.

Concentrate in turn on

(a) the face, eyes, ears, nose, chin, mouth movements or tensions

(b) then the body and tail, and

(c) the legs.

Exercise 7. Touch

1. The importance of weight changes and touching with the hands or the legs is all part of ordinary riding, so a good riding instructor will be able to point out many different things you can do to begin to cue into the individual sensitivity of your mount.

(a) just sit relaxed on the equine, close your eyes and try and feel his breathing

(b) feel and be aware of each of his legs as it comes to the ground. You should be able to feel exactly where every leg is at any time.

(c) with no reins or rope, even around the neck, try with very slight changes of your leg positions and weight on your behind to ask your mount to move in a particular direction. Practise this and eventually you will be able to do all the normal school movements with the legs or weight changes only. It is wise to start this in an enclosed space of course.

2. The importance of touch to the equine in his everyday life. One of the most sensitive areas is the nose and vibrissae (hairs) (one reason why they should *not* be cut off).

(a) Hold your hand to touch the vibrissae, and then gradually move it away until the equine seems no longer to feel it and does something else, alternatively gradually bring your hand, or an object nearer the nose and the vibrissae; watch when he appears to make some slight twitching of the face or mouth, or movement away or towards showing he is feeling it. It may help to have him blindfolded, but, remember, he will have to get used to the blindfold, so do not rush in and expect it all to happen in a few minutes.

(b) Repeat this with other equines, and you can even do something like this with a blindfolded human; how far away from her face and her top lip can she 'feel' something?

3. Another exercise is to test each of your equine's sensitive touch zones with different brushes, and draw diagrams of these. Make sure that any people handling or grooming them look at the diagrams before they rush in to scrub them with brushes that are too hard, or you will end up, as many stables do, with horses who hate being groomed, and have to be tied up or they bite and kick the people doing it!

Exercise 8. **Hearing**

1. Acuity of hearing. Arrive in the stables one day before the normal routine feeding time and watch the horses to see when they pick up the sound of others arriving. It will probably be before you do. Warnings of vehicles coming, or other horses, or strange events can often be picked up from the equine's responses of ear pricking, turning to look in the direction and remaining still while listening. Begin to cue into these in your everyday interactions with your equine.

 2. Hearing pitch range. Try playing a dog whistle which is above the normal hearing of adult humans and see what response you have from different equines, old and young. Infra sounds (very low sounds) are more difficult to test without equipment.

3. Equines are very sensitive to rhythm.

(a) When he is in the free school, or on a lunge, play a metronome to him at the rhythm of one of his paces (it doesn't matter which). After only a few days you will be able to make the rhythm slightly faster or slower and he will gradually follow it.

(b) You can then substitute the metronome with some music with a good beat and not far from their own rhythm and he will quickly follow the rhythm, even if you find it difficult. He also may syncopate, just to make life difficult for us.

Exercise 9. **ESP**

1. Some Russian scientists investigated telepathy with animals. They were very clear that this had to be learnt. Try concentrating on your horse and thinking/ willing him to do some very simple thing, raise his head, or walk a step left, etc. It is said that if you work at this you can get better at it. The Russians suggested that the best way to start was by sitting on a park bench, and willing the passers-by to scratch their heads. We have tried this a little, there does seem to be some evidence that one gets better with practice, but it needs a lot of practice. Worth a try though.

Learning to concentrate the attention on the subject rather than on human company.
The first and often the most difficult cognitive jump that has to be made by any animal teacher is to learn to concentrate with 100% of the attention onto the individual equine student, rather than (as we normally do) on the other humans who are around watching or talking to the teacher about the student.

Mental exercises of changing the consciousness can be useful here (e.g. yoga, shiatzu, reki, ti chi etc). However the aim is not to concentrate the mind on 'nothing' as in yoga, or on 'energy' as in Shiazu, but rather on the 'equine subject'.
Stage 1. Spend 5 minutes (time it) holding or standing near your equine subject while he is just standing resting or doing not very much. Look at him, concentrate on him (not what he is doing, why he is doing it, or what adventures you have had together) **concentrate on him just there as he is right now.** Do not try and concentrate on 'nothing' either. Look him in the eye, look at all aspects of his body, without assessing him or reminding yourself to do this or that to improve this or that, just looking and enjoying without judging. No talking to others.
Stage 2. When you have managed to spend a good 5 minutes doing this alone, then do it when others are watching you; this is more difficult. Discussion about how you managed to put your mind in a neutral concentrated zone on the subject may be useful afterwards.

Learning about the subject/student's consciousness, and what may be going on in his mind.
Many people jump in at the deep end and try and do this first. The problem is that one is always putting one's preconceived notions across rather than seriously looking and critically assessing what is going on. Thus, it is best to start with the first exercise, which really makes one concentrate attention before this one.
Stage 1 **Ecological knowledge**
1. Watch the equine doing things for 10 minutes (time it, it is quite a long time!). He can either be in a stable wandering around eating or, preferably (and easier for the person), take him for a walk on a headcollar to look at things, and eat something along the verges or wherever is convenient. Watch him carefully, and in detail. Use the way of concentrating on him that you have learnt to critically assess what he may be feeling. Take him through woods, rivers, trees, roads, up and down banks, whatever you have available, make the route as varied as possible.
2. The easiest behaviour to look at in detail is eating. Look carefully at what he is eating, how he is using his nose and what he is selecting. Find out which plants he is eating, which he is rejecting, what part of the plant and stage of growth of the plant he chooses, how he selects, what movement he makes, what he spits out and how. It will be a lot more interesting than you think. If you do not know what the plants are, then it is a good opportunity to learn something about them, and become a good 'natural historian' yourself, after all your equine already is! This does not mean you have to look them up in books (although having a name does help you remember) but it *does* mean you have to look very carefully, and remember.

There are many more exercises here in relation to his knowledge about geology,

Sioban and Shezam going for a bluebell walk in the woods. Expeditions help young horses as well as humans learn about the world.

topography, the weather, other species (zoology), that you can observe closely either as you walk about with your equine or ride or drive.

3. Set up little experiments testing his knowledge (e.g. different substrates: gravel, cement, tarmac, grass, tufted grass, boggy areas, surfaces in an arena, sawdust, soil in the woods, or ploughed land etc.) Watch and learn about his knowledge.

This can then be developed to help him learn more about different aspects of the environment: 'environmental learning'. You will be surprised how much natural history you learn too.

Stage 2. **Food selection/botanical knowledge**

The same grazing exercise (2 above) but this time you are trying to assess his choices in one particular sward or piece of verge. So first assess how common the different plants are in a square metre (so you have to count them: rare (1 plant), occasional (1-5 plants), common (5-10 plants), abundant (>10 plants)). Get him to graze in this square metre, and count the number of times he selects one of them, and make a note of this. How does this relate to how common they are? Which is he choosing particularly? Does this change a month later because of the season? How many different plants does he eat in, say, 5 minutes? How does this relate to your assessed frequency of them in your square metre?

The idea here is again to make you look and concentrate closely on the animal, (not on other humans or other animals around), and also to begin to appreciate the complexity of his selections. The same can be done with hay, silage, haylage or straw in the stable if it is too wet or cold to go out.

If this becomes a human social exercise, that is, several of you chatting together while trying to do it, it misses the point. This is not to ignore the importance of humans socialising with horses, but just to suggest that in this case it may be better to disperse to the tack room and drink a coffee and chat which is also an important part of stable life, but not the only one!

Having learnt to concentrate on the individual, without your mind jumping back to communicating with humans every now and then, and begun to understand his knowledge of botany and food selection, the next step is to try and begin to concentrate on how he might be perceiving and interpreting the equine social world; in other words his ability to be a 'natural psychologist'.

Stage 3. **Being a natural psychologist and communicator. His social knowledge.**
1. Take your equine on a halter, somewhere where there are other social equine things going on, horses or ponies are coming or going, members of his group are around, or strange equines are around of different sexes and ages. Keep him approximately 10 metres from the others and observe his social interactions. These may not be directly obvious. It may appear as if he is ignoring the others, but subtle cues will be there, for example, which direction he is pointing or progressing when grazing, whether he tenses or twitches any part of his nose or nostrils, movements of his head and where he appears to be looking. Look carefully at the movements of one of his eyes and you will be able to assess to a degree at least what he can see with that eye, and eventually the degree to which he is paying attention with that eye.
2. Try, without preconceived notions from other humans, to piece together the relationships he may be subtly demonstrating.
3. Then lead him nearer to another. Meeting others may be a time of squeal and throw a front leg forward, so do not stand in front, and have a long line to let them play out their greeting. This is particularly important introducing strangers or mares to stallions. But once they have met and greeted each other in this way, if they are well adjusted sociologists, they will then get back to eating and watching each other. Failure to let them greet each other leads to constant frustrations and excitement.

There will be times when you jump to conclusions about his relationships with another which are wrong or the result of something someone else has said to you, or that you have decided yourself, such as 'she hates him' or 'she is boss'. Critically analyse how you have interpreted the social relationships afterwards, you may find there are other explanations, and perhaps it is not really like that.

You can also do this with others and compare notes afterwards. Other people who are interested in equines but do not know these ones are also very helpful to put different slants on one's interpretation. Writing brief notes is often helpful as one can easily forget what one thought previously.

Stage 4. **Free interaction with others**

The next phase is to do this concentrating on one equine when loose in a field, or yard or pen with others. You will need at least 30 minutes before anything much will reveal itself, and don't be put off because you think nothing is happening, just look more closely. A cheap pair of binoculars is useful here, a thermos of coffee and a sandwich. Dress up warm too, there is no need to be uncomfortable. You may find they all come and interfere with you to start with, but eventually they will go off to do their own thing and you can start really observing what is going on. Take notes and gradually over a period of days, the 'soap opera' will unfold, and you may find you become an addict!

Stage 5. Here the task is to talk to other humans about what you are seeing, or think you are seeing. Do this as a running commentary while you are both watching. First do, and then discuss it. Be careful not to develop a particular human narrative based on what you think others want to hear, or interpreting the equine social whirl in an entirely human way (e.g. manipulating others, being deceitful, either to try and please, or to escape other problems). Make sure that you use the simplest possible explanation of what you think is happening. This is a difficult exercise, the first step in trying to be an observer of the subtle communication and complexities of equine social life (Stage 4 above). The second is to translate this into human language, which is of course important if you are teaching humans.

It can all be discussed after each of you have described what you think you saw, to see if you come to the same interpretation or quite a different one. Again it is important to write it down before giving your interpretation because otherwise you will find it changes as a result of other humans' ideas!

There are endless other exercises that can be invented, this is just a sample to try and convince the equine enthusiast that in order to understand equines and teach them well, it is necessary to observe very carefully and have some idea of 'what it is to be an equine', and not to take preconceived notions from others on trust, they may be wrong.

These exercises will have made you a better observer, and an interested participant into another's world view. It will have prepared you for the complex interactions necessary when teaching or educating some one of another species. Having practised these exercises, and arrived at least at some understanding of the importance of observation (even if they tell you not much more than how little you know about equines), the next step is to consider how you might begin to teach. One important asset you have is a voice, and we are good at using it, in fact often have trouble not using it, so perhaps we can use it to help with our equine teaching, as we do with our human teaching.

REFERENCES

Adam, C. & M. Bekoff. 1997. *Species of Mind*. MIT. Cambs USA.

Burghardt, J. M. 1991. 'Cognitive ethology and critical anthropomorphism. A snake with two heads and hog-nosed snakes that plays dead', in: *Cognitive Ethology*. ed: C. A. Ristau. Erlbaum. Hillsdale.

Chambers, T. 1993. 'Recognition of pain ad distress in horses'. Brit. Vet Ass. Roadshow. *Pain in Practise*. BVA. Plymouth.

Dantzer, R. 1986. 'Behavioural, physiological and functional aspects of stereotyped behaviour: a review and a re-interpretation', *J. Anim. Sci* 62. 1776-1786.

Darwin, C. 1868. *The Expression of the Emotions in Man and Animals*. John Murray. London.

DeGrazia, D. 1996. *Taking Animals Seriously*. CUP. Cambridge.

Fisher, J. A. 1986. 'Taking Sympathy Seriously: A Defense of Our Moral Psychology Towards Animals', *Environ. Ethics*. 198 p197-215.

Fox, M. W. 1968. (editor) *Abnormal Behaviour of Animals*. W. B. Saunders. N. Y.

Griffin, D. R. 1992. *Animal Minds*. Univ. Chicago Press.

Hickman, J. 1984. *Horse Management*. Academic Press. London.

Hughes, B. O. & I. J. N. Duncan. 1988. 'The notion of ethological "need". Models of motivation and animal welfare', *Anim. Behav.* 36. 1696-1707.

Imam, S. A. H. A. A. 1983. *Mis-en-Main without a bit*. Imam Hazaribagh.

Jackson, J. 1992. *The Natural Horse. Lessons from the wild for domestic horse care*. Northland. Flagstaff. Arizona.

Johnson, B. 1995. *The skilful mind of the guide dog*. G. D. B. Herts.

Kennedy, J. 1992. *The New Anthropomorphism*. Cambridge University Press.

Kiley-Worthington, M. 1977. *The behavioural problems of farm animals*. Oriel Press. Stockton.

Kiley-Worthington, M. 1990. *Animals in Circuses and Zoos. Chiron's World?* Little Eco-Farm Publishing. Basildon.

Kiley-Worthington, M. 1998. 'Competition and Cooperation. A detailed study of communication and social organisation in a small group of horses (*Equus caballus*)' *Eco Research Centre*. ISBN 367-2045, paper 024.

Kiley-Worthington, M. 1998. *Equine Welfare*. J. A. Allen. London.

Kiley-Worthington, M. 2000. *Right in Front of Your Mind, Equine and Elephant Epistemology*. M. Phil thesis in Philosophy. University of Lancaster.

Kiley-Worthington, M. & D. Wood-Gush. 1987. 'Stereotypies in Horses', in *Current therapy in equine medicine*. ed N. E. Robinson Saunders. London.

Masson, J. & S. MaCarthy. 1994. *When Elephants Weep. The Emotional Lives of Animals*. Jonathan Cape. London.

Meyer-Holzapfel, M. 1968. 'Abnormal behaviour of zoo animals' in *Abnormal Behaviour of Animals*. ed: M. W. Fox. W. B. Saunders. London.

Midgley, M. 1978. *Beast and Man: The Roots of Human Nature*. Cornell Press. Ithaca. N. Y.

Nagel, T. 1974. 'What is it like to be a Bat?', *Philosophical Review* 83. 435-50

Roberts, M. 1992. *The man who listens to horses*. Hutchinson. London.

Rollin, B. 1989 *The Unheaded Cry. Animal Consciousness, Animal Pain and Scientific Change*. Oxford University Press.

Salt. ,H. 1980. *Animal Rights*. Centaur. London.

Sainsbury, D. W. B. 1984. 'Housing the Horse', in *Horse Management*. ed: J. Hickman p63-91. Academic Press. London.

Selye, H. 1950. *The Physiology and Pathology of Stress*. Acta Inc. N. Y.

Svendsen, E. 1994. *Professional Handbook of the Donkey*. Whittet Books. Stowmarket.

Swift, S. 1996. *Centred Riding*. J. A. Allen.

Waring, G. 1983. *Horse Behaviour*. Noyes Press. N. Y.

Welsh, B. L. 1964. 'Psychological response to the mean level of environmental stimulation - a theory of environmental integration', in *Medical Aspects of Stress in a Military Climate*. US Gov. Washington.

Welsh, D. A. 1973. *The life of Sable Island wild horses*. Ph. D. thesis. Dalousie. Canada.

Wemelsfelder, F. 1993. *Animal Boredom towards an empirical approach to animal subjectivity*. Proefschrift Leiden.

3

NATURE AND NURTURE.
HOW EQUINES LEARN

Hominus dum docent discunt. Even while they teach, men learn. (Seneca)

• Instinct and intelligence
• The theory of learning
• Types of learning

It is vitally important to have at least some idea of what instinct is, and how learning works before we embark on educating either equines or humans. We all know that equines learn, but a false belief abounds that the way they learn is not the way humans learn, and that their behaviour, unlike humans', is always tempered by 'instinct'.

Instinct

What is 'instinct'? An instinct is a genetically pre-programmed behaviour that is inflexible, and is performed as a result of a specific stimulus without voluntary action and possibility of control. It is a term that was used widely by the father of ethology, Tinbergen, who published one of the first books (*The Study of Instinct*) to spark scientific interest in animal behaviour, and particularly its cause: why animals do what they do. Lorenz was studying mainly birds, and their behaviour. He came up with ideas such as 'imprinting', a type of early learning which is being used for horses today (see below). Lorenz also argued, in a popular book that had a considerable influence on the way people thought about emotion, that emotions, such as aggression (*On Aggression*), built up if individuals were not allowed to express them. He compared the relationship between instincts and emotions to an adaptation of a hydraulic ram, a notion that held sway for a decade or two among ethologists in Europe in particular. These ideas acted as a catalyst to interest people in why animals do things, and sparked off half a century of detailed experimentation in many laboratories throughout the world, and field studies on many different species. As a result, these conceptions have been severely modified or thrown out.

One of the problems with instinct is to explain how it could work; how could such elaborate behaviour such as sexual behaviour in equines, for example, be genetically pre-programmed and fixed, how can such complex behaviours be wired in the brain, and wired in from birth? An equine's head would have to be twice the size it is in order to have space for all this 'instinctive behaviour'!

Another problem is that pre-programmed behaviour is inflexible; clearly, if we look at sexual behaviour of equines, for example, it varies between individuals, and in different situations. In other words, it changes and adapts, which must involve some learning.

The nature/nurture argument controlled much of ethology for a couple of decades: how much of an animal's behaviour was controlled by instinct, genetically pre-programmed, and how much learnt as a result of experience? Eventually, ethologists agreed that such arguments were inhibiting progress on more interesting discoveries about the behaviour of animals, and agreed that all we could do is understand that all mammal behaviour, including human, is controlled by both 'instinct' and by 'learning'. The instinctive part takes the form of pre-programmed tendencies to perform certain things. Thus an equine or a human has a *tendency* to behave sexually, but when, where, how, or even if he does depends on his/her past experiences and the present environment ... that is learning.

Unfortunately, this development has not yet filtered through to most ordinary people, and animals are still believed by many to behave predominantly 'instinctively', whereas humans do not!

Most of us know quite a lot about learning and teaching, simply because we practise it with our children and in our human relationships, so it is useful to employ what we can call 'common sense', and not always necessary to understand all the terms. But sometimes we need to examine our understanding to ensure that we have not taken up some 'preconceived notion' which is not helpful. One of these is the widely held belief that needs to be dispelled, that equines (and other animals) learn by 'conditioning'. This is believed to result in some reflex response which the animal has no control over; a sort of 'instinct like' learning. Pavlov, who worked with dogs in the 19th century, showed that some learning was of this type, but this reflex-type conditioning has now become part of our popular cultural understanding of how animals learn. As a result, many assume that equines do not perform actions voluntarily. Although the same people do believe equines have emotions, most of the time, they argue, an equine is like a motor car in its response. It is just a question of 'pushing the right buttons' and the right response will result. We now know that learning is a great deal more complex and interesting than this, and it is of benefit to all those involved with equines if they have some serious understanding of how it works. As early as 1956 learning was categorised into different types, but with an emphasis on the overlap between the categories and the complexity within them.

First I will update and outline the types of learning both equines and humans display that most learning theorists would agree on today, but, remember, things change fast in our understanding of animal cognition. To bring it alive, I will give examples, which will be set in a different type for easy recognition. It is important to remember that learning was originally studied in rats and pigeons because they were cheap and easy to keep in laboratories. The findings of the early researchers, together with many since, were turned about and modified by continuing work with laboratory animals. In many ways these findings have been successfully applied to help understand how humans learn and should teach. In other words, it has long been recognised that *learning works in the same sorts of way for all mammals*, although some may be better at certain types than others.

First we need to define what learning is. It has often been defined as having occurred in any situation *where behaviour is modified by experience*. This definition was used because its effect on behaviour could be measured. But it is now understood that some learning in animals and humans does *not* make any immediate, or perhaps even long term difference to behaviour that we can measure.

Learning is influenced by the individual, the species and the environment. Are horses, donkeys, zebras and mules 'intelligent' is a question that is often asked, and most of us have strong views on this, particularly concerning our own equine! Intelligence is another tricky term and we will start by discussing it.

Intelligence

If I had £1 for every time I had been asked, 'Are horses intelligent?' I would be a millionaire. The relative intelligence of each species, or even individual, within a species, is a subject of endless discussion. Horse breed societies will recommend their breed by claims that they are particularly 'intelligent'. Comparative intelligence is something that some psychologists are now discussing. The most common position taken on this issue is that each species will have a different physique, different receptors, different emphasis on emotionality and socialisation and consequently live in different worlds. If this is the case, then comparisons between species are meaningless, each species will be the best, the most intelligent at living in *its own* world. A comparative cognitive psychologist's stock response when asked about the intelligence of one species relative to another is:

'Each animal is likely to appear very intelligent in the environment for which it evolved and may appear very stupid when faced with other kinds of demands. Comparing animals' intelligence is like comparing their abilities to move. Do fish move better than horses?'

One of the major problems here is that there is no agreed definition of what intelligence is. The common use of this term relates to 'ability to learn' or 'to solve problems' or 'to perform IQ tests', but IQ tests given to humans are generally based on language ability and consequently irrelevant to non humans. In any event what IQ tests measure and whether they are worth the paper they are written on remains highly disputed. It is beginning to be realised that there can be more than one type of 'intelligence' even in humans: for example artists have a different type of intelligence from musicians or academics. Males are now widely regarded of having different mental abilities: they are better, generally, at logical linear thinking, whereas females at multi-tasking and emotional understanding.

But rarely do we consider the even greater differences in world views there must be between species in relation to types of intelligence. 'Intelligence' is often used to indicate how similar an animal's behaviour is to that of a human (usually an adult male) in a particular situation – in other words 'how like a human male is he?'

So what could the general rules be for measuring one type of intelligence, say the ability to think and act rationally, to learn fast, to remember and to be able to put information together from different areas to solve problems? Speed of learning might be one, but if we are trying to measure this, how is it possible to be sure the act the subject is learning is equally difficult for different species, and how can we be sure that they have similar motivations? In the 1970s there was a fashion to test farm animals in mazes to see how their performances compared one with another. On this reading, horses scored badly; this confirmed the general folk belief that horses:

(1) learn very slowly, so everything has to be repeated again and again,

(2) have to learn everything on both sides of the brain because they do not have a *corpus callosum* (the part of the forebrain where information is transferred from left to right and *vice versa*). This is untrue.

(3) will not be able to learn anything at all difficult because they are 'stupid' ... a circular argument which is often used.

But there were many reasons why the horses might not have performed well in a maze:

(1) they were not interested in solving the problem,

(2) they were more easily distracted and cautious,

(3) they may have known the solution but simply not felt like rushing there.

Learning in the real world is a constant interaction between others of the same and different species and the environment. Testing animals in an isolated alien laboratory environment might be expected to cause changes. Indeed it is interesting that humans are not tested in such alien isolated situations: laboratory ethical committees would not allow it!

So, before having opinions concerning the 'intelligence' of your equine, remember that making this judgement is rather complicated; perhaps only another equine can make it! In just the same way it is not possible to consider donkeys more or less stupid than horses, who are more or less bright than zebras; and mules, well we all know they are stubborn – or are they? Perhaps this is just the way we like to interpret their behaviour. On looking through some of the military history where donkeys and mules have been used, one cannot but admire the donkeys and mules used by the military in every type of terrain, who had to put up with every type of harsh physical condition, their extraordinary toughness, but also their ability to come to terms with those conditions, and to learn about the physical, emotional, social and cognitive trappings and difficulties of human wars. Is this intelligence or adaptability?

The chapter is divided into four parts:

(1) We need to clarify the meaning of some of the terms that are widely used but whose meanings are not always clear. Unfortunately there is a tendency to use these terms too loosely, and then for others to use them without having much idea what is meant! Thus rather confusing language emerges which puts people off trying to understand any of it. This is not at all helpful for either clarity or

Extinction. The foal, Oryx, has had his hind leg held up without a fright, so that now his response to withdraw it is extinct. His mother, Omeya, watches.

understanding.

(2) The next step is to outline the different types of learning so that one can have more of an idea why that equine behaved in that way in that situation, as well as what a teacher may have done right or wrong.

(3) Finally, I will outline some of the co-operative teaching research we have been doing with our equines and other mammals over the last few years. The central idea here was to see if our subjects could learn to understand human language by using a similar interactive approach as we use when teaching young children to talk and understand language.

(4) Develop some rules of good teaching for equines based on what we know about learning so that we may be able to begin to educate our equines. (See page 67)

(1) The meaning of terms

Here I discuss briefly only the most important and commonly used terms. Not all theorists will agree with all I say, but to avoid lengthy discussions, I have tried to extract a working understanding for the everyday equine owner and others who are interested.

(a) Stimulus and response

A 'stimulus' is something that arouses an activity (the 'response' of the subject). This can either be internal in the body (such as changes in hormones, heart rates, etc.) or external (such as doing something): but it will be related to the situation with which the responder is faced.

The stimulus can be 'unconditioned', that is, nothing (in relation to what is being learnt) has so far has been associated with it, or 'conditioned', that is, it has been linked to some outcome, that is reinforced (see below).

> Shindi, our yearling, comes into the ring for her first free-school lesson. She has never seen the whip before (unconditioned stimulus, U-S) and when it is raised behind her, makes no response. She is touched by the whip and leaps forward (unconditioned response, U-R). Next, she is asked to walk on with the voice,

an upright body and the whip raised behind her (conditioned stimulus, C-S), she leaps forward as the whip is raised (conditioned response, C-R). That is, in one trial she has learnt to go away from the whip (the reinforcement is to avoid being hit and frightened by it).

(b) Extinction, habituation and desensitisation

Gradually, if there is no reinforcement (see below), a conditioned response will occur less and less frequently, until it no longer occurs at all: this is called 'extinction'.

> Naive equines do not like having their legs touched or held firmly because, presumably, as prey animals if their leg is trapped, they will be much more likely to be caught by a predator. Consequently the normal response of a naive equine to having the leg touched by a human is to withdraw it. If he is frightened, trapped or hurt while his leg is being held, then he is confirmed in his tendency not to allow his legs to be touched or held. If, however, nothing nasty happens, or, even better, something nice happens (he is given a food reward when he allows his legs to be picked up and held) then his tendency to withdraw the leg will become extinct.

'Habituation' and 'desensitisation' are a type of extinction where there is a gradual decline in the strength of a response that has been learnt the more times the stimulus is presented.

> Police horses are habituated or desensitised to crowds, to traffic and bombs. Cavalry horses were habituated to the noise of guns.

> Horses that live where there are many low flying aircraft, or very near motorways, become habituated to aircraft flying nearby or constant traffic, respectively. Humans too become habituated to traffic noise; often people who are, find it difficult to sleep when there is none. The same may well be true of equines.

Habituation to a stimulus may require no remembering or processing of the stimulus, but equally, there are occasions on which it may.

> Humans or other animals may be habituated to a particularly loud noise. When the noise changes tone the subject's attention is aroused, because comparisons are made with the previous noise, and it is recognised as different. In other words, mental events have taken place to compare the noise, even though the individual may not be aware of doing so.

> Lack of habituation of many ridden horses to traffic is the cause of many accidents and behavioural problems. To become habituated to traffic, the equine must overcome his 'instinctive' tendency to flee (unconditioned response to fear). To

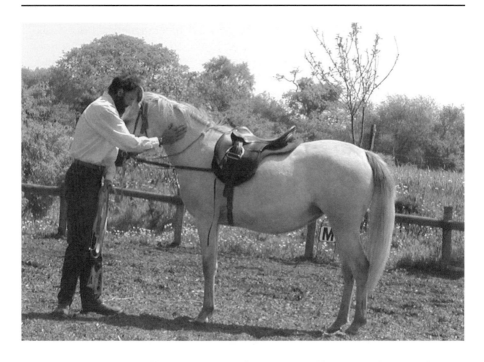

Chris rewarding Lilka: positive reinforcement, talking, touching, with a relaxed body and chuckling tone of voice.

do this, he has, initially, to be consciously aware of the object (see chapter 8) and of his own immediate response in order to be able to make a decision to change this, that is, *stop* himself from leaping away. After some repetitions (provided this behaviour has not been accompanied by some form of negative reinforcement: an unpleasant experience e.g. a fright or pain), standing still in traffic will not require a great deal of attention or decision-making. Here the equine is described as 'habituated' or 'desensitised' to the stimulus.

(c) Reinforcement

Reinforcement is the trigger that motivates (makes the individual do things) when behaviour has been 'conditioned' (pages 57, 58). It can be ' positive' (a reward) which will encourage the animal to do something for which he 'has an appetite'; or 'negative', that is to do something in order to avoid something aversive or unpleasant. When training equines, although **positive reinforcement** (food and other rewards) have sometimes been used, generally it is much neglected.

A horse moves about when someone is trying to mount. Instead of scolding him for moving, which will be a negative reinforcer and cause him to be more unsettled and consequently to move more, use positive reinforcement: reward him with some food and voice praise when he stands still. If he does not stand still all the time, do it again and again using the same approach until he does.

Remember, however, that you must always praise him *after* he has stood still when you have got on, and do not, initially, do it in difficult or scary places or he may not be able to resist moving around. A good idea is to give him a food reward and praise him before moving off. After a few trials he will have learnt by positive reinforcement to stand still and not to move off until he has had a food reward, and praise.

Equines are, unfortunately, today, more often trained by avoiding something nasty happening to him, that is **negative reinforcement.**

A naive horse is chased around in a round pen by a person throwing out a lunge line along the ground. The horse moves away from the lunge line in order to avoid being hit, and having an unpleasant or frightening experience: negative reinforcement used to get him to move away. If the lunge line continues to be thrown out after him, he may become so scared that instead of running forward, he rears up and tries to climb the side of the round pen. The wise approach at this stage is to stop throwing out the lunge line (stop the negative reinforcement). Failure to do this will result in the horse learning that the round pen is a scary place, and to try and get out of it or avoid going into it. This is not the lesson one is trying to teach.

There are also '**secondary reinforcers**'. A 'positive secondary reinforcer' will be praising the horse for doing the right thing because, in the first instance, he performed this act to get something he wanted: usually food. Then the food was paired with the voice saying particular things (e.g. 'good boy'). After several trials it is no longer necessary to give food, the word itself is reinforcing. In this case it is often the voice conveying not only the right word, but also a pleasant emotional response from the teacher: pleasure or approval. This speeds up learning because the equine responds to the teacher's emotional responses displayed by her body. Gestures and smiles can also become secondary reinforcers.

Traditional training of equines often does not emphasise how important it is to praise the horse for doing the right thing, it is often taken for granted, whereas the animal is scolded, or worse, for doing the wrong thing. This is one of the most important reasons why so many horses learn to do the wrong thing and thereafter have behavioural problems related to training.

A slightly different 'secondary reinforcer' which is becoming very fashionable is 'clicker training'.

Here, initially, the clicker is used at the same time as a food reward is given; after a time, the noise of the clicker itself becomes reinforcing (a secondary reinforcer). In order to encourage the animal (or it could be a human) to do something different or new, the clicker will be used as soon as he begins to do what is desired, until the final response is performed.

To get the donkey to walk across the stable and touch a bucket. Initially, the

Shemal putting her head down to a word and gesture.

clicker (which has already become a secondary reinforcer by being paired with a food reward) is clicked when he starts to move towards the object. Clicking continues as he moves towards it, but stops if he turns away. When he touches the object he will have to be given a food reward otherwise the reinforcing value of the clicker will gradually decline, it will become 'extinct'.

'Clicker training' has an important contribution to make to equine education for the beginner or someone who is confused about learning, and may otherwise end up with equines learning inappropriate responses. What 'clicker training' does is to train the teacher *to observe carefully, and respond appropriately.* If the clicker is clicked at the wrong time, or too late, then it will have a reinforcing value for a response that is *not* desired.

Learning to observe and act on observations when teaching equines is essential; if the teacher is having trouble with this, or making the wrong decisions when interpreting the student's behaviour, or having 'preconceived notions' (that is thinking that this animal is difficult, or stupid etc.) then a session or two with a clicker will help. However, the use of the clicker as an important training aid from the equine's (or dog's) point of view has disadvantages, which are:

(i) It is not possible to direct the student to what is required with the clicker. One might do this with gesture, with facial expression, and voice as well as using the clicker. If this is done, then what is the point of the clicker? Why not just concentrate on the appropriate use of the voice, gesture and facial expression without the clicker? A more useful lesson for the teacher that we use when running workshops is to have the teacher say 'yes' to the animal when he would be using the clicker. In this way, the teacher learns to observe, but the equine is also learning to listen to the voice and watch the teacher and interpret their emotion. In addition the teacher uses as many gestures as necessary to start with. Finally she can simply say 'go and touch the bucket' or whatever it is, without either gestures, clicker, or other physical restraints or aids, because the equine has learnt to listen to the voice. With the clicker this is not possible, all one can do is click or not click.

(ii) Another serious problem with the use of the clicker is that it tends to confirm the user in the belief that emotional interchange between the student and the teacher is unimportant, that learning, even operant or instrumental learning (see below) is just a sort of automatic series of responses without mental events taking place. This is an outdated approach that takes us back to the behaviourists. Skinner (a famous behaviourist) could eventually (using hundreds of trials) teach his rats to do a long series of agility acts or chickens to dance. He even maintained he could teach pigeons to fly aeroplanes or chimps to drive trains by clicker training-type conditioning.

The trouble with this 'clicker training' approach is that it is mechanistic; it denies the importance of any emotional input on the part of the teacher. The teacher is of no real importance, it could be a robot doing the teaching, which usually takes place in laboratories. The animal takes much longer to learn the desired response by this method than by listening to the voice and gesture. It also results in the subject going through a large repertoire, trying things out to see which one is right, which may be mildly amusing (although I find it distinctly distasteful).

It is very easy, in fact, *a lot easier* just to say to the animal, 'yes, yes, well done, good' when he does the right thing at the time one would use the clicker, and at the same time direct him with gesture (especially as horses use such a great deal of visual communication, as discussed in chapter 1) and particular words. Inevitably the voice and gestures will be used to direct the animal anyway, so the voice shows approval as a secondary reinforcer and the clicker is superfluous.

'**Partial Reinforcement**' is when the response is only reinforced some of the time. There are two characteristics of partial reinforcement:

(i) It tends to increase time to extinction. If the individual does not know if he is going to get a reward or not, he is more inclined to try rather than not to bother, particularly if he is working for a reward: positive reinforcement.

(ii) It increases the speed of learning new things because the outcome is not predictable. This may be one reason why with horses we can often get away with some very confusing teaching with fewer problems than one might expect; we have not reinforced actions because we have not noticed. Initially when teaching a new act to an equine it is important to motivate him to want to do it, consequently, continuous reinforcement is important. However, once he expects a reward, often it is sufficient *not* to give him a tit bit.

Shemal is learning the Spanish walk. To start with each time she lifts a leg she is rewarded with a tit bit and praise; after half a dozen times when she does it well, she is only rewarded with the voice, and finally she must do at least 10 strides correctly before she is rewarded even with the voice.

(d)'Delayed Reinforcement'

One of the characteristics of effective reinforcement is that it needs to follow the response immediately. If there is a delay before the reinforcement is acquired, then the subject will learn less fast.

In an equine learning workshop, the participants are asked to teach an equine a simple movement: to lift the left leg to a word command. They have 10 minutes in which to do this. They have been instructed to give the food reward as soon as the equine subject, initially at least, begins to lift a leg or even change his weight to the other leg. In one group, the person who has the cubes that are being used as the positive reinforcer keeps them in a pocket from which it is difficult to extract them. In each trial there is a delay of around 1 minute before the horse has his reward. After 10 minutes, the horse has more or less given up paying any attention, and does not perform the required response when asked at the final display. In another group, who had immediately given the food reward, the horse performs the response immediately when asked in the display.

(e) Punishment

This is when something unpleasant happens or is done to the individual *after* he has performed an act (a response) ... not at the same time. We all know about punishments in human education (a child being hit after he has run in the passage when he was supposed to walk, or criminals going to prison, that is, having their freedom taken away from them). We also know that the effects of punishment are more unpredictable than rewards for doing the right thing. In fact partly for humanitarian reasons, but also in order to improve learning, corporal punishment at school is now illegal in most European societies. It is less effective in improving learning than using rewards. But punishment is still very widely used when teaching horses.

If a horse shies or refuses a jump, he is whipped, rather than being rewarded when he does approach and praised when he *does* jump a jump, however small.

The use of punishment at the wrong time can result in the equine *learning to do the thing you are trying to teach him not to do.*

The horse spooks, he is kicked, shouted at and whipped to try and get him to approach the object he shied at. In this case the first thing to consider is why did he shy? Generally this is because he is excited and afraid. If you hit him or kick him as he looks at the object or shies, then you are negatively reinforcing him, that is, he is learning that the object he was slightly frightened of, is indeed, frightening and causes some pain or unpleasantness. If you hit or kick him after he has shied, he is also confirmed in his belief that the object *is* frightening, and consequently continues to try to escape. The more you do this, the more he learns to spook or shy.

The rider will often say that he cannot be frightened, he knows this place or object very well, and he is just being 'difficult'. He may indeed know the object or place very well because he has had similar experiences in the past there, that is unpleasant ones. It is often tempting to try and explain his behaviour in this way, but take a moment to let him stop and look, and 9 times out of 10, you will find he has a high heart rate and is unable to stand still, all evidence of something like fear and stress (page 23).

Consequently, the great majority of shying horses have been taught to shy by their unsuspecting riders! A little understanding of learning and thought can go a long way to help correct and avoid such problems.

A common explanation of why the horse is shying or spooking is that he is 'trying to get away with it', or 'trying the rider out'. This explanation must be examined with evidence *to see whether there is a simpler explanation* before you accept it. Suppose it were the case, then why would the horse bother to do anything with you, he is bigger and stronger and can avoid doing anything required when he really wants to. Why would he be trying to 'dominate' you and 'get away with it'? these are rather complex cognitive manipulative ways of interpreting a competitive world. This may be the way some humans view the world, but it is very unlikely to be the way that equines do from what we know of them today (see chapter 9 for further discussion).

Very often the equine is 'misbehaving' because he has been taught to by the human handlers and riders by inappropriate use of punishment, negative reinforcement and lack of reward for doing the right thing. Thus, in effect he has 'out done' you, but only because you taught him to do it, and he thought it was the right thing. The fact that you have taught him to do the wrong thing is hardly his fault! (see above example).

(f) Generalisation

In the real world, the stimulus is never identical each time. The horse can learn to respond, for example, to come when you call his name, even if each time you say his name, it is slightly different. Provided it is sufficiently similar to the word he has already learnt, he will come. This is called 'stimulus generalisation'. The closer the stimulus is to the one he already learnt, the more likely he is to respond. The more different, the less likely.

The relevance here, when teaching horses, is that initially, at least, it is important to be consistent with the stimulus; don't use different gestures or words to mean the same thing. This is something that we may often do without thought, even when teaching a child to talk. At least at the beginning of something new, it is important to *make things very clear and to be consistent*. After he has learnt what is required to one set of stimuli, it is possible to use 'generalisation' so that the same response will be performed to a variety of slightly different stimuli.

> In our experimental work we taught all the subjects to lift their right legs, to (i) a physical cue, (ii) a gesture, (iii) imitation and (iv) the voice saying 'lift your right leg'. Now they will do it to any one of these stimuli.

Equine and humans 'generalise' responses, and perform them with more or less speed and enthusiasm to different stimuli.

In this regard, consider, for a moment, how confusing one can be to an equine.

> The use of the arm and hand with equines. We put our arm and hand out when we want the horse to come up to us, or to touch him. But we also raise our arm and hand as a signal, sometimes accompanied by the whip to tell him to go away (in the free school for example). Now how is he to know when it means come here and when it means go away? You may think that you use many other gestures as well to make this clear, but if you video yourself one day, you will see how this is by no means always the case. It is again much easier to use the voice, paired initially with very obviously different gestures, postures and so on and then eventually, just the voice: 'come here' or 'go away'. There can be no confusion once he knows the words; they are too different to generalise — even if one's gestures and body movements are confusing.

Often a horse is blamed for what is in fact the human's inability and clumsiness. After a while of such confusion, he may give up responding at all unless things are very clear, and one may have to be rough; for example making a riding school horse (who has been kicked and pulled about daily, often for years) go forward will initially require some rough encouragement. However even an equine with years of such experiences can often relearn to respond quickly and easily when things are made clearer.

The human who does not understand how equines learn, often increases the strength of the stimulus.

> A horse does not stop or put his head in the right place. Different bits that hurt more, or pieces of leather to prevent movement such as martingales and drop nosebands to keep the horse's mouth shut, or spurs and whips to hurt him more are used to try and 'improve the response'. These are all negative reinforcers used because the horse has learnt *not* to respond in the required way, and it is, of course the teacher's fault, in one way or another.

(g) Shaping

Shaping can be called 'successive approximations'. This is what one does when one says, 'yes, yes, good boy' or clicks the clicker before the animal has performed the final response, but is starting to do what you are requesting. Thus, he is rewarded for an approximation to it. Gradually the reward is only earned by a closer and closer approximation. Shaping takes place in most of equine teaching.

Teaching a *piaffe* (trotting on the spot with the back legs well bent and an elevated stride). First, the horse has to learn to have his hind legs right under him, then to trot, gradually moving forwards and then less and less forwards until it is on the spot. The next set of 'approximations' are to ensure that he holds his head correctly without being held there. The next, to gradually increase how high he lifts particularly his hind legs, and then, to jump off the ground more so that the trot becomes more suspended, there is a split second when no legs are on the ground. Each of these stages must be taught one at a time successively, ' shaping' the movement. There is no way he will understand all the concepts involved in this movement at once, but he can if they are presented one by one, like a human learning algebra. Almost any equine can get there with good teaching, but not all will do it as well.

(h) Moulding

This is a type of shaping where the leg, or hand or whatever will be helped physically into the desired placing or movement. It is employed a great deal when teaching children, and primates to use AMSLAN (American Sign Language which is a gestural language used by the deaf and dumb).

Teaching an equine to stand with her front legs crossed. Shemal has learnt to lift her left leg when asked so she is asked to do this, and then she is asked to 'cross your leg' and the teacher places the left in front of the right leg and, initially, holds it there, while praising her vocally, and telling her: 'cross your legs'.

(i) Memory

How 'memory' works in the brain is not very well understood yet, but what is clear is that it is interwoven with perception, past experience and, possibly, imagination. In all types of learning where voluntary acts are performed, memory has to be involved. Retention of information or memory is now divided into 'short term memory' and long term memory. By remembering a series of recent events, decisions can be made on what to do next.

A zebra remembers the distribution of the *Acacia* trees at the edge of the water hole that he has frequented recently. As a result, he can dart through and around them to escape the cheetah chasing him.

A human remembering where she put down her book five minutes ago which she now wishes to read.

There is very little experimental empirical information on the extent of equines' short term memory, but we do have information on this from studies of the ecological and social knowledge they need to live as they do (see chapter 2).

Short term memory is very important when teaching equines.

The pony remembers when the reins were dropped onto the ground five minutes ago and he stood on the end of his rein as he tried to walk away, so he stands still this time.

'Shaping' Shemal's leg crossing. She has lifted her leg – but not yet placed it over the other, as her teacher has.

Equines have good long term memories, which can be stored, often for years. They can remember locations, food substances, individual horses and individual people, places and situations over many years. The importance of long term memory, the amount of information they need to remember and what this is in order for them to survive and live the way they do in wild or feral populations is outlined in detasil in *Equine Lore*. One thing is sure, that we do not need experiments to demonstrate this; we already know how profound their use of memory must be, because of the lives they live. Consequently it is no surprise to find that a mare recognises her daughter or son years after they have been parted, or that individual donkeys or horses will recognise humans who have been particularly unpleasant to them many years later.

Equines will remember particular unpleasant experiences all their lifetimes, and may require to be retaught, with care, before the undesirable response can be changed, even years after an event.

One winter's day we rode up onto Dartmoor, found one of the rivers was flooded, and decided to ride across a clapper bridge (a narrow bridge made of a large lumps of stone).Crystal was cautious but followed one of the older mares onto the bridge, but then looking down into the swirling water, panicked and fell off. We helped her out and she was not injured. However, she remembered this incident for years, and even generalised her memory so that she made a fuss before crossing any bridge thereafter. Eventually she unlearnt this experience, but it took us some serious re-teaching over two years of exposure to non dangerous bridges, accompanied only by positive reinforcement before she happily crossed bridges, even quite wide ones.

Memory is selective (one does not remember everything); there has to be some form of 'reflection'. Some events, situations, and behaviour of others are remembered, as a result of thinking about them.

Memories will be likely, in the first place, to be 'autobiographical': memories of what the subject has done, or what has been done to him and where he has been. After the establishment of an autobiographical memory, a biographical memory might develop; this involves a memory of what others have done or might have experienced. The social behaviour of equines indicates that these animals will have to have some form of biographical memory as they remember how another individual behaves.

Different species as well as individuals will remember different things. Sometimes individuals, even of different species, have similar experiences, at other times different ones. Sometimes this is the result of the combination of a selection of past experiences they have had or have witnessed, interwoven with previous information so that outcomes are predicted. This is what is called ' imagination' which is discussed more fully in *Equine Lore*.

(j) Motivation
This is the energy/will/emotion/need to do things. It is at the heart of learning, nothing can be learnt unless there is motivation to learn it. What motivation is, and how it works is a subject of deep debate at the present among scholars of learning and behaviour. Here all we will say is that motivation is necessary in some form for learning to take place, even if it only involves paying some attention. Motivation is most obviously important when understanding reinforcement: the motivation for learning to do something voluntarily is either to have pleasure as a result (positive reinforcement) or to avoid pain, fear, or displeasure (negative reinforcement).

This is not a textbook on learning theory, but because of the general belief that if you use jargon you know what you are talking about, the use of these sorts of terms often sounds grand and tends to give credence to certain statements, or methods employed with teaching equines without any proper explanation or understanding.

If in doubt, think how you might behave in that situation, or how you might try and get a child to do this or that: that is, use 'conditional anthropomorphism'.

You may never have to use any of these terms, but if you do, let us talk about the same thing or wires can get crossed, often with very unhelpful consequences, and it is usually the equines who are the losers.

The next stage is to identify the different types of learning, because there are a host of beliefs about them which cause confusion.

(2) Types of learning

(a) Avoidance learning

This is where an equine, or any other species, learns *not to do* something because it will hurt, give pain or problems of one sort or another. It is usually the result of negative reinforcement.

> The child learns not to put his hand in the flame of a candle because it hurts, the horse not to go through a gateway because it hurt last time when the human let it bang on his hips. The subject will then generalise this response to all candles or all gateways.

Many undesired behaviours in equines are of this type, but with thought, avoidance learning need not occur.

Avoidance learning can of course be useful too:

> A harness horse who learns to keep to the side of the road because he is hooted at when in the middle, and this frightens him, or an endurance horse in the western Isles of Scotland who learns to avoid falling into bogs by observing the vegetation where he places his feet.

Both humans and equines may use avoidance learning quite constructively much of their lives, but if they have a bad or traumatic experience, then they may develop a *phobia*, and devise elaborate strategies to avoid going to certain places, or doing certain things, even if the original frightening stimulus has long since been removed.

> A horse hurts himself when loading into a trailer. He develops a phobia about entering the trailer and becomes more and more hysterical the harder people try (using negative reinforcement, such as pulling him, ropes behind his legs, and noise and excitement) to make him enter.

What has to be done here is for him to unlearn his aversive conditioning, relearn slowly and quietly that all is well, and that going in can be pleasant. This may take many hours, *but is practically always possible*. Whether the human handlers will have the motivation and patience is another matter. What is important is not to try and frighten him into the vehicle, this will just enhance his fear of going in next time.

The halters presently being marketed which cause pain when the horse pulls back use avoidance learning. The problem is that once it has worked, the horse will often have other avoidance strategies either not to have the headcollar fitted or not to go into the trailer. His existing phobia has been re-enhanced, and he may be seriously traumatised.

Since equines are so easily frightened (see page 20), the problem is to stop them 'learning to avoid' the things you would like them to do, or the places you would like them to go.

(b) Reversal learning or 'unlearning'

This occurs when some response which has been learnt (and may even have become habitual) is reversed: the human or other animal learns to do something different, sometimes the opposite.

> A young horse has learnt, by instrumental conditioning (see below) to rear (stand on his hind legs) when the rider gets on. The *reinforcement* for rearing was that the rider fell off, or got off, and he was put back in the stable (which he preferred, as he had unpleasant and frightening experiences when he had been ridden out). He now needs to learn (be taught) *not* to do this when the rider mounts.

The first thing is that the people handling and riding him must not be frightened. A team approach is useful here, where at least one person who is not frightened at all is there, reassuring the horse. It is important to be relaxed and to have 'bonded' with the horse, that means to like the horse, and both of you recognise each other and have some confidence in each other. A mounting block and someone to talk to him and reward him to start with is also useful. But finally, the job is to teach him that being ridden is pleasurable rather than scary; that it does not involve fear, roughness, and general misery all around. First, the re-teaching is made pleasant by giving him food, pleasant tactile attention, and reward to remove the fear. He is praised and rewarded with food when he remains relaxed. Gradually over several trials, mounting is started. Each time he is rewarded with food and then returned to the stable before the rider has completely got on. This continues, until he stands all the time while being fed, and mounted. Gradually over the next couple of weeks, the food is withdrawn but verbal praise continues, and slowly, moving forward a step at a time, the goal (him standing still while being mounted) is achieved with voice praise. Eventually, movement around the yard following another horse is possible while keeping him relaxed and calm. After that, movement away from the stable can begin, again with another horse. There may be progress one day, and retrogressive steps the next, but he never goes back to his stable until he has remained relaxed even if this is only while someone stands beside him. The speed at which one progresses must be common sense, but the central idea is to rebuild his confidence in the exercise. The voice is invaluable here to help the horse relax, provided, of course, that he is already familiar with its use. When he does not rear, then he must be praised and rewarded.

Shouting at him, jagging his mouth, putting on more and more restraints will

only confirm him in his worry and fear. Force does not work very often because:
(i)   The horse is stronger than you are,
(ii) Someone may get injured,
(iii) It will re-establish the problem.
(iv) Anyone who is nervous should be sent off to make lunch, because they may, by their body language, frighten the horse further.

(c) Habit formation

After the initial learning process, **habit** can become an important component of learnt behaviour, and can obliterate the conscious processes. Once a more or less satisfactory way of doing something, or even thinking about things is established, it tends to be repeated in the same way. The more it is repeated, the more it becomes resistant to change. Some species and individuals acquire habits more easily than others. Equines acquire habits very rapidly which would seem to be a sensible strategy for a prey species. Trying a new series of actions might fail, and the subject would be caught by the predator. Consequently one would expect habits to form quickly in prey species and this tendency to be selected for, up to a point.

> When a horse is being free-schooled or lunged, he sees something suspicious at one point on the circle, and cuts in at that point. This is a voluntary action, the goal is to avoid the frightening object or event. The next time around, he is very likely to do it again, even though he has had no reinforcement to encourage this behaviour (has not been frightened) and he may well repeat this every time he trots around at the same place, even when the strange object has disappeared.

The way to change this habit is to:
(i) Remove the stimulus that started it first, if possible. If not, take the equine up to it and let him investigate it slowly and quietly, and wait until he approaches it by himself before allowing him to move off.
(ii) Walk him past the place on the ring 4 or 5 times on both reins. Praise him with the voice, and give him a tit bit when he does not jump or comes in less on the circle.
(iii) When he is walking past easily and quietly every time, start free school or lunging him past it. If he comes in, say 'no' and frown. Predict that he might do this, and raise your whip as he comes near that place on the circle.
(iv) Always praise him when he goes quietly past it until he has done it properly at least 8-10 times.

Strong habits are common in humans too: try cleaning your teeth, or getting out of the bath and drying yourself a slightly different way from normal. It is difficult. Unless there are very important reasons to change the habit (such as having an injured arm, for example), the old way of doing it will constantly be reintroduced. In this way, habits tend to inhibit innovation.

Because equines form habits quickly, bad habits can also be formed quickly, but let us not forget how many good habits are formed very rapidly too. Without this quick habit formation, we would find it much more difficult to look after and teach equines.

'Habits of mind' (forming mental habits) are also very important for understanding an individual human or a horse (discussed in *Equine Lore*).

(d) Imprinting

In order to survive, a foal must quickly learn to find a teat and suck some milk. To do this, he must rapidly learn who mother is. The term 'imprinting' was invented to outline this early learning which consists of the new-born having an innate tendency to go up to and follow moving objects. The usual first object is the parent, the mother in the case of equines, who is approached. The new-born then searches for a teat, and if he finds one and receives a milk reward, he learns rapidly to discriminate her from other mothers by using all his senses: vision, hearing, touching, smelling and tasting, and to stay close to her, follow and suckle her thereafter (see picture opposite).

In the earlier days of ethology, much was made of imprinting as a particular type of learning (e.g. Lorenz); however, it has since been demonstrated that **imprinting involves rapid association learning**, although it does have one particular characteristic. There is a 'critical period' after birth during which it is likely to take place. This in equines appears to be up to 24 hours *post partum*.

Originally, it was also considered that, unlike other types of learning, imprinting was irreversible. But this has now been shown not to be true.

> If the foal has imprinted on its mother, and then the mother dies or disappears, the foal can adopt another mare as its mother, although this may need some encouragement, skilful handling by humans if they are involved, and 're-learning' of the infant.

'Imprinting' a foal on humans has become a popular idea. Be warned, however, there can be many problems attached. A number of youngsters have been brought to us with behavioural problems; an attempt had been to imprint them on humans. Miller's idea was that if humans handle the foal very early in his life, that is, within the first hour if possible, the foal will 'imprint' on humans and not be afraid of them in the future, because, he erroneously maintained, imprinting is not reversible and imprinted experiences are not forgotten.

One of the dangers of interfering with the foal very early in life is that it interrupts the development of the relationship with the mother. This can cause considerable problems for both the foal and the mother. There are, in addition, many examples where the foal handled immediately after birth and therefore supposed to be 'imprinted' on humans does *not* behave differently towards humans from others who have been handled for the first time later in their lives, illustrating that imprinting is reversible.

Learning about humans is better done gradually by the foal associating with a sympathetic non-frightening human after he has already established his relationship with his mother, is feeding well and has been exposed to other equines. This is

Imprinting: Shereen with day-old Shindi following, all joints and legs. Shindi learning who mother is and to follow her. Shereen learning who Shindi is. The first step here is probably that she smells of herself when she is born.

some days after birth.

A week or so after birth, if you have the time and inclination, it is a good idea to begin to familiarise him with humans by fondling, handling and talking to him for short periods, as frequently as you like. Remember, equines, like humans, continue to learn throughout life, although the speed at which they can acquire information tends to reduce with age. Consequently, early familiarisation of the foal with humans and even starting to learn not only about humans, but with humans is a very good idea, if the foal is healthy, and all is well with his relationship with mother and learning about other equines. The handling must be done well though, or he will learn to avoid humans rather than have much to do with them (see Kiley-Worthington 2003, chapter 5).

> Druimghigha Osnan was handled all over (non invasively) for two hours immediately after birth, stroked, talked to and rubbed. Although for the next two days he approached a human when the human approached him in the field, and continued to be stroked, after three days he became wary, and only after handling his mother for 10 minutes would it be possible to touch him without his withdrawing. His handling continued for 5-10 minute sessions every other day for the next 3 weeks. By the end of this period he was familiar enough to come up and investigate and be stroked.

Thus, Osnan had to learn and become familiar with the humans even though he had been handled shortly after birth and had never had a rough experience with humans. During the summer we were too busy to handle him regularly. When the winter came and we had more time, he was as cautious as any of the unhandled foals with humans to begin with. Once he had begun to eat from the hand and a bucket, he rapidly progressed.

Two colt foals born within 1 week of each other to the same father (Oryx) : one, Liloni, was handled at birth The other, Shenandoah, was not handled for 15 hours after birth. Two months later, although both foals had been handled for 5 minutes a day, Liloni is much more wary than Shenandoah, although she should have been 'imprinted' on humans.

Two related foals, by Oberlix out of two half sisters, were born at the Druimghigha stud in 2000. One was gently, non-invasively handled at birth by humans; she was stroked, rubbed, patted all over the body, and exposed to the smell and sight of the handler leaning over her, and touching her. The other foal, born within two weeks of the first one, was not handled at all for the first three months of his life. When his mother was inspected or moved from field to field, he was never touched, and no effort made to handle touch or manipulate him in any way.

At three months old, the two foals were bought into the barn with their mothers, and the handling proceeded as normal. That is, the foal was gently touched when he was near his mother, and rubbed as he became familiar with this, while rubbing and brushing the mother. Whenever the foal avoided the contact, the handler returned to handling the mother, and waited until he came to her. The first session was 30 minutes. This was repeated for 10 minutes for 3 days, during which time a headcollar was fitted on each foal. They were then handled all over and their feet picked up. There was not significant difference in the behaviour of either of these foals. If anything, the foal that had not been handled at all at birth was a little more relaxed with being handled all over by the handler. The same handler (the one who handled the first foal from birth) was used for both foals to avoid there being a difference in the way they were handled.

'Mis-mothering' is a type of 'mal-imprinting' when things go wrong in early learning between the foal and the mother:

Druimghigha Baksheesh was the first foal of his mother and was born in a stable. Although after an hour he was standing and attempting to suckle, his mother had sore teats, was young and inexperienced, and kicked out as he tried to grasp the teat. Within another 2 hours he had learnt not to try and suckle her, and was suckling a bar in the stable. After expressing some of her milk which was causing the pressure in her udder and increasing the soreness of her teats, she was then held and fed food, while someone else manipulated the foal onto her teats. This was continued every 3 hours for the next 12 hours, by which time, the pressure in her udder had been reduced, he had learnt where to suckle, and she to allow him to. Thereafter things progressed without our interference.

Baksheesh became an easy stallion who was relaxed with humans and took part in almost every type of equine activity. Nevertheless, we have no evidence that this was related to his handling at this early stage as he was quietly handled fairly regularly as he grew up in his first summer.

Mal-imprinting describes the imprinting of one species on another, usually as a result of the infant being bottle reared or suckled by a mother substitute of another species. After this, the individual will preferentially associate with the other species, rather than his own kind, and even direct his sexual behaviour towards them when he matures. This can be embarrassing, or dangerous, and it is important to ensure that young equines, particularly hand reared or orphan foals, do not become 'mal-imprinted' onto humans.

A friend of mine in Kenya brought up a young orphan giraffe on a bottle. When, after a year, he was 12 ft tall, he started to direct play sex behaviour: mounting, neck twisting and turning, around my 5 ft friend! When you have a 12 ft giraffe jumping on top of you and trying to embrace you with his long neck around your body, you begin to wonder if raising him was such a good idea.

One year we placed duck eggs under a bantam. The mother bantam looked after the ducklings with all her considerable skill, but one thing she found extremely agitating is when they paddled off into the pond. She would run back and forth screaming and panicking, as their yellow forms bobbed happily out on the muddy broth.

There are many examples of bottle reared equines who become serious problems to humans, again because horse play is rough play. Remember it is very rarely aggressive, just over exuberant affection from a rather larger mammal, and the fault of the rearer. It is very important if hand rearing a foal to ensure that he also has contact with other equines for the majority of the time.

(e) Pavlovian learning

This is the conversion of an unconditioned stimulus and response to a conditioned one as a result of reinforcement (see above).

Pavlovian conditioning has often been taken *not* to involve the subject's voluntary participation, although the messages do pass through the brain. The classic example is Pavlov's dogs who were conditioned (i. e. they learnt) to salivate when they heard a gong. However, when the dogs were released from the experimental restraint, it became clear that they were 'expecting' food as well as salivating. To behave as if they 'expect' necessarily involves some form of awareness: it is not a kind of 'reflex'. Thus, this example of classical conditioning involved some form of mental awareness or conscious control, of expectations and decision-making, just as habituation does.

A better example of this type of conditioning which is *not* under voluntary control, is eye blinking when a gong is sounded because the human or animal has previously been presented with a strong light accompanying the gong. Here there is a physiological response of the eye to blink to protect itself, and neither humans nor equines can voluntarily control this. However, they *all* can learn *not* to blink the eye voluntarily on other occasions by instrumental conditioning.

(f) Instrumental or operant conditioning

This is defined as conditioned learning where the subject does something voluntarily, and the behaviour is thus under some conscious control. Instrumental conditioning is goal directed and the subject decides either to do it or not. The instrumental behaviour is the means to achieve the goal (the reinforcement). This type of learning is common in humans and other mammals, and is used when learning to perform any particular movement. It is the most important type of learning used in teaching both equines and humans. By definition, instrumental conditioning involves a series of mental events.

> On page 61, Shemal imitates me, placing her right leg on the pedestal. The conditioned stimulus is Marthe's leg movement, she performs conditioned response and receives a verbal reward (the goal). But she *chooses* to do this. It is voluntary.

Once voluntary actions have been learnt, then the individual who has learned has some idea of cause and effect. So they *believe* tightening the rope is unpleasant, they *remember* what happened last time they tried, and *decide* to follow. The *goal* is to avoid being frightened or hurt.

Learning does not stop there, however: secondary reinforcements, generalisation, habituation, extinction and all the other things we have discussed can modify what has been learned, and result in different behaviours being performed – or things can be unlearned.

One area of possible confusion here is that instrumental learning (otherwise called 'operant conditioning') can become 'automatic' so that it does not need direct attention.

Examples of this type of learning are – for humans, such things as the ability to ride a bicycle, or drive a car. An example for a horse might be the response to the riding aids. Although these behaviours have been instrumentally conditioned, and have therefore required voluntary decision-making by the learner, thereafter they can be performed without this conscious decision making as a result of becoming **habitual:** well practised and performed without attention.

But, if there is a problem with the response for some reason, the conscious attention will be redirected to the doing of the action.

> When driving your car and thinking about your latest boyfriend you are dangerously overtaken near a corner – your attention is immediately directed away from your thoughts to your driving, which previously had been on auto-pilot.

Zanape having one of his first leading lessons with Chris in Zimbabwe. He has followed Chris for 100 metres and is now allowed a snack. This is three days after he was captured and brought into an enclosure.

A horse pulling a milk cart around a well known route stops and starts at the appropriate houses in an automatic way, 'without thinking about it'; but if the road is obstructed by a lorry, which has to be negotiated, the well known route is bought back into conscious control, he becomes aware of where he is on it, and where to stop next after negotiating the problem.

I am stressing this here as people tend to assume that animals are very different from humans when they learn to do things in what seems to be an 'automatic' way. But in fact humans do the same.

(g) Associative learning

This is S-S (stimulus – stimulus) learning rather than S-R (stimulus – response); it involves associating one object, or situation with another, without the observer making any response. This involves causal links, that is some understanding of cause and effect, in other words, there has to be a recognition of an association of *this* object with *that* situation or object.

In the winter, our horses are kept in yards where they can come and go to the field. In the morning some of them (the young, the pregnant, the old, and those working hard) are given a small feed with some minerals in it. The feeds are made up in the food store, in view of the horses from the yard, and then presented in buckets. When they see me coming out in the morning, they all call, and stare at me over the rails, that is, they have an expectation of having their food(S) and they associate me with giving it to them (S-S).

These associations may be formed without any consciousness; but when necessary, the association *can* be brought to the conscious attention such as when (as a result of making an association) voluntary acts are performed.

Oberlix is tied up outside the tack room as usual before working. He is aware that he will be doing some form of exercise at this time and will be tacked up accordingly. He sees the collar being prepared and sighs. It is put on and he moves off quietly to the garden to do some hard work pulling a spring tyne cultivator. He returns and we untack him. Next we bring out the small racing saddle, he perks up, looks at the saddle and begins to jink about as it is fitted. Here, he has made an association between:
(i) Being kept outside the tack room at that time and going to do some work.
(ii) The harness and hard slow work in the garden which requires pulling and walking only, that is, going quietly and slowly.
(iii) The small racing saddle which requires short bursts of fast work.
He has already done some hard work quietly, so it is not that he is just excited to be doing anything, he 'understands' that the small saddle means fast exciting work. He demonstrates this by the difference in his behaviour associated with the different tack.

Equines are particularly good at association learning, but it can take some analysis of what is and has happened to that animal before the range of associations can be disentangled. It may not be just stimulus-stimulus, but may be stimulus-stimulus-stimulus-stimulus and so on.

(h) Observational learning, social learning and culture
Observational learning is a type of association learning and involves the ability of an animal to acquire information or skills by observing. This can be watching events, even those not involving other equines.

Equines have to grasp simple physical principles, like gravity, for example. Shemal hears a noise on the roof, looks up and sees a tile slipping. She leaps away, knowing that the tile will fall down and if she stays where she is it may hit her.

Equines often observe things in the natural environment which give them information on where to go or what to do. For example, if they observe a land slide or a rock fall in one area, they will be very cautious of visiting it even days or weeks later.

More commonly observational learning is used when one equine is watching another and learns something from this. This type of observational learning is

Operant conditioning by imitation. Shemal voluntarily places her right foot on the pedestal, imitating me.

called 'social learning'. It is extremely important in a social mammal, as much information necessary to survival can be acquired by observing others, for example, how to behave in certain unfamiliar situations, where to go, what to eat and so on (see chapter 5 & 7).

Druimghigha Shereen's mother was called Sheba who, when we bought her, aged 18, was difficult to catch, particularly for the students. Shereen learnt the same behaviour from observing her mother, although she had never had any worse experience as a result of being caught than any of the other horses we have bred and owned, and all of them have been easy to catch.

This ability has often been harnessed by humans to help equines learn:

To familiarise a horse to do draught work on the land (or many other things) an experienced horse will be used while the youngster walks beside and watches. One equine will often follow another; having one equine who is familiar with the routine will make a great difference to how easy it is to get the rest used to it or enter a certain place. The follower, by observation and association, has learnt that nothing terrible happens.

Social learning gives rise to differences in behaviour between populations, this is called 'culture'. There is now much evidence that animal societies, including equines, have different 'cultures' just as humans have (e.g. Bonner, and *Equine Lore*).

Shereen has had 5 foals, all of whom learnt from her to be difficult to catch when they were with her. So we take them away at 9 months and put them with some of the other older mares and stallions who are easy to catch. These youngsters then learn the 'approach humans and be friendly' culture, rather than the 'keep away when the humans have a headcollar' culture.

On the stud we do not like horses with bad manners, such as stepping on one's foot, barging through gates, kicking or biting a human or another horse when a human might get hurt by being in the way. We taught the first youngsters these simple manners with care. However, four generations later, we find we hardly have to teach the new youngsters, they appear to learn how they behave in relation to humans from their elders: a 'culture' has been established.

Each yard /stable/stud which has had some residents for at least a 10 year period will have its own 'culture', the result of (i) the behaviour of the humans, (ii) the humans' expectations of the other horses, and (iii) the horses' expectations of the humans: all of this is social learning from their own and other species. It is worthwhile taking the trouble to understand that social learning is likely; it will help with understanding the horse's point of view, enable you to establish the equine culture you would like, and, of course, help to educate him.

Proving whether or not different species learn by observation and social learning is a current vogue in ethology. Having some empirical results here is interesting, and particularly finding out the limits of what can be learnt in this way; but really we can deduce that social learning must take place or their societies would not work. Equines learn much by observing what happens to others, as we know.

But what is particularly interesting is that social learning also works between species: between people and equines. People learn to behave in different ways as a result of their contact with different equines, and different equines behave in different ways as a result of their observation and contact with different people.

(i) Imitation

A particular case of observational learning is imitation: learning to do something novel by copying another. Imitation has been much discussed among those interested in animal minds because of its relevance to whether or not various species have an awareness of themselves (true imitation, rather than just imitating as a result of learning to do this by instrumental learning. Records are only just beginning to be kept of true cases of imitation in equines. Here is one.

Shindi (middle) *learning what to eat by observing Shemal* (left) *and Lilka - social learning.*

One day when I was showing a scientist around, we went into the field where Shemal (one of the experimental subjects we had been studying learning with) and Shukrune (a yearling gelding at the time) were living. I asked Shemal, verbally, to paw when she came up to me. She did, but, most surprisingly, seeing her paw, Shukrune also did it. Shemal had been taught to do this, but Shukrune had had no teaching at all of this type. It was out of context, since he had no expectation of a reward and was not frustrated (when pawing takes place naturally) and he was performing a novel act by imitating his elder sister.

The subjects of our studies learnt to perform leg lifts, head shakes, head up and down, to paw, and many other behaviours partly by imitating the teacher. At the beginning of the research programme I would perform the act I was asking for, as one does when teaching a child, for example, and found that this was a helpful teaching aid, together with gestures and verbal command. As a result we used imitation to help with the teaching. The interesting thing here is that the subjects were learning to imitate, not just another horse, but a similar movement made by another species. This means they had to be aware of what bits of my body were equivalent to theirs. This does imply a considerable amount of self awareness; I had not heard of it being reported for equines before. I will discuss the implications of this more fully in chapter 8.

(j) Trial and error learning

Thorpe places this in a different category of learning because it combines both associative learning and instrumental learning, or operant conditioning. He defines it as: 'the development of an association, as the result of reinforcement ... between a stimulus or a situation and an ... action'.

The classic examples of trial and error learning are rats learning to run mazes or to open problem boxes. Rather than a stimulus leading to a particular response (S-R) as an explanation for learning a maze, a simpler explanation could be in terms of the animal having what is called a 'cognitive map'. This implies some form of understanding of 'what leads to what', and the need for some form of conscious involvement by decision taking and memorising .

A donkey is presented with a box with a lid on it in which there is some relished food. Only by pressing a button on the right side of it will he be able to open the box. He pushes it with his nose, attempts to lift the lid with his prehensile upper lip, unsuccessfully. Finally he pushes and bashes the box so hard that it breaks. He eats the food. The next time he is presented with the box, he immediately breaks it and eats the food. He has learnt by trial and error to break the box, which was not the intention of the experimenter!

(k) Cognitive and silent learning

This is a type of associative S-S (stimulus–stimulus) learning which allows information about the world to be acquired. As an individual travels through the world, he notices things in it. This may be done by directing conscious attention of those objects or just by picking up cues about objects and their places in the world. There is a recognition of objects, shapes, places, species and individuals without any stimulus attached to any particular response and without any immediate reinforcement. Silent learning is often involved particularly in route finding, cognitive maps and ecological knowledge.

Some maintain that cognitive learning is a different, more complex type of 'reflective learning' than association learning, but, as we have emphasised, the boundaries between each type of learning are moveable, one drifting into another.

A zebra, walking on her familiar way to the water hole, sees a peculiar shaped Acacia tree with a' rock' at its base. That evening as she walks back towards the centre of her home range with her family, the 'rock' has disappeared. She snorts, ears pricked towards the tree, showing a recognition that it is different.

The stallion Oberlix has previously once been ridden over part of the island of Mull to the other side, a distance of some 15 miles over which there is no marked trail. Two years later he is ridden over the same route and allowed to choose the way. He follows almost exactly the same route as before, even remembering a particular stream crossing which we had had to choose carefully the first time.

Shemal has learnt to kick the football forwards. Here she has kicked it, and is following it up to kick it again. She has an understanding that 'kicking leads to movement and therefore following the ball.'

(l) Insightful learning

That an animal can solve a problem by understanding the problem and resolving it was first shown by chimpanzees in a classic experiment designed by Wolfgang Kohler. He placed the chimps in an area where there were some hanging bananas that they could not reach by jumping, and some pieces of furniture. They solved the problem by 'insight', having some idea (i) of the problem (can't reach the bananas), and (ii) its solution (pile the furniture underneath until they can be reached). None of the other types of learning was used. Previously, it was considered that only humans would be able to do this.

> A young stallion can understand a problem and behave in a way to avoid it. He must ensure that he is not attacked by an older one when they are living together. He has to make clear:-
> (i) That he is not a threat to the other stallion even though he may be a post pubertal male.
> (ii) He is not sexually attracted to the stallion.
> (iii) He must never show he is attracted to any of the mares and behave sexually to them when he can be seen by the other stallion.
> He may manage all this; since when he sees that the stallion is boiling up to try and attack and chase him away, he behaves like a much younger colt, and manages to reassure him that he is no threat, 'champing' and squatting. In this way he may be able to continue to live with his family group. He may even occasionally copulate with one of the mares, provided the stallion does not see.

When riding on Dartmoor we had a two-year-old gelding, Druimghigha Shirac (now an international endurance horse), running loose with the three mares and a stallion whom we were riding. We rode across a clapper bridge over a deep small river. The youngster had been left behind as we came to the bridge because he was grazing. He came rushing to catch us up, but went past the bridge along the wrong edge of the ditch. After 300 metres of following the ditch on the other side, the rest of the party turned away from it. Shirac neighed and became frustrated rushing up and down the ditch. Instead of turning back, we left him to it. After around two minutes, suddenly he turned and galloped 300 metres back away from us to the bridge, came across and joined us. He had apparently had a flash of 'insight' of how to solve the problem.

Sometimes it is difficult for us to leave the equines to try and solve the problem themselves, and it may well be that the motivation has to be very high before they do have these flashes of 'insight', but of course in the wild situation, there is no human there to help them out; perhaps it becomes quite common, at least in some individuals. Possibly we keep our horses in a state of such protection that their intelligence is not used.

Insight learning has been neglected when considering equines and what they may be able to do mentally. But we must be very cautious not to jump to conclusions when there may be simpler explanations. I would not say that equines use 'insight learning' a great deal, but I certainly would not say they *cannot* solve problems in this way.

There are, of course, a number of controversies among learning theorists concerning all this; I have tried to be accurate but simple. The main controversy is the degree to which these types of learning may require mental events and what these are. Are non human mammals, in this case equines, conscious or not, and if so, when? Many people have argued that consciousness does not need to be involved in learning so equines are not conscious. But the main type of learning that we use in teaching – whether children or equines – is instrumental conditioning, which involves conscious decision-making, because it involves voluntary action. The individual has a choice to do something, or not do it. If your equine demonstrates choices (if he decides *not* to do something, for example, to run out at a jump, rather than jump it), then he has some awareness of the environment and what he is doing within it.

Another important point I would like to emphasise is that even though we have compartmentalised these types of learning, it is very important to realise that learning is generally not so simply compartmentalised, that all types of learning are occurring simultaneously in most situations, although one or other may be most important at any one time.

Shemal is having one of her lessons in learning to kick a ball when she is asked. First, it is crucial to obtain her attention, this may not always be easy as she is going to be aware of her environment and absorbing information from all around her all the time. For example, the sparrows in the barn are making a racket as usual, and she is clearly aware of them; when there is an obvious change in the noise, she reacts; at the same time, Chris is about to go and turn the hay with the tractor that is parked outside the ring, but first he has to fix new blades on the mower, so she is aware, and to some extent watching him (silent learning) at the same time as listening to me trying to teach her by instrumental learning. She kicks up some dust when she kicks the ball, and after a couple of times, as she kicks the ball, she shuts her eyes and turns her head away (Pavlovian conditioning).

To start with I kick the ball and say, 'Kick the ball,' she watches me kick the ball, and then has a go (imitation); she has also been watching Oberlix just before kicking the ball (social and observational learning). After a few trials all I have to say is, 'Kick the ball,' without gesture and she goes to the ball and kicks it (association learning). Then I say, ' Kick the ball to me,' and when it comes somewhere in my direction, I praise and reward her. After another five tries, she has more or less got the meaning of, 'Kick the ball to me,' rather than just kick it randomly anywhere (further association learning of direction). She listens to my words, and the emotion involved in them, and, although she would like to follow her sister, Shindi, who is being led back to the field, she continues to remain calm and get on with the work required (cultural learning).

There are some basic rules of learning despite this.

(1) There has to be motivation, that is, an awareness or a need/want/desire: a feeling or wish to respond appropriately. Learning thus has to involve emotions or feelings.

(2) There must be directed attention. Attention by definition involves some form of awareness and recognition of objects or situations.

(3) In the case, particularly, of voluntary behaviour, there are decisions to be made: to do this, to do that, or to do nothing.

(4) During learning, the behaviour may be modified by experience, thus there must be experience.

(5) Experiences in their turn require perception (things to be perceived), and analysis, things to be ordered and related to others in some sense.

(6) Some form of personal feeling results, in other words some form of 'conscious memory'.

Although some forms of learning may be induced without any conscious involvement of the mind (by Pavlovian conditioning for example), most learning requires **memory**. Some learning will be done at a conscious, decision-making level, but may afterwards be transferred to a less conscious level from which responses, even quite complex ones (such as performing a dance routine for a horse, or typing for a human), can be performed in an automatic way.

These are general rules of learning which apply to all species, including of course humans, and they do not depend on obtaining information from others through language, although language may help the acquisition of more information about the past or the future. There are clear individual differences in behaviour both between species and within one species. This is due to the different sensory information they acquire and different physical, emotional and cognitive experiences they have. There are differences in the use different species make of these different types of learning; even different individuals of the same species vary.

We do not have enough information yet on what equines can and cannot learn because, to date, the question has not been seriously asked.

One thing is clear: learning inevitably involves the *interplay of the physical, emotional and cognitive worlds of an individual, and a recognition of the causal links between events.*

How can we apply this information to our dealings with equines? And will it enable us to understand them better? In the first instance, we should now be better aware of why an individual may be doing something unexpected at any time. Using this information, we can formulate some general rules for teaching our equines.

GENERAL RULES FOR TEACHING AND LEARNING

(1) Ensure you have the attention of the pupil.

(2) Ensure that the situation is conducive to doing whatever is required.

(3) Use positive reinforcement rather than negative: it is more effective in motivating the pupil to do it willingly and with good humour.

(4) Do not use punishment, its results are unpredictable.

(5) Be clear and simple with the conditioned stimulus (the 'aid', see page 57).

(6) Be consistent.

(7) Use less of the conditioned stimulus as time progresses, and ensure associations, e.g. a gesture with a voice command over time.

(8) Use the voice. Both equines and pre-verbal children can understand a considerable amount of language. Language is much easier for us humans to use; its use is clearer and relatively more subtle than gestures, smells or even touch.

(9) Adjust your teaching to the individual.

(10) Do not underestimate the equine's speed of learning, or his ability to learn complex series of actions, or even concepts.

(11) Be aware that the equine is aware and learning about the world around him, as well as the event that you are concentrating on, and build this knowledge into your teaching.

(12) Be innovative and creative in your teaching.

Knowing or learning 'that' and 'how'

Ryle, a philosopher of mind, made an important contribution to the understanding of how knowledge is acquired, or learning, which is relevant here. He divided the task into two phases or types of learning. The first one is to learn 'that' or 'what to do' and the second is to learn the 'how'. Ryle's classic example illustrates this point: a human riding a bicycle. You may know that bicycles are for riding: 'that'. But can you ride one? Do you know 'how', the practical side of how to do it?

Teaching a more complex movement to a horse, the Spanish walk. The front legs are to be thrown up in an exaggerated way forwards one after the other, and the hind legs follow as he walks forward. Now the equine may quickly learn 'that' with the appropriate words and gestures, including imitation and watching others, he knows he has to lift his front legs right up as he walks. But can he do it? What usually happens is the novice horse finds it difficult to do in sequence while continuing to move forward; the hind legs keep getting left behind! This demonstrates learning 'that' for a horse is one thing, but learning 'how' to do it is another.

An understanding of this distinction can be very helpful when teaching equines. Generally, he will not manage the 'that' and the 'how' all at once, any more than a human will. He will have to learn 'that' first, followed by 'how'. If one takes account of this and structures the teaching to allow for this, praising when first the 'that' and then the 'how' is acquired, rather than just being disappointed that it is not happening right, it makes a great difference to what can be learnt and how fast it is learnt, it helps greatly with the 'shaping' of the response (page 48).

Recently Oberlix has been doing advanced dressage tests. In his learning of the various movements and how they are to be done, I omitted to teach him the 'that' of lateral movements: that is, 'go sideways, and cross your legs ', thinking (as most are taught) that this would just come out of other exercises. His low marks and the judges' comments brought this to my attention. Thus, we did exercises going sideways, almost anyhow, but without going forwards (learning 'that') so that he grasped the concept of the movement ('go sideways and cross your legs'). The next step was the 'how' the movement had to be done for this discipline. This requires that the horse bends in the direction of movement, keeps going forward as well as crossing his legs and not leaving his quarters behind. Once he had the concept of 'go sideways', it was relatively easy to teach him the rest, although we do not always do it very well of course! This learning took three sessions not three months or years.

With equines, though, there is a third type of distinction to be made. This is 'knowing that and how, but not feeling like doing it'. Equines do not always tell us in an unambiguous way (like humans may) that they do not want to do something. So it is sometimes difficult to understand whether they have understood 'that' and 'how', but just don't feel like doing it or if they just have not understood. The only way out of this is to try to increase their motivation. Sometimes stopping, having a break and doing something different is useful; sometimes rather harsher methods involving negative reinforcement for being idle, which, in my view should be avoided if possible. Many of the old masters of equitation suggest that the best reward for a horse is to get off and take him back to the stable. This is a sad reflection on their teaching. Despite the teacher's efforts, the equine *still* does not like doing whatever it is, presumably because he was taught mainly by negative reinforcement (whips and spurs and pulls in the mouth). If you have to reward him in this way, in other words he dislikes doing it and consequently the reward is to stop, it cannot be co-operative teaching.

There are by contrast many horses who get frustrated and excited when asked to do things they do not understand, and may indeed even panic. If negative reinforcement is continued here, far from them learning what you are teaching, they may learn not to do it, and panic more and more. For this reason it is always sensible to assume the horse does not understand the 'that' and/or the 'how' before assuming that he just does not want to do it.

Teaching Shemal a *piaffe*. She is asked to collect, something she already knows, but then not to go forward at all, but continue trotting. She finds this difficult and begins to jump and becomes very excited, a general panic. This she does with any new activity where she does know 'that'. Rather than continuing, which will lead to a great panic, with the result that she will not settle down to do anything right for a while, the solution is to recognise this, and take her very slowly through it all, praising her for the slightest improvement. Anyone riding her who is to bossy and firm causes her to become panic-struck, not because she does not want to do, but because she does not understand.

By contrast, Oberlix is extremely laid back about learning new things, in addition, he really does not care too much to do flat work with any enthusiasm for more than around ten minutes, and his piaffe will be performed on the spot with the minimum of effort. He knows the 'that' and indeed the 'how', but does not really feel like putting the effort in. Touching him with the whip makes little difference to his energy and enthusiasm, all he does is kick out backwards. The only way I have found to motivate him to put more effort and lift his legs higher is to scold him verbally. If I get very cross, verbally, he usually begins to make an effort, but of course I cannot do this too often or his response to this will extinguish!

The distinction between 'knowing that' and 'knowing how' will apply when the equine (or human) is learning a mental skill, a 'habit of mind'. There may initially be difficulties with learning both 'that' and 'how'.

Learning to comprehend some simple human language. First he needs to learn (i) that he must listen, (ii) he must learn the meaning of individual words, (iii) he must learn the meaning of the combination of words presented to him. This is an area we have been working on at our research centre, and there are some remarkable results coming out of the short periods of time we have been able to spend with our pupils: we have been teaching in the same way as we generally teach pre-verbal infants. Once they know that they must listen, then the 'what is the meaning', is easier, that is, they have developed a 'habit of mind', at least up to this point.

(3) Interactive or co-operative teaching of equines and other animals

At the research centre, we determined to set up some learning experiments for a variety of species, including equines, not in isolated experimental boxes, but in an interactive teaching situation as used for children. Such interactive teaching situations have been used traditionally for equines, but the point of our experiments was to try and measure the performance of the different species, and learn more about how the animal learns, and the similarities and differences between the species.

Of course these difference might be related to the different behaviour of the teacher with the different species, so we were particularly interested to measure the behaviour of the teacher and see if this were the case. We also wanted to see if we could develop some 'general rules' for improving the teaching of equines.

Because of the physical, emotional and social differences between species, it is difficult to find problems of equal challenge between them, even when teaching them to do some simple action.

> Horses do not have hands, trunks or paws, and rarely fetch, lift and carry things around like humans, elephants or dogs. Consequently teaching them to hold, lift and carry objects might be expected to be more difficult. It might be like teaching an elephant to trot, or a human to canter on all fours!

We were also faced with the question of what are the limits of their minds, and what can they learn? Making assumptions about the way animal minds work and the inability of certain species to learn certain things has been shown to be highly suspect (see *Equine Lore* and Chapter 1). Negative results will tell you very little. If only one animal of a species can learn to do whatever is being tested, it means that we can no longer conclude that that species *cannot* learn that task. Tests indicating that a species cannot do it (negative results) may just be that the experiment has been wrongly designed, and with further tests, the results may be shown to be incorrect. Haangi, for example, showed that equines ' transfer learn' (transfer some general rules about shapes to slightly different shapes); previously it had been concluded that only primates and humans could do so. We have shown that equines can learn to perform new acts by imitating a human, something that was not considered possible before.

To try to overcome these problems, we chose to teach our experimental animals of five different species (a filly, a heifer, a pup, a young guanaco/ llama, and a young African elephant) some very simple movements that none of them should have much difficulty performing to a word command. The activities were: (i) to shake the head, (ii) lift the right or left front leg as asked, (iii) to put the head up and down. The teacher accompanied the use of the words with (a) gestures, (b) physical restraint to stop them walking off, (c) shaping and moulding (d) imitation to start with, much as if they were children. No negative reinforcement was used in any of these experiments, and food as well as verbal (' good girl' etc.), physical (patting, scratching and stroking), and gestural praise (smiling and laughing etc.)

were used as positive reinforcements to help motivate the individual towards the correct response. In addition to the responses of the animal student, the behaviour of the teacher was recorded to see if there was a difference in the way she responded to one animal versus another, and whether this affected the subject's learning.

The species differences emerged after these simple movements. It was easy for the filly to learn to paw when asked (something that they often do when in some form of frustrated situation), but difficult for her to learn to kick the ball forwards (picture on page 65).

Some of the results of this work comparing the learning of these different species were expected but others were unexpected.

This is only a beginning of the 'science of animal educational psychology', using interactive teaching, but the results are very interesting and together with information about learning that we have already covered, allows us to outline a list of 'general rules' for good teaching of equines (and other animals, including human infants) (page 67).

Some might counter by saying, 'This is all very well, equines may be able to learn a lot more than we thought, and even learn some simple human concepts, like some numbers, the use of symbols and so on, but what they *never* will be able to do is to understand some of our uniquely human concepts'. Again, the jury is still out on this issue. We have only just begun to consider what the mind/body of the equine might be about and what it might be able to learn with good teaching, so let us not jump to conclusions at this stage, although I am prepared to admit that equines would probably never design a space shuttle or send a man to the moon! But they may be able to teach us something about 'feelings'.

One thing is clear: studying learning and teaching these species will give us a much better handle to further our understanding of the world they live in, the knowledge they have of the world, enrich our thinking and perhaps help us improve our teaching of them ... help us all to become better educated.

Summary

(1) All behaviour is the result of both nature and nurture, that is both the genes and the past experiences of the individual. To describe equine behaviour as 'instinctive' (genetically programmed and consequently unalterable) is unhelpful and wrong. We all have 'instinctive tendencies', but how, when, where, and if they are performed is the result of the individual's lifetime experiences. This applies to all mammals, including humans.

(2) It is helpful to have a good grasp of learning theory to teach any mammal, including humans. To do this we need to agree on the meaning of words that are used when discussing learning as well as how it works. This has been outlined and an attempt made to simplify it and, in particular, make it relevant to equines.

(3) How learning operates is often divided into a series of different types, these are outlined and examples given relevant to equines. However, it is very important to understand that these types of learning interweave and overlap, they are not distinct or mutually exclusive.

(4) Learning to do voluntary acts generally involves complex mental events. These include an understanding of cause and effect, having goals, desires, beliefs, memories, making decisions and choices – consciousness of a type.

(5) Mammals, including human mammals, learn to do voluntary actions by reinforcements of various types, but also by acquiring information from the social and physical environment in which they live.

(6) The measurement of 'intelligence' between species is fraught with difficulties, but not impossible to overcome. Different species will have different mental skills as well as physical ones. There may also be some general rules concerning 'intelligence'.

(7) One important aspect of learning is to be aware of the difference between learning 'that' (learning what to do) and learning 'how' (how to do it). An understanding of this is particular important when teaching more complicated actions or mental skills to equines.

(8) Early experiments with 'interactive teaching' of equines and some other species involve teaching animals in the same way as children, i.e. (a) by emotional involvement with the teacher, (b) use of associative, observational, silent learning and imitation as well as instrumental conditioning have shown promising results. The equines learn fast when this method is applied, and in particular, when taught carefully, can begin to comprehend not just commands, but language.

This has considerable relevance for improving their teaching and education.

(9) The limits to what equines can learn are not clear. There is much more to learn.

(10) That all the answers to training equines are not known is illustrated by the large number of problems exhibited by equines as a result of bad teaching.

REFERENCES

Bateson, P. P. G. 1966. 'The characteristics and context of imprinting', *Biol. Rev.* 41. 177-220. ch8,p2.

Bernstein, I. S. 1981. 'Dominance: the baby and the bathwater', *Behav. Br. Sci.* 4. 419-29.

Bonner, J. T. 1980. *The Evolution of Culture in Animals*. Princeton Univ Press. Princeton.

Burger, U. 1959. *The way to perfect horsemanship*. J. A. Allen. London.

Dickinson, A. 1994. 'Instrumental conditioning', in *Animal learning and cognition*. ed: N. J. MacIntosh. Academic Press. San Diego. p 45-79.

Galef, B. J. Jr. 1986. 'Tradition and Social Learning in Animals', in *Animal Intelligence. Insights into the Animal Mind*. ed: R. J. Hoage & L. Goldman. Smithsonian Institution Press. Washington. p149-163.

Haangi, E. B. 1994. 'Serial reversal discrimination learning using shape cues in horses' (*Equus caballus*). *Equine Research Foundation,* California.

Haangi, E. B. 1996. 'Conditional discrimination learning in the horse (*Equus caballus*)', *Equine Research Foundation.* California. Houpt, K. A. 1979 'The intelligence of the horse', *Equine Practise.* 1. 20-26.

Howe, J. 1997. *IQ in question. The truth about intelligence.* Sage. London.

Iwanowski, G. 1987. *You and Your Horse.* Shutter and Shooter. Jo'burg.

Jerison, M. 1973. *Evolution of brain size and intelligence.* Academic Press. London.

Johnson, B. 1995. *The skilful mind of the guide dog.* G. D. B. Herts.

Kiley-Worthington, M. 1998. 'Competition and Cooperation. A detailed study of communication and social organisation in a small group of horses (*Equus caballus)'Eco*

Research Centre. ISBN 367-2045, paper 024.

Kiley-Worthington, M. & H. Randle. 1997. 'Animal educational psychology. A comparative study of teaching 4 mammals of different species' *Eco Research Centre.* 013.

Kiley-Worthington, M. 2000. 'Right in front of our minds. Elephant and equine epistemology'. Thesis, Lancaster University.

Koehler, O. 1951. 'The ability of birds to count', *Bul Anim. Behav.* 9. 41-45.

Lea,S. & M. Kiley-Worthington. 1996. 'Do Animals Think?' in *Unsolved Myseries of the Mind.* ed. V. Bruce.

Lilly, J. C. 1961. *Man and Dolphin.* Gollanz. London.

Midgley, M. 1978. *Beast and Man: The Roots of Human Nature.* Cornell Press. Ithaca. N. Y.

Miller, R. 1999. 'L'impregnation comportementale du poulain nouveau-ne', p13-21. in *L'equitation, le cheval et l'ethologie.* Colloque du 18 Sept 1999 a l'ecole National d'Equitation. Belin. Paris.

Pearce, D. 1987. *Introduction to Animal Cognition.* Harvester. Hove.

Pojansky, *My horses are my teachers.* J.A. Allen. London.

Romanes, G. 1883. *Animal Intelligence.* Kegan Paul & Co. London.

Ryle, G. 1949. *The concept of mind.* ch8, p7 Penguin. London.

Schjelderup-Ebbe, T. 1922 'Beitrage zur Social psychologie des Huashuhns',*Z. Psychol.* 88. 225-252.

Tinbergen, N. 1951. *The study of instinct.* Oxford University Press. Oxford.

Thorpe, W. H. 1963. *Learning and Instinct in Animals.* Methuen. London.

Toates, 1994. Motivation. CAEC meeting. Provence. France.

Tolman, E. C. 1932. *Purposive Behavior in Animals and Men.* Century. New York.

4

DON'T WHISPER, TALK!

For equines rarely is any one sense used in isolation from the others. Thus visual signals are important but their meaning is tempered by the smells around, being touched or touching, noises, and/or tastes. In addition, the meaning of messages to equines is generally 'context dependent': the specific meaning is interpreted from the context. This is unlike human language which is largely 'context independent', where the meaning of the words is the same whatever the context. They can learn that signals have particular meanings, independent of the context, but this does not come as easily to them as to human language users.

There has recently been much emphasis on the use of visual cues to help train equines; the use of 'body language' this is often called. This involves making the human trainer conscious of the importance of body posture. It is a first step to increasing the awareness of how the trainer behaves. The fact that the horse responds so quickly to these cues underlines how important they are, but it is not new. It has been known and used for centuries by good equine educators world wide. What is new is that attention is being drawn to it. The result of this is, however, not always helpful. So much attention has been drawn to the use of 'body language' that the use of the voice (something we humans are particularly good at) is almost entirely ignored by the exponents of body language (e.g. Roberts, Parelli and their followers). Over the last twelve years or so at the research centre we have been studying not only the use of visual cues, but also the importance and potential use of smell, touch, taste and in particular the voice in communicating with horses and other equines to develop further our mutual abilities to communicate for two reasons:

(1) So that we can educate them better, rather than just train them for particular chores.
(2) To discover more about their mental abilities.

Many people argue that it is not 'natural' for the equine to listen to the voice and comprehend the meaning so conveyed, and consequently it is not a good way of training. This approach needs very careful assessment. What is 'natural'? If one really believes that one should only do to the equine 'what is natural', then why are we educating them at all? It certainly is not 'natural' for them to learn to carry people on their backs, wear harness, bridles or saddles, or have much to do with humans at all. If we sincerely believe they must only be taught to do what they do naturally, then we should have nothing to do with them (except hunt them perhaps); leave them to live their 'natural' lives. There are some who take this stance, but they will not be reading this book.

Various justifications for training and using equines are used. The main ones are:

(1) That equines are sentient feeling creatures, but very inferior to humans both mentally and in terms of moral concerns; consequently we are justified in using them as we like, provided we do not cause suffering. Equines have the same kind of status as valued slaves. This is the view held by most people who own, love and have to do with equines. As I have argued elsewhere, there are problems both for the humans' rational thought and the equines' well-being with this approach. But here, what concerns us is whether or not they are seriously 'inferior' to us mentally.

(2) Even though it is not 'natural', it is necessary for the equine to be educated and live with humans otherwise he will become extinct because of the pressure on land and resources. If we were to open all the gates and doors and let equines gallop off into the wilderness, they would quickly become extinct (as their wild cousins have become in Europe and are in the process of becoming in Africa and Asia) because of the demand for land by human beings and the shrinking of 'the wild'.

(3) Learning is natural. It is not 'natural' for humans to learn to write, but considered useful for the individual. Similarly, limits do not have to be imposed on teaching an equine: we do not have to only teach movements that he may occasionally do in his 'natural' life. If he learns new and different things he may be able to have a life of greater quality and a greater range of experiences as a result (see introduction); just as it is believed humans do as a result of learning new things. But, he must not suffer or have unhappy or a more difficult live than he would if he were still wild as a result of this.

'The wild' is not such a marvellous place sometimes. We can improve on it by, for example, ensuring that no equine dies of starvation, or is hunted and eaten and that their wounds and diseases are treated. But to ensure that they have a life of quality, a better life than they would have in the wild, we must ensure that all their needs are fulfilled, whether they be physical, emotional, social or cognitive/intellectual ones. It is not good enough to assume that the way we have developed to keep them (often in an over-protected environment), sometimes for our own convenience, sometimes for our own inconvenience (which makes us feel we are doing the right thing), is the best, or even good enough.

However, we need not dismiss using something that may not have been in the species' evolved experience, provided it does not cause suffering. The use of the voice is not going to cause the animal to suffer physically, and rarely psychologically, and then only after he has learnt a considerable amount about it, but will it be helpful? From our human point of view it certainly will be useful because we are good at it, and therefore it is much easier for us to use the voice than to learn to use subtle visual cues. But, if it is very difficult for the equines to learn to understand it may not be useful. First then, we need to think about how and what equines can learn about the voice and language comprehension. There are four questions here:

(1) Can we use the voice to convey emotions to the equine, and consequently

messages about how we wish him to behave? The answer to this is generally agreed to be 'yes'. Expression in the voice can convey emotions such as pleasure, displeasure, anger and fear from a human to an equine.

(2) Can we use the voice to convey particular messages about what he should do using particular words? Here again the answer is generally agreed to be 'yes', although some would argue that it is not the word command alone which conveys the message, but other cues and the expression in the voice. Equines can learn to respond quickly to particular words, provided they are well taught (see Equine Lore).

(3) Can we use the voice to convey other messages that are more language based? For example, can he learn to identify more subtle words and their meanings such as positions 'on', 'off', or adjectives such as 'prickly', 'big', 'small', concepts such as 'yellow. This is possible but takes a lot of time (see list of words on page 79).

(4) Can he learn to comprehend the difference in meaning of phrases as a result of word order: that 'the bucket is on the mat' means something different from 'the mat is on the bucket'. We do not know the answer yet, as no one has tested it.

The answers to the questions above are at present a qualified 'yes', although few experiments have been done using the voice without any other cues so far. The proof will rest with further experimentation similar to research with dolphins and chimps.

We know the use of the voice is important when teaching equines to :

(1) Indicate to him the pleasure or displeasure of the teacher (page 41).

(2) Teach him to do something particular when asked by voice, rather than always using visual and touch cues as well.

(3) Make communication with him easier for us humans.

(4) Possibly, to widen his cognitive/ mental horizons by exposing him to language and the various mental skills that go with it.

The sensible starting point for this investigation may be to use the same techniques as are used with infants when they begin to be taught and to comprehend language, including using techniques developed by a psychologist to help preverbal children learn to comprehend language. Here the word is used first in association with visual cues and sometimes with shaping (page 46) and imitation. Verbal praise is also conveyed by using the appropriate words and intonation in association with tactile messages (hugging, chuckling, stroking, patting, etc.), or visual demonstrations of pleasure by the teacher, such as facial expression, smiling and so on. We have found that equines (and other species) learn the emotional import from the expression of the voice and the meaning of particular words for the performance of simple actions very quickly.

Many of us have an equine because we want a companion and friend, and one of the functions of this companion is that we will tell him all our problems and in some sense, he may act as a psychotherapist for us ... appearing to listen and sometimes even responding to our chatter. There is nothing wrong with this of course, the only thing we must be aware of is that if we also want to use language in order to help him understand simple concepts, ideas and commands, we must make a distinction in how we talk to him on these different occasions.

Few people really believe that equines can understand or learn to understand language, consequently they do not take the trouble to use it initially simply and consistently. We are much more likely to do this with a child who, we believe, will, eventually, learn to understand, but even here there are plenty of parents who tell their troubles to their preverbal infants assuming that they will not understand! We talk to each other about our horses, ponies and donkeys in their presence, and we may address them with long soliloquies of our problems without taking any trouble over the use of the language, tacitly assuming they will not understand. As a result, many equines learn not to listen to language or word commands, but rather to wait until they are visually or physically (e.g. led, pulled or pushed) asked to do something. A similar thing happens if you are initially trying to understand an unknown language, say mandarin. After a while, if nothing is explained and you are given no help with your efforts to understand what is going on, you, like the equine, will not bother to listen any more, and as a result not learn the language.

Consequently, if you want the equine to learn to perform movements, or listen carefully to language, a distinction must be made between :

(1) Talking to him about your problems, and what not, or to other humans around. We must make a clear distinction for him between, 'Now I am going to rant on to you my pal,'

(2) And, 'Now, my pal, I would like you to listen carefully to this simple statement or request, and react to it': and talking to him directly, expecting him to listen, understand and perform. Here, the first job of the teacher is to ensure that the equine is listening, help him develop his attention to what you are saying by making it simple. The words used must be to the point, direct and always the same.

We will now discuss the three uses of the voice and language we have been using with our equines.

(1) The use of the voice to convey emotions to the equine

Most people consider that this is useful and use their voices in this way, even if they are not thinking about the consequences. Here it is the intonation, the emphasis, rather than the individual words which convey meaning to the equine. Consequently, it does not really matter what you say, it is how you say it. Thus to get the horse to move on, the tone will be shorter and sharper, to quiet the horse a calm, leisurely use of the voice lengthening the words, and repeating words in a sing song way. To praise the equine, the voice has to convey the speaker's real pleasure, not just a 'good boy' but 'goooooood booy' chuckle, chuckle, smile and nod.

In the first instance the voice and the expression you wish to convey must be paired with visual clues about what you are feeling. At the beginning it is helpful to be over demonstrative with the emotion. If you are pleased, show it with your body, your movements, facial expression and voice. As the horse learns, cues can be reduced. In a little time, just an expressive voice when out of sight or even on a tape recorder may suffice.

Using the voice is particularly useful when beginning to harness train a lively youngster. Here the constant voice from behind, calming him, telling him you are there and he is not alone makes a considerable difference to his ability to keep fear in check and to calm him. This will be more effective if he has already learnt to listen carefully to the voice.

> Much to my surprise, the other day by using my voice with force and expressing my fury, the two adult stallions, who had managed to get out together with the mares near by, stopped in their tracks before seriously attacking each other. They stopped long enough to allow us to go up to them and lead them away. I did not think that in such an intense emotional state they would listen, but they did ... that time at least!

This again illustrates how we tend to underestimate the potential for utilising the voice in our relationships with equines.

As with all learning however, it is vital that the voice is used consistently and directly, and not just repetitively. Constantly shouting at horses switches them off so they no longer listen, just as with humans. The opposite – constant praising, patting and cuddling them – also loses its meaning, again just as with humans.

(2) Words to convey particular messages or commands

Equines can rapidly learn the meaning of around 200 words. Start with commands – 'walk', 'trot', 'canter', 'halt', 'come here','go out', 'go left', 'go right' and so on. It is remarkable how quickly they will learn these words if they are initially carefully paired with visual clues. Within ten minutes of starting a youngster on the free school (going around in an enclosed area without a lunge line), if well taught, he will understand walk, trot, halt and come here. Of course he may not remember all these words for a while, but he will be hearing and learning them in association with the visual cues, which can then gradually be reduced.

Expression in the voice is useful, just as with a child. As usual it is important to be clear and concise, to ensure the same word is used for the same activity each time, thus 'go right', not sometimes 'go over there'. This is quite difficult for us humans to do, as we often do substitute different words which have the same meaning. It requires some thought and attention just as it does when talking to a young child to help them understand.

Two important words are 'yes', and 'no'. When the equine understands these – and they are really not difficult to teach (although a little exaggeration in one's emotional response is initially helpful) – then an enormous stride has been taken. All you have to do when teaching even something difficult and advanced is to say 'yes, yes' when he begins to do the right thing, and he will continue to do it, and 'no' when he tries something else, so he stops doing it. The 'yes' and 'no' have to be used immediately he starts to do something, almost before he does what you

LIST OF WORDS USED WITH THE EXPERIMENTAL ANIMALS

Names: Horses: Shemal, Oberlix, Oryx, and other names of horses they live with
Humans: Chris, Marthe, Hayley, and other students
Dogs: Pepsi, Mishwi, Rupert, Sadie, Kaz, puppy
Other animals: Rambley, cow, bull, calf
Objects: machine, tractor, van, flower, grass, plant, tree and names of different plants (particularly those they like to eat, or will not eat): dandelion, cow parsley, nettle, dock, thistle, violet, barley, oats, sugar beet, minerals, oil, rug, blanket, bag, shoe (horse and human)
Parts of bodies: head, neck, eyes, nose, nostril, lip, mouth, chin, ears, hair, coat, mane, shoulder, front leg, back leg, knee, hock, hoof, foot, ankle, tummy, quarters, rump, tail, back, ribs
Trees (again, particularly those they eat or don't eat): ash, oak, beech, pine, hazel, lime, willow
Other animals: cow, bull, calf, puppy, llama, sheep, horse, donkey, geese, chickens, ducks
Things: bridle, saddle, rope, traces, rein, bucket, injection, vet, medicine
Places: stable, field, hedge, bog, moor, track, road, manege, ring, bedroom
Verbs: come, go, lie, lift, drop, take, give, touch, smell, hear, see, taste, smile, like, rasp, cut, nail, trot, canter, walk, halt, back, forward
Adjectives: nice, nasty, good, bad, big, small, green, red, blue, brown, black, white, yellow, soft, hard, prickly, smooth, rough, easy, difficult, left, right, near, far, beautiful, ugly
Prepositions: in, out, on, off
Pronouns: yours, mine, his, hers, theirs
Adverbs: then, before, now
Commands: come here, go over there, touch this or that, smell this or that, life your left/right leg, paw, bow, lie down, cross your legs, walk, trot, canter, gallop, go faster, go slower, steady, careful, yes, no, stand still, halt, go backwards, turn left and right, pirouette, *piaffe*, *passage*, extend, collect, go sideways, half pass, shoulder in, travers, renvers, go straight, circle, volte, figure of eight, listen, keep time, stop it, eat, don't eat, drink, don't drink, head down, head up, head shake, head nod, head turn, look, wait, Spanish walk, Spanish trot, stop it
Other: please, well done, very good, bad and clever (with name)

Approximately 75 commands and 179 words

think he is going to do. Consequently observing and predicting behaviour makes teaching equines a great deal easier and faster.

Learning to perform simple movements to word commands requires no particularly advanced mental skills, it is instrumental or operant conditioning: learning to perform a voluntary act in order to achieve a reinforcement (pages 57-61). However it helps a lot if the teacher is aware of exactly what the horse may be feeling and his next likely action, and takes this into account so that she can ask at the right time.

> A young horse beginning on the free school is unlikely to walk quietly around the ring to start with. He is much more likely to walk about sniffing the ground and then start cantering and leaping around. He may stop and turn and rush to and fro, trying to find a way out. The teacher's job is, not to ask him to walk around quietly but, when he starts to move, just to keep him going around in the same direction at whatever pace he chooses, and praise him when he does. When he has used up his energy and become more relaxed is the time to ask him to walk, but only when, by looking at his body posture and behaviour, you can see he would like to walk. If the teacher picks the right time, when the horse wants to respond, he will respond correctly, and then is praised. Consequently he begins to learn the meaning of the word 'walk'.

In this way the horse learns because he wants to, and he can find the whole process fun rather than an exercise in obedience which can end up with a 'tussle of wills'.

Good circus performers, for example, act on the messages they are receiving from the liberty horses or other animals they are working with. They are doing a show, and it must be seen to work and to be impressive; it would not do for an animal to be seen to be disobedient, so movement or behaviour which is not a scheduled part of the act must be included as part of the act. Consequently, the format may change in line with what the animals want to do at that time rather than the presenter insisting on submission and obedience, at least when in the public eye. In fact it is possible to teach animal performers to be innovative, so that eventually they develop their own act. This approach could be more widely applied in other types of performance and would be likely to improve the quality of performance rather than the robotic performances that are often displayed in dressage, the cavalry and today's equine 'dances'.

It is quite remarkable how few people praise their horses when they have done the right thing, but nearly all of them tick them off for doing the wrong! The voice is, perhaps, the best way of doing this, once they have learnt about how the voice expresses pleasure, joy and so on, because it can be done at a distance, anywhere, any time, in sight, out of sight, it is the easiest reinforcer (way of supplying a reward).

We have learnt a lot recently from educational psychologists concerning the education of children using a positive, non confrontational, interactive approach to teaching. We should be doing this much more with equines, if we want them to go further faster with their education and learning. By contrast, there is a general belief, when training horses on the lunge for example, that it is vital to get the animal to do what you ask at all costs. If he does not want to walk, then you go on and on at him until he does walk, often becoming frustrated and irritated along the way; the horse reads this and it makes him less likely to want to walk! The time to insist on gait changes when you ask is later in the individual session, or another one. The teacher's job is to assess when the equine is likely to want to do what you ask; and consequently to ask then and obtain the correct response, then everyone is happy!

Using such a co-operative approach does not mean that you allow disobedience or will not have a quick response when, perhaps for matters of safety, you need it. In fact if the equine has been taught in such a co-operative interactive way, he will quickly recognise urgency and necessity in one's voice and act accordingly, see the example above where the voice stopped the two stallions fighting.

To summarize: firstly, the word is used to denote exactly what response is required; secondly, postural and physical cues are used; thirdly, the teacher does the action. Gradually, with repetition, all cues except the voice are reduced.

> Teaching a donkey to lift a front leg. First, one arranges the situation so he is likely to do this. In this case it will be when one touches the leg lower down if he has had experience of having his feet cleaned. The word command is given simultaneously with the leg being touched. When he does the movement, or even begins by shifting his weight to the other leg, he is verbally praised. The next time he has to lift the leg right off the ground before he is praised, and given a food reward perhaps. Then the teacher only gestures towards the leg but does not touch it as she gives the verbal command. The next step is she stands in front, and simply looks at the leg as she gives the verbal command, and finally all she has to do is say the words, 'Lift your left leg,' and he will understand it, even if she is looking in another direction. Whether he will do it will depend on if he wants to, he always has a choice! So the teacher's job, as we have repeatedly stated, is to ensure that he does want to.

Head shaking, leg crossing, lying down, Spanish walk and trot, *piaffe*, *passage*, flying change what ever else you like can be taught in this way. If it is not done exactly as you like or the dressage rules demand, then all that is necessary is to teach him by 'shaping' and 'moulding' exactly what you require (page 47).

> Oberlix is not lifting his hind legs enough in the *piaffe*, so I ask him to lift them more with the voice, and touch the hind leg with a whip. He lifts a hind leg higher at once. He is praised. We start again, and only with the voice used with urgency to encourage a lively action, he lifts both hind legs higher for two strides. We stop and give him a food reward, and then ask him to do it for three strides. This is then enough for one session and we do something different.

It is not necessary to have had years of learning about teaching equines, or to ride very well before you teach your equine these types of movement; all that is

Shemal being asked to go and touch the green colour.

necessary is that you observe and act appropriately, and that you understand and apply the rules of good teaching (page 67), and you can make strides teaching almost any horse these movements in as little as half an hour. A young horse may try them out at times when you do not require them, so be warned, and of course, just as important is to teach him *not* to do them at the wrong place or time.

Teaching must be progressive, the important thing is for the teacher to set the situation up correctly, observe the pupil closely and change her approach as required. React positively as soon as he begins to perform the correct response. The next time he will have to do it a little more completely, the next more and so on. Once an equine has learnt to learn and listen to the voice, it should not take him more than about thirty minutes' teaching time before he understands some simple command words, at least when paired with slight visual cues. If it takes you longer, then it is because the teaching method is not as observant and reactive as it could be, so analyse your own behaviour. This way rapid improvements can be made.

The next stage is to introduce positional words such as 'left' 'right' 'on' and 'off', 'in' and 'out', 'behind' 'in front' and so on in relation to doing particular things. It will take many repetitions in different situations before the equine has grasped the general meaning of these propositions, but it helps both the teacher and the pupil if these lessons are started. One of the most important things about this is, it really makes one concentrate on what one is doing and what messages both visually and verbally one is giving to the equine; never a bad idea for a good teacher to think about.

Whether or not your equine ever grasps the exact meaning of the words, what he will grasp is that you are paying much attention to him and trying to communicate seriously with him, rather than just bossing him around in a rather confusing muddled way. We have three horses now with whom we have worked with carefully in order to see if they can recognise words and their meanings, and they certainly can do this without us consciously using any visual cues, but whether they are responding to some subliminal visual cues we do not yet know since we have not done the 'double blind' tests. To do this we must not be seen, so we must either be behind a blind, or use a tape recorder.

There are some things that are very important, which we human language users do not often consider. The context in which they are asked to do something – particularly something rather difficult, such as to lie down or to do the Spanish trot – is important not only from the point of view of having everything conducive for the equine to do the behaviour, but because they will quickly associate a particular action with a particular context, and then it will works well there, but not in other places. Consequently there has to be a second stage included where they are taught to generalise the response to different situations.

> Shemal was taught to lie down when she was around 9 months old, and until last year would do it to the word command, without any visual cues in any ring or manege, stable, paddock, anywhere we asked with a soft surface and enough room: her response was 'generalised'.

But things can also go awry if not enough attention is paid, and lessons can be unlearned.

> During a rehearsal for the ballet 'Sleeping Beauty', Shemal was the beauty, Oberlix Prince Charming, who had to come up to her and smell her face as she was lying flat on the ground. On this occasion he struck out with his front leg (because there was another stallion near, and I had failed to take this into account), and cut her lip slightly. Now 9 months later, she may take over 15 minutes before she will lie down at all, and as soon as she is down she will be up again. Here I made a very silly mistake, and it will take many hours to reverse what she learnt in one trial: 'lying down when asked is dangerous', even after 4 years of having no bad experience. However, she has no problem lying down in the field or stable when she is with Oberlix. It is lying down *when asked* that is the problem.

(3) The more complex comprehension of language by equines

We devised a series of tests to see whether horses associate a word and a picture of the shape with the actual concept of number. The equines were asked to paw out the number associated with the symbol of the number; thus if they touch the two, then they must beat out two with their hoof, and so on. It is very early days with these experiments, and it would be better to have more subjects, although if

Shemal touching the green while I look away so as to give her no visual cues. She was right 80% of the time in over 200 trials.

one horse can do it, there is no way we can then maintain that horses cannot do it any more.

The other question here is whether the equine can learn to understand concepts defined by language. For example, the name of 'yellow' for yellow objects. We have tested this in the same way by interactively teaching them to go and touch the correct colour on the board displaying four different colours (see picture above). The next stage is to test the understanding of 'same' and 'different' using colour. If we give him several yellow objects and a red one, can he pick out the red one as different? So far we have not done this experiment. There is a problem here, though, as green can be of many shades, so he has to acquire our understanding of what is green and what is not before we will consider he has learnt, even though he may see many more or many fewer shades of green.

Whether they can understand other aspects of human language (e.g. word order) needs more research, but by using interactive co-operative teaching, we may be able to answer such questions a lot easier than in a laboratory, and have a lot more fun doing it too.

By teaching this type of thing, can we learn more about equines and their view of the world? This has indeed been the case for me at least. One thing that is very evident is how fast the equines learn such 'unnatural' things in an interactive teaching situation. Each subject has to date had 350 trials for each action, whereas rats and pigeons in a laboratory situation will take very much longer to learn these discriminations (sometimes thousands of trials for one act). This does not tell us that equines are particularly bright (see page 37), but it does tell us that this type of teaching is successful and quick.

Summary

(1) The use of the voice and language can be helpful and important when teaching equines.

(2) It can be used to indicate the teacher's emotional state to the horse, and as a result be a positive or negative reinforcer.

(3) It must be carefully used, initially paired with visual messages and the equine helped to listen and understand. This can be done by being consistent and starting simply.

(4) It is important to separate talking to them for other reasons from asking them to do things.

(5) If one gets into the habit of using the voice and teaching equines something about language, it is remarkable how quickly they, and other mammal species, learn; this makes the teacher's life much easier and the whole process more enjoyable.

(6) There is some evidence that equines can learn to understand individual word meanings, including adjectives, prepositions and concepts, but further work is in progress.

(7) Don't whisper: assume your horse understands and talk to him as if he were a young child. You will encourage him to listen and understand more language.

(8) It is not necessary to have had years of learning about teaching equines and to ride very well before you teach your equine all sorts of movements and responses using the voice and gestures to start with. All that is necessary is that you observe and act appropriately, and that you understand and apply the rules of good teaching (page 67).

(9) You can make progress teaching horses all sorts of movements in as little as half an hour if you use the voice. A young horse may try them out at times when you do not require them, so it is just as important to teach him not to do them at the wrong time or in the wrong place.

(10) Teaching horses to comprehend language simplifies our life with them, is fun and teaches us more about them.

REFERENCES

Fowler, W. 1990. 'Early stimulation and the development of verbal talents', in *Encouraging the Development of Exceptional Skills and Talents*. ed. M. J. A. Howe. 179-210.

Hearne, V. 1987. *Adams Task Calling Animals by Name*. Heinemann. London.

Hermann, L. M. 1987. 'Receptive competencies of language trained animals', *Advances in the study of behaviour*. 7. Academic Press. New York.

Hockett, C. F. 1960. 'Logical considerations in the study of animal communication' in *Animals Sounds and communication*. (ed) W. E. Lanyon & W. N. Tavolga. American Inst. Biological Sci. Washington. DC. (p392- 430).

Kiley-Worthington, M. & H. Randle. 1997. 'Animal educational psychology. A comparative study of teaching 4 mammals of different species' *Eco Research Centre*. 013.

Lea,S. & M. Kiley-Worthington. 1996. 'Do Animals Think?' in *Unsolved Mysteries of the*

Mind. ed. V. Bruce.

Linden, E. 1986. *Silent partners. The legacy of the ape language experiments*. N. Y Times Books.

Roberts, M. 1992. *The man who listens to horses*. Hutchinson. London.

Schjelderup-Ebbe, T. 1922 'Beitrage zur Social psychologie des Huashuhns',*Z. Psychol.* 88. 225-252.

5

FOAL HANDLING
AND NURSERY SCHOOL

- Early handling
- Leading
- Farrier and veterinary experience
- Learning to be tied up

Unlike the human infant, the foal is at an advanced stage of its development when it is born. So precocious is the foal that, even as it dangles out of its mothers vulva, it may be looking around, blinking and beginning to take in the world into which it is being born. The trauma of collapsing onto the ground can then cause the new-born to switch off from the external environment, onto pains and other sensations of his own body. We studied the first three hours of life of 22 foals and their mothers. For a period of several minutes (up to around 30) the foal's new world is self-centred. This is demonstrated by his coughing, sneezing, shaking his head in order to free the sensory organs of the mucus and liquid of the uterus he has been living in. This ends when he demonstrates that he is beginning to watch objects and pay attention to the world around rather than just his own body.

By this time his mother is, if all is well, licking him, which stimulates his skin and dries him. At this time she begins to learn something about what he looks, tastes and smells like. Initially this will be mainly of her since he is covered in secretions from her body. This is probably an important stage in her learning about who he is. She is initially attracted to him rather than other foals, *because he smells of her.* This fact has been known for centuries; another foal can be easily accepted by a nascent mare provided it is covered by her own amniotic fluid and afterbirth when it is introduced to her. In equines, this is a brief stage. The amniotic fluid and afterbirth has little effect in helping the mother identify her offspring or a substitute after around ten hours *post partum.* Presumably because by then, the foal has started to be recognised as an individual as a result of secreting his own smell from skin glands, and his mother is starting to recognise him by sight, although the mother may be attracted to other very young foals for a day or two after giving birth, and may mistakenly identify others as hers from a distance.

Equine mares, unlike cows, do not eat their afterbirths. The mother will move away with the foal as soon as he can walk, leaving the afterbirth behind. This is typical strategy of a species that is very mobile. The youngsters can be up and running so quickly after birth that the afterbirth can delay the predator while he eats it. This delay allows the youngster to have a few more precious minutes to get all his muscles working, learn to walk and gallop in order to be able to stay with mother and escape being caught by smaller predators who will not take on an adult mare.

At the same time as the mother is absorbing his taste, smell, feel and appearance, so the young foal will be absorbing all these individual cues from his mother – what she smells like from her breath and close body, what she feels like from her tongue and nose on his body, and at least what the close-up parts of her body look like. She may give her own individual nicker to him, particularly when he makes a large or sudden movement, thus he becomes familiar with her call.

So, immediately *post partum*, the mother and foal are mutually absorbing information about each other. This rapid mutual learning to recognise each other early in the foal's life has been called 'mutual imprinting'. One of its characteristics is that it is very rapid, which it needs to be if the two are going to be able to stay together in a herd.

The foal is precocious (advanced) mentally as well as physically. When he is born he has a well developed fore brain or cerebral cortex (primarily concerned with mental events such as learning, consciousness and so on) which is highly convoluted (that is, has a large surface area giving space for more cells and greater mental abilities). He has a great deal to learn very fast if he is to survive, so his brain is around 80% of the size of an adult's, although it has yet to be filled with information. By contrast, the altricial (less well developed at birth) human infant is born with a relatively small brain and undeveloped body and spends several years learning to do what the foal has to learn within the first few hours. It has often been argued that the altricial young will end up cleverer as he has time in which to learn, but there is just as good an argument to suggest that it is not the stage at which the infant is born that is important to the eventual mental development so much as *the speed at which he can acquire information and physical and mental skills*. This, in the foal, is extremely rapid. He is born with a large fully functioning brain and sensory receptors and an able, athletic body to go with it so he can acquire an enormous amount of information very fast. This rate of learning may gradually fall off as he matures, although if he has acquired a 'habit of mind' to learn and have mental exercise (page 52) he will continue to acquire information throughout his life. When the infant is less well developed at birth (as is the case for human infants, rats or puppies), the rate of learning is initially slow, but becomes more rapid as their bodies mature, and then drops off again when they are mature.

Having cleared his sensory receptors so he can become aware of the world around him, the next task for the young foal is to clamber onto his feet, balance, walk and find the teat. It is important that all of these behaviours are managed within around three hours from birth, or the infant will not be able to absorb the immunoglobulins in the mother's first colostrum. Colostrum is composed of very large molecules, which become more difficult to absorb as the foal's intestines mature. A healthy foal will consequently begin to make efforts to stand up within half an hour of birth. He usually stretches his front legs out, and tries to push himself up with his hindquarters and then balance on his long wobbly legs. He often pushes up and collapses, falling up to forty times within the first three hours, but, because of the plasticity of his whole body and bones, he is very unlikely to cause himself damage at this stage – unless of course he is falling onto concrete (even if it is covered with a thin layer of straw!). Even with deep bedding foaling mares inside on concrete increases the chances of the foal hurting himself as he falls in his normal efforts to stand and walk; the foal's hooves also slip more on the straw than on earth or grass. In our experimental subjects, the number of times falling was significantly greater when they foaled inside than outside (average 10 outside, 19 inside). The time they took to stand up for the first time was also greater inside than outside (average 25 minutes outisde, 42 minutes inside). Another factor that affects the time taken for the foal to learn to stand when born in a box is that he can become stuck against a wall or in a corner so that he does not have space to stretch his front legs out, or hits his head against the wall as he falls. Thus, *it is best not to bring the mare inside to foal if the weather is at all reasonable*, but rather keep an eye on her outside, or ensure an earth floor and a large area if she is to give birth inside.

The foal of course has instinctive tendencies to do all these necessary things as soon as he is awake and born, but *when* and *how* he does them, as we can see, is controlled by his environment, just as with humans. He has to learn how to get up and balance, how to move as well as how to find the teat. Moving forward is difficult. First, he manages to lift one leg, then sways and collapses. He has to learn to co-ordinate the muscles to move these long uncontrollable limbs to progress in the direction he wishes, usually towards the vague body of his mother. The young foal can be seen learning this skill, often lifting one and then the other leg, in an exaggerated way, and out of sequence, but improving all the time, until, after a few minutes, he more or less gets the hang of it, and wobbles up to his mother to search for the teat.

Here another major hurdle has to be surmounted. He has an instinctive tendency to search for the teat under something, and something warm, but the chest is just as good a place as the hind legs. It is only after he has achieved a reward (reinforcement) from managing to suckle some milk that he begins to learn where the teat really is. He might be searching the wrong mother too, if there are others crowding around, as there often are in the wild, feral or group pasture situations. A quick negative reinforcer, such as a slight kick, sudden movement, squeal or movement away, brings this message home.

Even when he has found the teat, which takes from 5 to 30 minutes in healthy foals, he then has to grab it and suck something out of it. He has an instinctive tendency to suck, but he will often suck on a loose piece of skin at the elbow or on the hind leg for example. What stops him continuing with this is the fact that he does not receive a reinforcer: milk. The teats are often sore, very swollen and the milk is very thick and gluey to start with making it difficult to suck out; none of this helps the foal, but it does ensure persistence! He must continue to try and try before he has his reward! If the mare kicks (which, if she is a first-time foaling

Sioban talking to Shindi, aged one, in the field, naming her mane, neck and just spending time with her, handling quietly and with pleasure for them both.

mare or a mare with sore teats, she does frequently), then he may well be put off and will return to sucking something else, which satisfies his need to suck although it does not satisfy his hunger. Once he has had milk, his finding and getting hold of his mother's teat stops being such a chancy affair as he has learnt where it is, although he has not learnt how to suck it out well yet.

The foal takes very little milk to start with, a few drops of the thick first milk (1-5cc). Over the next few weeks foals take many small drinks, suckling around every half hour. These suckling bouts are much more frequent than for babies or calves, and ensure the strengthening of the bond between mother and foal, and that the foal stays very close to mother (page 55).

Many young inexperienced mares do not like the sensation of this young thing nuzzling around their undercarriages, they squeal and either move away or lift the hind leg, and if he persists, may even kick. A few kicks, even when the foal is looking in the right place, is enough to cause him to give up (negative reinforcement) and to try somewhere else. Having had a bad experience with mother, the foal can quickly become fixated on a particular place in the stable and often will be suckling on a piece of projecting wood, or even a piece of dangling baler twine. The hungrier he gets, the more he sucks on his chosen object; he has learnt to suckle in the wrong place because his mother hurt him when he tried the right place. *Mis-mothering* of this type may have its origin in the mother learning that when he suckles, it hurts because of her sore and extended teats. To correct this, the task is for the mare to be positively reinforced when the foal suckles, either by being fed and fondled by people she likes so she is reassured and relaxed while the foal is manipulated onto the teat and his suckling is overseen so that he does not become rough. The relief of the milk pressure in the teat is itself reinforcing for the mare, so it is important to ensure that her udder is relieved (pages 55-6). If the foal does not take enough, then some milk/colostrum can be expressed so that she has relief and begins to associate the manipulating of the teat and suckling by the foal with pleasant sensations (human mothers can have the same problem). It is wise to keep a close eye that all is going well with the suckling for the first few days.

It is also a good idea for a first time mother to have had experience having her teats handled gently, and her tummy rubbed. We generally start quietly handling all these parts when the filly is a few months old, just to get them used to it so if it comes to having a foal, or even an injury in the area which has to be treated, it is not such a new and terrifying experience. However, it does have to be done with tact – horses have private places, just as humans do.

Recently, there has been much written about 'imprinting' the foal on humans. It is important that people realise what is happening here, rather than rushing in and trying to handle the foal too early and causing mal-and mis-mothering which can be a frequent result. *Imprinting* is otherwise known as early learning (pages 53-6).

It is true of course, as we have pointed out, that the young foal learns very rapidly as soon as he is born, but it is equally true that he continues to learn throughout his life. Occasional, careful handling from a few days old is important in order for him to learn to associate humans with pleasant experiences. As a result, he becomes more familiar with them as he grows up.

As the young foal grows up, he has much other information to acquire too; he begins to acquire ecological knowledge and learn how to integrate with the group (become a good 'equine sociologist'). This commences almost from birth as he learns about where he is, where he is going, what to eat, where to run, how and where to climb, to duck, to jump, to shelter and so on as well as about his mother and the other members of his group (chapter 6): who to follow, who to avoid, who to play with, who to annoy and so on.

When raising the Druimghigha stud horses, we usually do not handle the foals at birth; partly because of time constraints, and partly because it is not always easy to be there, and, importantly, because in less experienced mares, it can cause problems with the development of their own relationship with the foal. We begin to handle the foals when they are a month or two old, provided all is going well with them. First, to begin to establish an emotional bond between the foal and the handler so that there is some mutual familiarity and respect for each other. We will then begin to teach them the type of behaviour that humans like, that is, coming up when called and nuzzling, standing still when asked and when having any part of the body inspected. Also, we will begin soon to make it clear to the foal the type of behaviour that is not required, such as jumping around when handled, or kicking, turning the quarters to a human, nipping or biting of any type. This is done by showing disapproval if they perform the behaviour, scolding with the voice, or just going away and ignoring them, not by hitting or restraining them. We want them to know what to do and what not to do themselves, and make choices – not be restricted and physically prevented from doing the wrong thing. By the time he is a year old, the types of behaviour towards humans that are desired and those that are not are well known by the yearling, and as he gets bigger and more adolescent, he is easier and pleasanter to be with. The yearling has not only learnt to understand what equine behaviour is acceptable to other equines and how to integrate into the group as a result (equine ethics), but he has also learnt what humans require in terms of their good behaviour (ethics towards humans for equines!). Whether we are talking about a Shire, a thoroughbred, a donkey, zebra, mule or pony, the same applies.

What is even more important is how the handling is done. Nursery school for the foal or naive adult equine starts with handling.

One thing that is not appreciated enough is that good handling of any animal requires as much skill as riding really well and unfortunately it is usually not taught. Many professionals – competitors, trainers, veterinarians, farriers, as well as amateurs – handle equines badly and as a result have equines that behave in undesired ways. Instead of thinking how to improve their handling, or the conditions in which they keep their animals, they excuse themselves by allocating the cause of the behaviour to 'past experiences' or 'genes', the breed, the type, which clears them of any responsibility, and which they can do nothing about. We know enough about handling now for us to *have no handling problems in the next generation of equines*, if we really want to. This is not only the breeder's responsibility, but also the responsibility of all the professionals who may have to do with equines. Unless they start to question their methods there is little hope ofimprovement.

Nursery school

The best age for the foal to start 'nursery school', as we have already mentioned, is as soon as he is growing well, fit and actively curious. Nursery education involves the foal in beginning to 'learn to learn', accustoming the foal to humans and the things that he will be expected to do, such as to be led, have his feet rasped, go to new places, leave his mother and friends for short periods, or be left by his mother but remain with other members of the group and aunties.

> Four equines, Oberlix, Shemal, Oryx and Shindi, were foals whom we have studied in particular in this regard. Now they are all mature, they quickly grasp new movements, concepts and symbols, and adapt rapidly to different situations compared to their relatives who have had as much attention as most horses, but not quite the same amount of attention and teaching when young.

It is important to begin the process of educating the foal correctly, and particularly to allow the foal to educate himself about the world around him in order to help develop his mind, establish the right mind habits, and learn to learn. There is nothing unnatural about this, he has evolved to be able to do this, and acquires an enormous amount of knowledge even when he is living without humans. We must give him the chance of acquiring plenty when he is living with humans too, albeit that this will sometimes be a different type of knowledge. Consequently, to have a well balanced co-operative horse and delightful companion later, it is necessary to structure his life so that this will be possible. I cannot emphasise too much the importance of allowing the foal options to develop an ability to observe others and learn from them, and to make decisions and choices rather than over-protecting him, restricting his physical or social life and disallowing him to do things by keeping him stabled, or alone with his mother, or not working with him when he is young. Just living in a field with mother may not be sufficiently stimulating: let him mix with other youngsters, ponies, donkeys, mares, stallions of different ages if possible in order to learn equine etiquette. Also, encourage meeting other species such as cattle, sheep, goats, dogs, llamas – whatever is available.

Ecological knowledge can be acquired from taking him on rides with or without mother. We take our young foals out for rides running loose where they safely can, or led from another horse (see pages 11 and 115).

One of the most important things to consider is over-protection. Because we want our equine not to be injured, cold, or too hot, or covered in flies, we make judgements for them about this, and restrict them so they cannot get cold, slip, have flies over them and so on. Such anthropological judgements are inappropriate. They are not 'conditional anthropomorphism' (pages 19-20), they are 'inappropriate anthropomorphism' and often cause the equine to suffer a great deal more than without the 'protection'.

Just as with the early education of a child, if the child is never allowed to put his hand near the fire, even to hurt his hand slightly in the fire, how will he ever learn that fire is hot and dangerous? Over-protection can have disastrous results, for both humans and horses, but the problem is where is the line to be drawn; what is over-protection and what is not? Of course one does not want the foal to have accidents and to injure himself severely, but he must experience things going wrong in order to be able to avoid problems in the future. For example, not allowing the mother and foal to gallop out and around in the field excitedly because it is hard or wet and he might slip and hurt himself will not allow him to learn how to control his footing and to avoid accidents in the future. The older he gets, the more serious the accident may be if he has not learnt about substrates, balance and slip. If you look at your horses galloping around in the field, you will see how quickly they learn that particular places are to be avoided, or that certain speeds or turns in certain places are necessary. They may rush around and fall in one area once, but next time they will be much more careful in that place. They will gallop up to a fence flat out and stop before it if they know about fences. They will even adjust when they stop relative to the slipperiness of the ground.

We recently measured one youngster's slip marks in a particularly slippery field: he had put the brakes on three metres from the fence and slipped right up to it, but on a dry day, without slip, he stopped only one metre from the fence.

Of course sometimes mistakes are made, but without making mistakes, how can learning occur? It is all part of being a prey species, and having to learn fast by experience. The predator gets another chance if he misses the prey, but the prey does not if he is caught!

Sometimes it is very difficult not to fuss about the youngster when you see him madly galloping and slipping. If you cannot stand it, go away and have a coffee, and talk about him with other humans, but don't go out and interfere with him. It is particularly important that when the individual is already excited and unwisely moving or leaping about, he is not further excited by people rushing in, themselves excited, often screaming and throwing their arms around. That can certainly lead to excessive excitement and hysteria and then the youngster, whether horse or human, may do almost anything without thought. This is when the serious accidents occur.

> The most common example is when dogs begin to fight. In the nature of things if left alone they may have a tussle with a great deal of noise and saliva, but rarely (unless one of the dogs has been taught to fight by humans) is there any serious injury. It *is when people shout and scream and try and separate them that the injuries occur.* The sensible thing is to keep calm, and try to deflate the excitement by diverting the attention of the dogs, but also that of the humans watching them, rather than stirring it up.

> When a horse gets loose at a show ground, usually people will rush around, often throwing their arms about and screaming 'loose horse'. The result of this particularly balmy behaviour is to excite the horse very much more, and eventually (if these people are not controlled) an accident may occur, which would not have happened if everyone had remained calm and quiet, ignored the loose horse and eventually, one person had approached without threatening or exciting him. Even better for the person to attract the horse to her.

So consider carefully your behaviour before you restrict, restrain, or try and teach a young horse. Remember, he will learn the wrong thing just as quickly as the right, and relearning the right after the wrong takes much effort.

There are some rules of behaviour which are worth knowing if you want to make life easy for yourself and the youngster. Not all handlers and educators are good at articulating these, but the rules are easy to learn, although they are not always so easy to put into practice! What these rules are, and why they are there is explained below.

Handling
The definition of 'being handled' used here is that the equine does nothing when things are done to him. He must stand still. He has to learn to do this because his

initial response to anything slightly unusual, frightening, or painful is to run. A test of 'handling' in a horse is when he will stand still, even though the procedure may be causing him pain, or he is very frightened.

> Oberlix at the age of one was attacked by a llama who pulled the muscles of his forearm down almost over his knees. He was tied up at the time, and the llama had jumped out and attacked him when he could not get away. Our treatment for these serious wounds was to play a high pressure hose on them in order to get rid of any infection, allow him otherwise to live his normal life with his social group rather than be shut up in a box, stitched up and fed antibiotic which it was felt might increase his distress and prevent good healing. The cold hose caused some pain of course, but after the first time, he did not try and run away or avoid it, but stood still, even though he was obviously having to control himself, and showed this by his tenseness. The wounds healed remarkably well, and he grew up to win in international long distance as well as many other competitions. Here he learnt that standing still, even though it hurt, was the best option for him. Presumably it felt better afterwards too!

This learning to stand still when things are not going right is important too in harness work, particularly when using a dangerous agricultural implement (see Chapter 11); the equine must overcome his first impulse to run, and consciously hold himself still ... Equines have to learn to do this, but the handling must develop to give them confidence that this is the best thing to do when things get tough, even terrible.

Despite the importance of having a well handled animal in any situation to reduce risks of accidents as well as be able to treat sick animals easily and keep all parts of their bodies healthy and well, handling is rarely given the attention it needs whether from the zoo keeper, sanctuary manager, weekly rider or the serious professional. Humans have to learn it (as well as equines); like riding, skiing, writing, or playing music, it is not something you are 'born with', although some may find it easier than others. But to learn to do it well, you have to think, and work hard at it.

If you do not have the motivation to learn to handle well, then my advice, in all seriousness, is give up having to do with horses, and go and do something else. Equines, and other mammals, are emotional beings, just like humans; they form relationships and like and dislike others. If you do not have the motivation to work at your relationship with an equine from the ground, not just from a position of power on their backs, then you will not do either the equine or yourself any good by continuing to have to do with them. Even the immobilised or handicapped can enjoy handling equines.

> A seriously handicapped woman wrote to me once telling me that she had found a way of managing to saddle up her horse, even though she was chair bound.
> (1) She called the horse over to a particular place where she could, by pulling

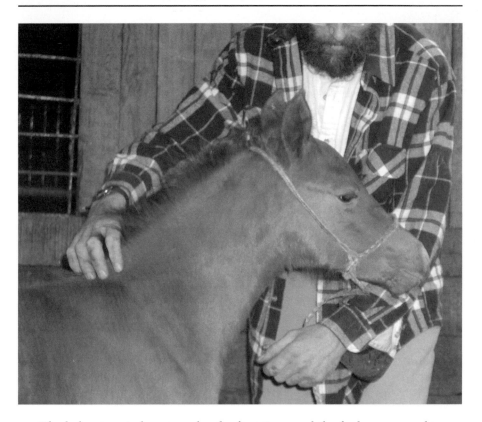

The halter is quietly put on for the first time, and the foal encouraged to investigate Chris.

a lever, lower the saddle onto the horse's back.
(2) Her dog then ran around the horse and passed the girth to her in his mouth, She fastened the girth, and then rolled herself up onto a mounting block from which she could slide onto her horse who had learnt to stand like a rock until asked to move on.

We were studying the donkeys in Lamu, East Africa, where they do all the heavy transporting work as there are no roads. They live freely the rest of the time, obtaining things to eat from the rubbish tip and stealing from vegetable stands. There was a family of donkeys who had taken up residence below my house, and not far away from the local corner shop that had a vegetable stand outside where all the old men met and chatted while drinking their tea for hours every day. Frequently, one of the donkeys would walk indirectly up to the vegetable stand, and, when the owner was looking away, gently snatch a sweet potato or a mango. He would turn back and give the donkey a heavy cuff. This seemed to have no effect, and the donkey soon returned for another snack, until the owner gave up even bothering to cuff him. The donkey by this time had had enough and fell into a drowsy sleep next to the stand, together with most of the old men!

Sequence of handling a young foal and teaching to lead for the first time. This is the first scratch. Chris with a relaxed body scratches the foal on his back, which he is enjoying. It is difficult for foals to walk and scratch their backs, so the back itches!

First walk with Socrates – Chris relaxes the rope and gives him a scratch and a chat to stop him becoming worried. He is already learning to stand still when things are scary, when with humans. His chin and nose are tense, he is worried.

Some resistance is necessary and inevitable for Socrates to learn the basic physical principle: pull against the rope – it is unpleasant; go towards it – it is more pleasant.

There are many ways of handling, and a host of things you can learn to do; you can teach your horse to help you be able to handle him better, it is up to you. Equines can learn of course to be handled very badly, often unfortunately the case in many teaching yards because teaching to handle is not taken seriously.

Learning to handle should become an end in itself. Equestrian schools and centres should have classes for their students in handling and working horses from the ground, rather than just riding. There are very many people, of all ages, who would love to do this, and who do not particularly want to learn to ride, but just love horses and want to have to do with them. Classes and competitions could also be developed to test people's ability to 'handle', particularly for professionals, veterinarians and farriers this would be very useful. It cannot all be learnt in an afternoons class, it requires as much skill and ability as to learn to ride well.

RULES FOR BETTER HANDLING

(1) The most important thing is to consider carefully *what* you do before you do it. Until you have a great deal of experience, it is very foolish to act without consideration. The reason for this is because both the horse and the human are good natural psychologists and the equine will respond to the emotion the human is feeling, and *vice versa*. Thus, if the horse is excited and rushing about, the first thing the human is likely to do is the sort of thing that adds to the horse's excitement. More usually, it is the human who is nervous and conveys this nervousness to the equine (whether zebra, mule, donkey, pony or horse), who then becomes nervous.

(2) It is very important to be self-critical, and analyse your behaviour. If you do something and it does not seem to have the desired effect, reappraise the situation and try another approach.

(3) Posture, movements of parts of the body and muscular tension are very important in conveying to the equine what you are feeling. Convey pleasure in his company, delight in the appropriate responses, and above all relax. Any tension will indicate wariness and this will keep all away and make them restless.

(4) Use the voice with expression to convey your delight, to calm him, and to attract his attention away from something you are doing which may be slightly scary or new for him, for example touching the legs or rubbing his stomach.

(5) Positively reinforce appropriate behaviour.

(6) Be sure you are in control of your emotions, whether this is fright of a large leaping about youngster, or irritation because he will not hold his foot still. If you lose your temper or become irritated, things will only get worse. If frightened, only do as much as you feel confident doing, and make sure you do not get hurt. If you do get hurt, it makes your and the equine's problem worse. There are no 'brownie points' for gritting your teeth and carrying on regardless. (Heroic behaviour is not necessary.) If you are really frightened, recognise it and go and do something else until both the equine and you have calmed down. Then try something along the same lines, but not so difficult. Similarly, do not reward him with a positive emotional reaction, like smiling or laughing, if he doesn't do what you want – even if it is funny. If you smile or laugh, this endorses the behaviour.

Go in the direction he wants to go in – towards his mother – and it will be much easier for him and you. Notice Chris's relaxed body throughout.

A suckle reward.

(7) Make up your mind how you would like your equine to behave and then work towards that aim. If you don't mind him dancing around as you get on, or jumping about afterwards, then he can easily learn to do these things. On the other hand if you have difficulty getting on and you really dislike this sort of behaviour, he can easily learn to stand still whenever you ask and stay there until you ask him to walk on again. It is up to you to teach him though!

(8) Make sure you have a schedule for advancing his learning about what you would like, don't just repeat old things; go on from there to another stage. For example, if you like him to stand still while you mount, and he does this, then go to the next stage and make him line himself up to a gate or a mounting block (so that you can get on easier) or stand still in more difficult conditions when others are coming and going. There is no end to education, and the point is not only to make your life easier, and for both of you to enjoy yourselves more together, but also to ensure that he has sufficient cognitive/mental exercise, the need most often neglected in equines (page 19).

(9) Do not rush in and try and do everything at once. For example, if teaching him to lift up his foot, rub his legs first and get him used to this, then pick a leg up, hold it only for a second and tell him how marvellous he is, gradually increase the time he has his leg held up, and don't hold on for dear life and turn it into a fight; the horse will learn that fighting wins, so don't fight, instil confidence instead. This applies equally to farriers and veterinarians who are often in a hurry, and also don't always know or think much about handling. If they are trying to rush and upsetting your animal by restricting him/her, shouting, hitting, twitching, grabbing, drugging, etc., then stop them. Take a little time and show them that it is not necessary. It is quicker for them and nicer for everyone in the long run another way. The first time it may take a little more time, but thereafter it will be easy. There are very very few occasions when a twitch or severe restraint is really necessary if you handle well, even when the treatment may cause pain.

Handling and first education of older naive equines

There are many equines who are not handled as foals, such as animals caught from the wild, or those that have been left alone at pasture. Handling these equines is of course more difficult than teaching them about humans when they are young, but it is not particularly hard if approached properly. The same general rules apply, but the first thing is often to get the animals used to the presence of humans without trying to avoid them. This is most quickly achieved by the handler doing nothing. The best way is to have them in a small enclosed area where there is nothing to eat or drink. Take a good book and go and sit in the middle together with a small pile of nice hay and a bucket of water. Take no notice of the equine, even when he comes up to the food or water, and, gradually, through curiosity, he will begin to want to investigate you. Lucy Rees made an interesting TV film in the 1970s comparing her co-operative approach to handling and training a wild caught mustang in the US with that of a Western cowboy. She sat and waited until the mustang came to her, and there were pictures of the wild horse coming up to smell and investigate her. Meanwhile, the cowboy and his horse where having a bad time while he threw blankets and sacks on him, the horse pulled back and cavorted around in terror. Here was a case in point where the cowboy admitted what he was trying to do was to 'break his spirit', that is, obtain a level of 'learnt helplessness' where the animal just gave up and anything could then be done with him as he behaved like a robot. At the end of the programme Lucy Rees' wild mustang was wandering in a headcollar along a river bed in the sunset with her sitting bareback on him, while the cowboy had given up! The moral here is to excite curiosity in the equine, without fear.

This approach is particularly important with animals that have never been domesticated and are captured when they are mature, such as zebras, rhinos and elephants. First they must get used to the small enclosure they are kept in, then to the humans and their activities around them. This means that people must continue to go about their daily business outside the enclosure, rather than creeping about trying to be quiet or not seen by the animals in the pen in case it frightens them. What frightens these animals much more is frightened humans concentrating on them! If they can see, hear and smell them, they much more rapidly adapt to the conditions of their captivity and are not so easily frightened. It is when they are frightened that they will do damage to themselves or to others. Eventually the handler can sit on the barrier and slowly descend into the enclosure as he continues to be apparently paying attention to something other than the animals in the enclosure, and gradually the animals become curious and will approach.

At some point it will be necessary to teach the equine about restraint so that he can be tied up and led for example, but only after he has become familiar with humans.

Once the previously un-handled adult equine can be easily handled, and enjoys it, his further education can be tailored to the required skills so that he develops the right 'habits of mind'.

Handling for farriery

Because handling is not properly taught, whether farriers (and veterinarians) learn to handle well depends on the individual. Some are good, but unfortunately, many could be better, and some are very bad.

> Aderin, at the age of 29, was loaned to a friend's daughter to ride. She had been shod on and off ever since she was 3, and was 11 hands. These people called in a farrier who handled her badly, terrified her and finally used a twitch to make her stand still! They asked us about this; we insisted that she was bought to the centre to be shod by Chris in the future. He had to spend half an hour calming her down the next time before she stood still as she always had before.

Twitches are frequently used by farriers. They often say this is to 'save time'. It only reflects on their bad handling, and possibly fear or short temper. Farriery is skilled hard work, and very bad for the back, so one can be sympathetic to a farrier with a difficult, particularly large, horse. However the approach that will make life easier is not to twitch, use drugs or other restraints, but rather develop the equine's confidence and reduce his fear of the operation by taking time; maybe not shoeing at all the first few times. If the owner will not spend the time getting

Picking up a front foot is no problem, although she is paying attention.

him used to all the various procedures of the farrier, then the farrier should charge for his teaching time, like anyone else, even if he does not shoe the horse.

Even if a horse is difficult, he can relearn.

Baksheesh's mother had a terrible accident while I was away in Africa, and was put down. He then went to stay at a livery yard. He was a 2 year old, 15. 3hh very reactive Anglo-Arab stallion, who, although he had been handled as a youngster, had not been handled for the last year. The livery owner was frightened, and he was hardly out of his stable for three months, before I heard of this and returned from Africa to rescue him. The result of this treatment was that he had to relearn to be handled quietly, in all conditions. This seemed to progress well, but I omitted to think enough about shoeing where he would be handled by someone strange. When the farrier came, although I held him and chatted to him, he became hysterical. The farrier lost his temper, hit him and said he would not come again. The next time another farrier would only come if he were tranquillized. We tranquillized him and, as sometimes happens, the drug was not effective and he was as bad. No farrier would come after that, and I needed him shod in order to teach him, work him and to ensure he did not become more difficult. I had noticed that the real problem with the shoeing was the noise of the hammer and the feeling of the nails going in. I therefore spent the next month hitting his feet with a hammer, bashing a loose shoe on the foot, in all positions until he became very familiar with it. Then it was a question of finding a sympathetic farrier who would take time. Eventually, I found one, I held up the foot and talked to Baksheesh, he bashed the shoe and eventually hit the nails in. Baksheesh stood still, and after four visits he had a set of shoes on, and had stood still throughout. Ten years on, he could be shod anywhere by anyone (as long as they did not lose their temper of course) – in the middle of a race, at a show ground with people and horses coming and going all over, and without being tied up.

It is often only in exasperation that one begins to think and structure the learning for the equine appropriately. It all seems so obvious afterwards!

Now we are lucky as we have a resident farrier at the centre, Chris, so the youngster's first experiences are well thought out and quiet. They are first habituated to being tied up, and having their feet lifted and held, their feet cleaned out, and, sometimes, shoes held and hit with a hammer on their feet with their feet in different positions.

The first shoeing may involve having someone the horse knows handle and scratch his head and neck, give him the odd tit bit or even a bucket of food to take his attention off his feet from time to time while Chris chats to him, and quietly works away at the feet and shoes. He is heartily praised when he stands still, and when he jigs around, first we decide if we have held the foot up too long, and so predict jigs and drop the foot first, or we rebuke the pupil and show displeasure. The back feet are often slightly more worrying for the young horse, so more care is taken with them. Shezam has just been shod in front for the first time, and with Chris's careful handling alone, stood like a rock. Provided he is not frightened in future there should be no problem with setting up the right habits, but if he is every frightened or mishandled during shoeing, it can go downhill very fast at any stage.

If you are paying a farrier to shoe your horse, you should not only examine his behaviour but also make sure you know exactly what he is doing for that particular horse and why. It is surprising how little people know about balancing the foot and farriery. Generally farriers are happy to tell owners what they are doing and why, and are delighted that they show an interest in what is after all a skilled and interesting profession; it must be soul destroying to go around shoeing horses without any interest or comment from any of the owners.

Chris has started 4-point shoeing to try and ensure that the horse's feet and legs are less distressed with hard work, and we are having some success with this. It becomes extremely interesting the more one learns about it all, and how skilled some people are. Little is really known about the best possible way to shoe a horse, and why. Farriery goes in fads, just like anything else.

Handling for veterinary reasons

It is a seriously good idea for every equine that is around humans to be easily handled when he has to have some veterinary attention, such as injections, having the teeth looked at, or the legs moved into curious positions. If there are problems doing these things, the chances are that the inspection will not be thorough, the veterinarian will get injured and or lose his temper, and things can go quickly from bad to worse. Most veterinarians today, partly because they are given almost no instruction on handling, and because many horses they see are badly handled and not able to be easily inspected, will quickly give a sedative drug. Not only is this expensive, but it can cause serious problems. Some tranquillizers do not work with some individuals, so the outcome is not always reliable.

The first thing is to accustom the equine to having injections. This really is not difficult if he already has a trust in the handler and it is done quietly, with his attention directed elsewhere while it is happening – giving him something to eat, scratching him, or otherwise distracting him. Praise and reward afterwards, so that you can almost see him grow in response, is also very important, particularly if something hurt; even if the equine did not stand all that still, if in your eyes he tried, that is enough, praise him throughout, and talking to him is also helpful. It is particularly important that the first time he does not have a fight with the vet. It is better to inject him yourself if you have any experience and can do it well, rather than have someone he does not know and who may be hurried, frightened and rough. If things go wrong the first time, the next time will need much time and patience to ensure that this does not become a habit. Equally, if it goes quite well the first few times, one can become too confident and not take the time to reassure and talk to the horse; then things can go wrong!

> Shindi is a very reactive mare who easily gets worked up; because she has been carefully handled since she was small, she was very easy to shoe the first time, to take in a trailer and to take almost anywhere even by herself. She was given a contraceptive injection in the neck and she stood still without a fuss. Two months later, she needed another, and, without thought, we approached her with the hypothermic to inject her in the other side of the neck. She puffed and blew and became very agitated, even leaping around. It took ten minutes of quiet handling and reassuring her while talking and then giving the injection which luckily was intra-muscular quickly but without fuss. She stood still well, but she is still suspicious sometimes when we pat that side of her neck, as she probably had a local reaction to the injection. If we had taken a few more minutes the second time, we would have avoided the problem; now we will have to be very careful when injecting her not to scare or hurt her the next few times, until she forgets this incident.

We have established the right habits in Oberlix and Shemal so that they stand still for the injections, even when rather incompetent vets inject them, or cannot find the vein and wobble the needle around for an intravenous injection.

It is all in the handling and taking a little trouble, thinking about what is

Lilka going for a walk with Sioban, coming out of the tack room. It is useful to get a youngster used to following the person leading anywhere she asks at this stage, including through narrow doorways, but be careful she is not hit by the door.

happening and how one can improve one's handling for that individual in that circumstance.

I always insist that, however hurried the vet is, they must come up to the horse and greet her, and take at least two minutes just stroking and talking to her before launching in to try and do something which may hurt, otherwise the horses quickly learn who is a vet and won't let them anywhere near – quite rationally.

We had just sold a two-year-old colt when he leaped over a fence and wounded his testicles at the stud before leaving. These swelled up and were clearly painful. Because we had sold him, I felt we must have a veterinarian check him out. A tall good looking young man came, and rather arrogantly went up to the colt and immediately tried to grab his testicles and see what was wrong. Quite rightly, the colt lashed out at him with a hind leg. It was not going well, and above all I did not want the youngster to get the habit of kicking out when he had already learnt that this was never done to humans, whatever the provocation. I had to banish the vet, and quietly approach the colt and show him how the colt would stand still if he was thoughtfully treated quietly without fear, arrogance or aggression. He did, and, to give him his due, the young vet caught on and made a good job handling him thereafter. He subsequently became a close colleague of ours, well known for his good handling of equines!

It is often difficult for people to point out to the vet that their handling is not good, particularly in the UK where vets are held in high esteem. But sometimes it is necessary, and it is also the vet's job to assess the owner, and whether or not they know something about handling and indeed veterinary procedure. It is very annoying to be treated as mentally undeveloped or incapable by veterinarians, even though they have very little education in learning how to handle animals. But of course there are also vets who are good at handling and, because they have to handle all sorts of equines every day, they have a great deal of experience.

The way to learn to handle well is to watch what those who do not manage are doing, as well as those who do.

We usually take a lot more trouble when handling our children when we take

Kahloon, a three-year-old black Arab gelding, who came for education, learning about being tied up, saddled and so on. Note we have not removed all the various other ropes on the ground, so that he learns about these too. He is impatient to get going (pawing), so we are watching and waiting for him to encounter the rope on the ground ... not rushing to pick it up. We will be there if real difficultires occur, but he must teach himself about such things.

Shindi being tied up next to Shemal, who is experienced.

them to the doctor or the dentist and so do the nurses, the doctors and the dentists, because we know that, otherwise, there will be trouble the next time: the same is true for equines.

Start with easy exercises and gradually progress at your and the equine's own speed, and without being watched by others if possible.

Exercise 1. Handle your horse all over, including his tummy, elbows, hocks gently and quietly, penis and testicles, ears, get him to open his mouth so that you can look at first his incisors and then his molars at the back. Praise him when it goes well, repeat actions that are not liked, but more gently while praising him. If something is really upsetting, go back to something that he does not mind so much and then try again more carefully and gently, even if it is just a question of holding your hand over the area rather than touching it. Each day repeat the exercise and make notes on how far you got until it is all very easy.

Exercise 2. There are a series of exercises invented by physiotherapists to help stretch and relax various muscles. These involve lifting the front legs forwards and up and far as possible, and holding them there; the back legs back as far as possible, lifting them out sideways and as far forwards as possible. These again are good exercises to do to accustom the equine to get used to unusual handling. Gradually you and your horse will be able to improve these exercises, and at the same time be stretching and relaxing various muscles. Eventually you can teach him to do them when you ask too, if you bother! Quite impressive when the physio comes to visit ... but then you probably won't need one!

There are many other exercises you can invent yourself to practise handling, with different equines in different situations; take every opportunity you can just to practise on other equines, wild or not, old or young, nervous or docile, but remember never do something that frightens you, things will only go downhill thereafter. Make sure that your confidence is built up as well as the equine's.

Once the youngster has been taught to be handled (that is, to do nothing when handled), the next thing he begins is to do *something* when asked. It does not really matter what he is taught, as long as it is simple. One thing that needs to be learnt early is to be tied up.

Teaching to follow, be tied up and 'ground tied'

The first stage of following is to follow mother as he is led along with a headcollar and lead rein. The teacher can put pressure on the lead rein every so often to teach him to come. The next step is to follow the person rather than mother. Use of body language is useful here, encouraging him to walk towards you by adopting a relaxed and low posture, and not looking directly at him. When he does come, reward him with food, chuckles, praise and scratches (see pictures page 99).

To follow: If mother is in front it is possible to teach him about going towards pressure on the rope immediately. If mother walks, he will tend to follow, so if pressure is put on the rope at the same time, he will associate going forward with the pressure on the rope.

Sooner or later, he will not want to follow; in this case, continue with the procedure but avoid a conflict. If he pulls hard against the rope, hold it, but if he begins to panic, slowly relax it and praise him when he quietens down. Encourage him to move forwards and when he does, reward with food and praise.

Reward him when he stays close to you as you walk about with a relaxed

Ground tie. Chris gives Shemal a word command and gesture to 'stay'. Shemal is rather bored of this – and shows it!

A school outing - over Dartmoor.

posture and if he stops or goes another way, you say 'no'; if he follows as you walk again, praise and say 'yes'. The foal is learning to follow you as though you were another horse, or his mother.

Eventually it is possible to keep your foal with you 'at heel'; it is useful for your horse to learn to turn up when you call and then follow you about until you tell him what else to do. It is perfectly possible to teach him to follow without a lead rein.

To be tied up: He must also learn 'when a human pulls a rope, go towards it, but when the human goes away and you are attached to an inanimate object, stay with the inanimate object'. At first, when he is tied up, he will suddenly realise he cannot follow, and will pull. Unless he is tied up with something strong, he will break it and learn to pull back, because if he does, he can get away. The practice of tying a horse to a piece of baler twine encourages this.

It is possible to teach them to be tied up first, and then to follow. Once the concept of 'when the rope is tight, you go towards it' is learnt, it can be applied both to the inanimate object and to the human.

Use a quick release knot (a half hitch that, when you pull the end, will release), and leave him quietly with some hay (nothing too delicious). Preferably with relatives or friends close by. You should watch, but without being seen. After a while he will realise that he is attached when he moves off and he will pull back. He may sit down, or thrash about for a while, but as long as you are watching to make sure he does not get in a tangle, he will teach himself that it is more pleasant to go forward and stand quietly.

Extra care must be taken with a horse that has learnt to pull back. In this case, when the rope does not break, he may try harder and harder and build himself into a hysterical state. Follow the rules below and ensure that he cannot hurt himself. Then leave him to sort it out and teach himself: it can always be done.

Once he has mastered the concept (and has moved forward for a few minutes on a slack line) then reward him with food and praise. The next day he can be left a bit longer. If he gets too worked up, you can approach and calm him before leaving him again, but do not untie him, or he will have taught you! Once he has learnt that it is not worth pulling back, he will generalise this lesson to every situation. Whatever happens, you will be able to tie him up somewhere sensible (not for example next to a busy motorway). He will gradually learn to be tied up for longer periods until it will be safe to leave him for hours, or even tether him overnight (see page 227).

Ground tying: This is when the horse is left, untied, but with the rein dangling onto the ground, and told to stay. He should stay put until asked to move, or is led away (see picture page 108). Many donkeys and other draught animals learn this. A riding horse standing without a rider can be taught to stay still, either with a voice command, or some particular signal. The usual sign in western riding is to drop the reins, which fall to the ground either side of him. Or you could teach your horse to stand still when you use a gesture. Ground tying is usually taught after the equine has learnt to be tied up to a post or other object. It can be taught by word command, but it is easier to attach a weight to the end of the rein that is dangling to the ground. As the equine moves, he is restricted by the weight of the object. If he has already learnt not to pull against a tight rope, he will give up and stand. After a few trials (provided you don't leave him too long, or in an uncomfortable place, like in the hot sun when there is shade nearby) he will learn to stand for some time. If he is frightened, moves the weight and then runs with the weight attached, he will become extremely frightened and anything may happen, so ensure that initially at least you are there in case he moves the weight.

RULES FOR TEACHING A HORSE TO BE TIED UP

(1) Tie up using something that will NOT break.
(2) Use a headcollar that will NOT break (if you are worried, pad under the head piece)
(3) Use a length of rope he cannot get his feet over.
(4) Practise on a soft surface.
(5) Do not use a post in the open, in case he leaps forward and crashes his head into it. Preferably use a solid ring set into a wooden wall higher than him.
(6) Do not use a strange place in the beginning. It can be his stable (but not if a cement floor as he may fall or throw himself down).
(7) Give him something to eat to keep him busy initially. Later this can be dispensed with, if people are around and he has learned not to panic.

SUMMARY

(1) Early education is important. The central message is not to be frightened of humans.
(2) Teach him to do nothing when being handled.
(3) Following, being tied up and being ground tied are all useful first lessons.
(4) Education should involve equines teaching themselves, learning by observing others and learning from humans.

(5) Do not put yourself at risk, as fear will convey itself to the equine.

(6) Give the youngster as much ecological and social experience as possible from the start.

REFERENCES

Anon. 1999. *L'equitation, le cheval et l'ethologie. Colloque du 18 Sept 1999 a l'ecole National d'Equitation.* Belin. Paris.

Brady, E. 1999. 'Sniffing and savoring: the aesthetics of smell and taste', *Philosophy & Geography*. 4.

Kasselle, M. & R. Hanway 1995. *Touching horses. Communication, health, healing through Shiatzu.* J. A. Allen.

Kiley-Worthington, M. & H. D. Randle. 1997. 'Animal handling and Animal Educational Psychology. Symposium Comparative Psychology'. Montreal. & *Eco Research Centre* 012a

Lea,S. & M. Kiley-Worthington. 1996. 'Do Animals Think?' in *Unsolved Myseries of the Mind*. ed. V. Bruce.

Parelli, P. 1999. 'Natural Horsemanship' in *l'Equitation, le cheval et l'ethologie*. Colloque du 18 Sept 1999 a l'ecole Nationa d'Equitation. 23-34. Belin. Paris, and Demonstration.

Roberts, M. 1992. *The man who listens to horses*. Hutchinson. London.

Syme, G. T. & C. A. Syme. 1979. *Social Structure in farm animals*. Elsevier. Amsterdam.

Tellington-Jones, L & S. Taylor. 1992. *The Tellington - Touch*. Cloudcraft Books. Berks.

Wright, M. 1975. *The Jeffery Method of Horse Handling*. Williams. South Australia.

Wright, M. 1983. *The thinking horseman*. Edwards printing. Tamworth. N. S. W.

6

SCHOOLING FROM THE GROUND

- The benefits of working from the ground
- Primary school
- Equipment
- Secondary school

There are many different things your equines can learn from the ground, if you teach them. Remember, almost every equine can learn almost every type of activity that is done by another, and much more besides, so don't ever say, 'He is the wrong sort. ' It is not *him*, who cannot do it, it is *you* ... Neither you nor he may be the best in the world, but surely the point of it all is in the doing, not in the winning! Certainly for work from the ground. It really is not difficult, as you will see, when you start trying. You do not have to have an athletic body, a good figure, an imposing presence, a light weight, a heavy weight, an ability to balance, courage to take physical risks, or lots of money and equipment. . . you just have to want to do it and work at it. It's the mental ability to enjoy your work with equines, self analyse, and think about *how* and *what* to do. The great advantage is that you learn to communicate and co-operate with your equine, it stops being a 'he' and 'I' situation, and becomes a 'we' co-operation, and a delight in doing things together.

Very rarely, with the exception of liberty acts in circuses, or occasional long reining displays, is educating from the ground considered an 'end in itself'. It is usually considered just a 'training technique'. Text books on training horses say the horse must be lunged and long reined before being ridden, although it is not often explained why. That this is clearly not always necessary has been shown by the displays of the new breed of horsemen such as Roberts who demonstrates how a horse that has previously only been led can be ridden within half an hour of being brought into a round pen. The way this is done may not always be the best from the horse's point of view, but nevertheless, it clearly *is* possible for a horse to become a nice ride without previously learning to do anything from the ground except perhaps to be led.

There is no need to feel you have to ride or drive your equine; you can develop handling and working from the ground to a high level of sophistication, and it is not that difficult. There are many people who would like to have to do with equines, but do not want to ride, or may not be able to, for one reason or another,

Stopping for the view on the top of Dartmoor. (Right to left) Young (three years) Kadoon, older Gaynor, little Shindi (loose), her mother Shireen, Aisha, Shemal and young (three years) Shanti with Vicki.

but they can work the equine from the ground. Such people and their equines can demonstrate great skill and a level of communication with the equine which is just as sophisticated as that of the very best rider. In other words, working equines from the ground is not a 'second best', it can become an end in itself, an art form of its own. I would define this as 'harmonious, aesthetically pleasing communication between equine and human which results in actions'. Dances with their own and other species can be developed as a result (see 'Farm Fantasia', 1994, Channel 4). At present there is little emphasis on ground work, and as a result, few really skilled teachers.

In this chapter, I will suggest ways to help the human and the equine (whether donkey, pony, zebra, mule or horse) learn to work together on the ground. In the later part, I explore how 'working from the ground' can become an end in itself.

The first step is, just as in any form of teaching, to ensure that you have the attention of the student, and then use the natural tendencies of the animal to respond to different visual signals used in conjunction with the voice, as we did with handling. Gradually more sophisticated visual signals can be taught. It is very much easier if the voice has been used (chapter 4) with the youngster or naïve adult so that it can be used to praise, to correct and even to ask for particular actions: for example, asking the equine to stand still. The voice is particularly useful as much of the time working from the ground the teacher is at a distance and may not have any restraints, so it is not possible physically to stop the equine doing some things, or make him do others. We verbal creatures already know something about using our voices for communication, but even here there are things we need to learn in order to make it easier for the equine to learn what we are trying to communicate. A few hints here:

(1) Make sure that you believe he will understand; you will then use your voice much more carefully ... and he will!

(2) The voice is important in conveying emotional messages to the equine (the

body can too of course). For example, quiet talking and even singing can help an equine to relax. The voice only needs to be used in conjunction with an appropriate posture (a relaxed body and not looking at the equine to encourage him to relax) for a few times before he will begin to respond appropriately. After a few more repeats, it appears almost as if the gentle talking is an anchor of security.

(3) I find it easier to talk about something to the equine, tell him a story, for example, or sing a song with lots of verses that you have to remember. Perhaps this helps because it requires some of the teacher's attention to tell the story or sing the song, thus stopping her becoming tense or reacting to the horse's feelings inadvertently with the body.

The body of the human teacher also conveys many messages. As the equine becomes more familiar with humans, he rapidly becomes more able to interpret slightly different postures or movements of parts of the human body; the problem is for us to learn how to move and use our bodies to this end.

Working an equine of any type from the ground teaches the teacher to observe. You must learn to read the visual signals he is giving you so that you can choose the best time to ask him to do something different, and also know whether he is having a good time, is frightened, fed up, bored, over excited, lethargic, paying attention or not, and so on.

Coming back from a ride around Dartmoor. Shindi, aged 18 months, in the lead. This is a very small country lane. If a car comes, Katerine, on Aisha behind, puts her on a lead.

Shindi following her elder sister into a pond.

As you become better at visual communication, and he becomes more familiar with humans, much smaller signals will suffice for the equine to grasp the message. A good teacher appears to be giving very few, and very slight cues to even a naïve equine, at least to someone who has little experience. This is why it makes for good entertainment. It looks like magic but it is skilled mutual communication and other methods of communication which are used when riding, such as rhythm, balance, changing the weight in the saddle, use of the reins, and different parts of the legs on the sides (next chapters) which are admired in communicating with the ridden equine, are not available.

We start from where we left off in the last chapter: the youngster has now had a good nursery school education and can be handled (has learnt to do nothing when touched) and understands being tied up, can be led and will walk towards a person when he is asked with appropriate visual or voice cues. The youngster has also had the opportunity to continue to acquire ecological and social knowledge as a result of being taken out and about with or without others on expeditions, and living with others of different ages and sexes, so he is growing up a normal well balanced equine.

The age at which this should start is a matter of considerable debate. Many people say that since the youngster is still growing and his bones are cartilagineous, he should not do very much at all or it will stunt or damage his physical development. It is surprising how often one comes across articles which exude outrage at a youngster learning to lunge as a yearling.

(Above) *Shanti all tacked up is a little scared of the string. Vicki shows it to him. Then* (below) *she waggles it – and he has grasped it is not frightening.*

The rational approach, it would seem, is to consider whether or not learning new things, learning to use the body in different ways, and developing muscles and skills is beneficial. If one trains a child of ten, say, to perform Olympic athletics (female gymnasts for example) this involves the very young growing body being over stretched and working for hours every day. When the women mature their bodies are often severely damaged. On the other hand, learning to do some of the gymnastic movements slowly, exercising the mind and body for an hour or two a week is generally considered beneficial for children of all ages and is included in their school curriculum. Just the same applies to equines: too much physical work accompanied by excessive feeding and all sorts of chemical additives in the diet and applied to the skin is likely to cause problems as the equine matures. A small amount of work learning the ins and outs of different tasks is both mentally and physically beneficial to development. Consequently, we start our youngsters on the free school or lunge, walking, trotting and, when they can manage it, cantering for one circle, for a total of up to ten minutes on both reins at nine months or a year old, depending on the youngster's growth and behaviour, and the time we have available. It is particularly important to give young colts things to occupy their minds as they often become rather bumptious and try things out in order to have a reaction from the human handler. If the individual is badly grown, weak or sick, or we are just too busy, then they will not start further learning work until later.

Lilka on a 'school outing', learning about walking over a series of logs.

Shanti, aged three, is driven out on free school by Vicki with her body upright and the whip behind him.

Primary school

The equine's primary school can be divided into stages described below.

Stage 1. The youngsters are taken on different, longer walks in order to acquire further experiences of the world. Gradually, as they become used to everyday things, more different things are introduced, for example going into ponds and swimming, walking over tarpaulins, ducking under trees, climbing mountains, jumping ditches and so on. It is just as much fun taking your equine for a walk as it is taking your dog or your friend, in fact you can all go together if you like! The youngster can either be led by hand or from a ridden horse, or from a horse-drawn vehicle if another equine is being driven. If there is open, traffic-free ground, then they can be let off and allowed to follow the others freely, exploring as they go (see page 113).

Stage 2. The next stage of primary school is to begin to learn to do more simple movements to a word (or gesture) command, such as to lift a leg, or put a leg on a pedestal (see page 60). The youngster is learning more about the teacher as well as to listen to her. Just as important, the teacher is learning about him. It is fun teaching many little movements and rewarding the youngster when he gets it right, as well as an extremely important step in the equine's education.

Stage 3. Getting used to the equipment, such as ropes, bridles, saddles, harness and so on. The equine must stand still while such things are fitted, willingly take the bit, if one is to be used, or have the various straps and girths tightened without

Here he is going forward with a lengthened trot, although his head is too high for a conventional dressage stance. Note he is on the free school and is circling around the teacher in the middle in a 20 metre circle, although he could go right down to the other end of the manege where Lilka and others are standing. This is genuine 'free school' and it is remarkable how quickly they will learn this.

worry. He must get used to pieces of rope and leather around his legs. All the fitting must be done quietly and progressively. Remember, if he does not like something or becomes slightly bored, then return to simpler things he does not mind, and progress again until he is completely quiet with each phase. Rushing through something to achieve something else does not pay off in the long run and often teaches the equine to be difficult with particular procedures.

Stage 4. This next stage is learning to move when asked at different gaits. You can either (a) free school,(b) lunge or (c) no restraint school. It is not necessary to choose one only, since your youngster (or older naive equine) can learn by doing some of all three of these. We will point out the advantages and disadvantages of each of these, and how to begin teaching your equine to do them.

Equipment

Many people are put off working their equines from the ground because they do not have all the equipment that is recommended in the establishment handbooks, and cannot afford it all. This is very unfortunate and gives rise to welfare problems for horses that could easily be avoided if more ground work was done before riding.

All sorts of boots and bandages are recommended for ground work, and many spend more time putting on this equipment than actually working their horses! Even if this is done in order to reduce potential injury to the horse, one needs to ask whether, if the horse is so likely to get injured doing such work, he should be doing it at all. It is also overlooked that being aware of his body and legs and how they can be controlled is part of what he is learning during work from the ground. If he treads on one foot with the other, or brushes two together, trips and even grazes himself, he is much less likely to do it again. He has a chance of learning to adjust his movements so this does not happen, rather than because he is over-protected. If he is handicapped and will hurt himself anyway, then there is of course a reason for protecting him, but only the handicapped horse needs bandages, boots and so on.

A headcollar which is strong is recommended, and a lunge line or rope around 6 metres long with a clip on the end that can be clipped around the front of the noseband and onto itself if you are beginning with lunging. Cavessons (noseband bridles with pieces of mental around the noseband which are traditionally used for lunging) are heavy, expensive and restrictive and there is no need to have one.

A long whip is advisable. It is possible when free schooling or with non restraint teaching to use the lunge line as a whip and throw it out at the horse, but it is less accurate, slower and consequently more difficult to use well than a whip which can be flicked out wherever required to encourage both pace and direction of movement.

Shanti coming in on free school; teacher has dropped whip and slouched body.

Neither whip or lunge line should be necessary after a lesson or two, but they are helpful for the beginner in particular.

If the youngster is going to learn to be ridden, we usually tack him up with a bridle and saddle for these lessons. This allows him to become used to the bit, the saddle, stirrups and things flapping around while moving. But of course it is not obligatory.

When starting energetic ground work we also use **side reins**. These are reins/ropes attached to the bit and then to the girth or a band around the belly. The reason for the use of this extra restriction are several:

(1) The restriction of the head prevents the equine looking around all over the place, and makes it easier for him to pay attention to the teacher.

(2) The constant pressure of the side rein teaches him another basic physical principle he must learn: to give to the rein because it is more comfortable than to resist it.

The idea of free schooling or lunging is that the equine will move around the person in the centre (who turns, but does not move his position from the centre, so that the horse can describe a circle, not an oblong or some other irregular shape). The equine can learn all the same things as when free schooled. He will, in order to stay in particular gaits and rhythms, have to balance himself carefully on the circle. He will learn about tack, equipment, ropes, and about human reactions. Since equines like to move, and will move away when uncertain of anything, it is an ideal way of allowing them to move but also ensuring some continual contact with them. In other words an important step in their learning to learn.

(a) Free schooling

This requires an enclosed pen of some sort. It is easiest in a round pen around 12-15 metre diameter (which is why demonstrations are always done in such pens). But this is not essential. Any enclosed area will do around 20 metres x 20 metres, round, rectangular or square. This can be made up in almost any field with an electric tape. The youngster must know and respect an electric wire and he must not be too frightened otherwise he may charge through it or jump it. It is easier if the ground is even and flat, but again not essential. If it is muddy and slightly up and down, it will be harder work for both pupil and teacher, but it is always possible.

The advantage of teaching the equine to move around you on the free school is that he learns to listen to your voice and watch your gestures, and the teacher learns how to use her voice and her gestures, so the communication between the two can quickly improve. However, it needs a little skill to get started if you do not have a round pen, and it is particularly important to be able to get the equine to move forward without frightening him too much.

The equine is let go in the pen and allowed to wander around investigating it for five minutes or so. Then the teacher withdraws to the centre and, using her body language (see opposite), her arms, a length of rope, lunge line or a whip behind him, encourages him to move forward. There is little to choose between

Gestures, accompanied by the voice, directing the two-year-old Shukrune in his first free school lesson. 'Off you go', when he was inclined to hang around me, an upright posture.

'Come in please' to a lower posture. These are gestural and postural changes that the youngster will learn by instrumental learning within a few minutes in his first lesson, provided they are clear and consistent.

A food reward follows.

lunge line or whip from the horse's point of view, and those who call whips 'wands' in order to excuse the use of a whip (e.g. Teddington Jones) have their heads rather high in the clouds (from the horse's point of view). From the humans' point of view, there is an advantage to the long whip, as it is easier to place exactly where you want, rather than flapping about with a lunge line that goes in the wrong place.

You first teach the equine to go away from the whip, by flicking it behind him; if he has not had any exposure to a whip before, you may even touch him with it. As he goes forward he has to circle around the teacher. The teacher, who should stay as still as she can in the centre, should ensure that he keeps going, so if he stops or turns, she must raise the whip behind him and even walk up behind him if necessary. She uses an upright stance, looks directly at the equine to keep him away on the perimeter.

Many of the people who demonstrate free schooling do not make the most of its potential. One common fault is that they run along behind the horse flapping their hands, the whip or lunge line instead of standing still and using the equine's quick ability to learn visual signals to go forward away from the whip and later a raised hand. Another fault is they often allow the horse to turn around and go the other way on the circle whenever he wants. Usually he will do this by turning his head to the pen fence and his quarters to the person in the centre; as a result he does not learn to keep going in a constant direction, but may stop and turn frequently when something worries him. They also allow him to go at whatever speed he likes and some of the less skilled chase the horse relentlessly; I have seen horses, even in public demonstrations and teaching programmes (where it should have been stopped), so terrified that they try to climb the walls of the pen! Three opportunities are missed here:

(a) Firstly, the lesson to keep the horse going in one direction with the teacher still in the middle simply calling a word, or performing a slight gesture, to keep him going at the desired gait and in the desired direction, until he is asked to change, rather than stopping or randomly changing direction at will. Properly done, the exercise encourages the horse to watch you and to gradually learn to respond to a series of gestures or word commands for particular gaits and direction. It also makes the teacher think much more carefully about her positioning, posture and word commands.

(b) They learn to turn away from the teacher by turning out. After, it is more difficult to teach them to turn towards the centre when asking for a change in direction, or a *volte* (small circle and continuation on the same rein). If they are then frightened, it is not unknown for the equine to turn his quarters to the centre and towards the human, and kick out. It takes very few occasions of this happening with an unskilled teacher before it can become an unpleasant habit.

(c) Lessons about different gaits and even different types of one gait (e.g. lengthening or shortening of the stride) can be learnt by the equine, often in the first couple of lessons, but only if they are taught.

The most important educational aspect of free schooling or lunging is to familiarise the equine with going forward at different gaits, to balance himself on

Lilka following Sioban around the manege - 'join up'.

a circle, learn to keep an even cadence (rhythm) and to learn the word commands for different directions, different movements and different gaits.

The use of the whole body by the teacher, initially, will encourage the animal to go away as far as he can from the teacher (see page 123), or to come towards her.

The first thing is to keep the equine going around the ring consistently. When he is relaxed, starts to look towards the centre, and comes in slightly off the fence, is the time to then ask him to come in by adopting the opposite stance and using the voice: relax your body and not looking directly at him. When he comes in he is rewarded with tit bits and the voice before again being sent out with the upright body position. It is important to remain slightly behind him in order to direct him forward and in the required direction. After a few times of coming into the middle when asked, provided the teacher's body posture is kept relaxed, the equine will tend to keep with the teacher, and follow her around. This has been called 'joining up' by Roberts. He is more likely to follow if, when turning, you turn to the side he is - i.e. if he is on your right, you turn to the right. Consequently, start with this and as he falls into ' following', introduce turning away from him, and having him follow. He may stop, catch sight of something else or just wander off, in which case you must attract his attention and start again, rewarding him well when his attention stays with you. If he is not being very co-operative about coming in when asked, or not following, then send him out and keep him going until he keeps turning his head in and wanting to come in, then ask him to and praise him when he does.

One of the signs that the equine is relaxing and more or less at ease with the movement is when he licks his lips or chews. This is what is called a 'transitional activity' because such movements occur between bouts of doing other movements. Chewing in this way often occurs at the end of a period of slight fear, anxiety or uncertainty. When the teacher sees it, it is a good idea to praise him with the

A student learning about free schooling in a conventional round pen at a college where this was being taught. She is throwing the lunge line out behind the horse, who is frightened, and is about to climb the fence rather than go forward, not a satisfactory development. With a young horse, reducing fear is extremely important.

voice, indicating that this type of behaviour (which signifies that the uncertainty and worry are over) is acceptable. This will then help him to relax.

A young reactive horse will learn the gait changes, to come towards and go away from the teacher, to go left and right, to change the rein, and even to lengthen and shorten the trot stride when asked in around 15 minutes from the beginning (page 123), if a skilled person is doing the teaching, using appropriate gestures, body placements and voice commands. In fact to test this out I did this with Shukrune aged two, when a TV company came to film (shown page 126). He had only been handled and led before (TV film 'Great Western Women', 1998).

How far all this is achieved in the first lesson will depend largely on the teacher, although the past experience and personality of the horse is also important of course. Most important is to observe the general rules for good teaching (page 67). In particular:

(i) Learn to observe and act appropriately.

(ii) Self analyse so you can learn from your mistakes.

Remember, if things go wrong, it is *never* the student's fault. It is the teacher's for not presenting the problem and its solution properly; this is one reason why teaching can be such fun, but hard work. As time goes on, the teacher will develop her own more sophisticated methods to develop communication with the equine student further. Here there is no dogma, no way or order in which things must be done. Let your own common sense dictate; only bear in mind the general rules of teaching.

Of course, if you are a beginner, it is better to practise on a horse who knows what he is doing, and can teach you. But even a complete beginner who has never had to do with equines before can have a go at free schooling and sometimes they can get further than people who have preconceived ideas. The exciting thing is how quickly both teacher and taught will enter into it all, and how much communication really does take place; there are no restraints, no pushing or pulling, the equine does it because he wants to and he understands.

If you get confused or troubled, and have tried unsuccessfully to overcome a problem, then analyse your behaviour and think carefully. Generally with a little thought and a lot of observation, it will be possible to solve the problem yourself. Talking to friends and family, and airing the problem may help you see other possible solutions which you can try.

Once one has achieved gait changes and direction changes and so on with the youngster, the challenge then is to ensure that he continues to learn new things otherwise he will become bored and it is then that he will mess about and may develop behaviour and habits that you do not want. For example, start to teach him to do a *volte* (small circle and continue on the same rein, page 119) instead of just coming in to you (page 120), or to lengthen and shorten his stride at the different gaits, and be sure that you are reducing your signals.

In the first place remember that when he first starts going around, he will probably be full of energy and want to travel fast. He may lose his balance and that will make him leap about (particularly when he goes very fast around the circle). It is very important to let him do this, and expend some of his energy so that he will be more interested in listening and trying to understand what you want. Insisting on blind obedience at all times is bad teaching, because it does not help, reduces the pupil's decision- making and choices, and consequently hinders learning.

When the horse and human are working well together, there should be hardly a sign that anyone watching can see. I find that the position of my feet, and whether my hands are stretched or hanging loose can be used as signals. Where one is looking becomes a signal, even an eye blink can become an invitation to do this or that. In fact there seems to be no end to how far one can go with this communication. Perhaps the most interesting, though, is when the horse does the movements with only voice commands when the teacher is not visible at all.

As far as more conventional movements go, one of the reasons for lunging or free schooling is to allow the equine to be able to balance himself well on a circle, something gangly youngsters have to learn to do. When this is established, then work towards an even cadence of his paces. One way of helping him form the habit of a graceful, even cadenced gait is to call out the beat to him or even have a metronome or clap in rhythm, to encourage him to listen to the rhythm and associate that with the rhythm of his legs. This helps him to slow the tempo and even lengthen the stride. It is easiest at the two time trot, but it can be done of course with each gait.

Another requirement, if he is going to progress in his movements and teaching in the classical school, is that he should be equally active with his hind legs as his front ones. Most horses tend to lift their front legs higher than their hind, and leave their hind end spread out behind to start with. The 'engagement of the hind legs', as it is called, involves getting them to lift their hind legs up higher and place them further underneath so that their whole body does not appear to be so spread out; they seem to be using their hind legs and quarters to give them the forward movement: impulsion. Voice, in association initially with the whip flicked out towards the hind legs, often helps here. Sometimes they rush off fast, before they manage to lengthen the stride, slow the rhythm, and keep the same ground covering speed. When this happens, if you watch the hind legs, you will see that they are now lifting up higher, although not necessarily coming further underneath. Praise at this point and bringing them in will reward them for the movement which is one step further towards what you are after.

Ten minutes' hard work at one gait for a 2-4 year-old is probably as much as he will be able to attend to before needing a change. For a younger horse, with a shorter attention span, five minutes is enough, and in any case all one will require is quiet movement forward at the required gait, and coming in when asked.

As soon as some even minor improvement is achieved, stop and teach something else; for example: to go backwards when you asked a step or two, to begin to learn to cross over his legs, or to lift one or other leg in the first stages of a Spanish walk (see page 191). The teacher may have to push him into position to show him what is intended; for crossing a leg you may have to place the legs in the desired place (moulding), for example, or use imitation (see page 61) and voice to ask for the particular action. Reward as soon as he starts to do what you

Lilka having a first lunge lesson with Chris. Note the whip behind her, but low, and Chris's position to keep her out, away from him.

want. The next time he must do a little more of what ever it is before he obtains the reward, and after a few days of 5 minute sessions, he must make almost the complete movement ('shaping') before you praise him or give him a food reward. It is very useful to use the voice here to encourage him, so that when he begins to do the right thing you quickly say, 'yes, yes, good, well done' with plenty of expression. If he does the wrong thing you say 'no, no', frown slightly and shake your head or look away. He quickly learns these gestures in association with the word. Soon all you need to do is say 'yes' and 'no' to teach him new things!

After a break, another short spurt of balance and rhythm work may be in order, but it is vital to observe what your pupil may be feeling before deciding what would be the best thing to do next. There is no instant formula, there are only suggestions, just as when teaching a child. If the equine persists, for example, in stopping at a particular place on the circle, or trying to jump out at a particular place, then your job is to predict this, and act. Ensure that by voice command, gesture and the appropriate positioning and use of the whip he does not do the same the next time. It is vital to praise him when he does not stop or jump when you thought he might.

Sometimes equines who have started being over-reactive become relatively unresponsive to the whip. The cause originally for their over activity is often confusion and unfamiliarity, consequently when they are clear about what they are supposed to do, they become extremely laid back. The best solution, I find here, rather than using the whip or lunge line more firmly, is to indicate with the voice that you are displeased, or you would like more action. This sometimes can have much more effect than the whip.

If, by contrast, after a few sessions, the horse continues to be extremely over-reactive and panic easily, then you should question the way you are teaching.

Chris calls Lilka in; although she has a lunge line, she should come in without being pulled on the line. She is not coming in straight, but Chris continues to ask her to come with a relaxed body.

Perhaps your aids have not been consistent enough and the equine is just confused (this is very common unfortunately). Whatever the reason, the teacher's job is to adjust her teaching to suit the individual, so that he does improve. There is no soft option such as, 'He was so badly "broken" before.' If you know that, then it must be built into your teaching.

(b) Lunging

This is the most common and easiest method since the equine has a rope attached to him and can consequently easily be turned and stopped. The lunge line is not a rein and using it on the bit causes the equine to become much less sensitive to the bit thereafter.

The advantage is that it requires very little equipment (a headcollar and a long rope) and a piece of ground some 6 metres x 6 metres. A headcollar and a long rope or lunge rein which clips onto the noseband (preferably around the front so that it can slide over when the direction is changed) is something most people will have. It is easier of course if the ground is flat and soft, but not essential, although it should not be done on concrete or tarmac! If you are inexperienced and the naive equine is large, it is wiser to do this in an enclosed space to start with, but it should not take more than a couple of successful lessons for you then to be able to lunge him without a safety enclosure.

The disadvantage of lunging is that it takes a little while to get used to not getting tangled in the line, and keeping yourself in the right position – that is, behind him to drive him forward. A whip is usually held in the other hand from which the equine should move away. Many people find they cannot keep him going around, as he turns in to face the person lunging. For this reason equines are usually taught to lunge first by having someone leading them around. Lunging should (but often does not) teach the person the importance of the body in communicating with the horse. It can also be a useful way to give him a little exercise when there are no other possibilities and no enclosed area. Lunging has the advantage that it can be done almost anywhere and does not require an enclosed area. This means that even the one horse owner who keeps her horse in a field on the outskirts of town can lunge her horse, and get to know him better, communicate with him more astutely and exercise him when it is difficult to go out.

There is a surprising amount of mystique concerning lunging. It can take a little while to get the hang of it, but anyone can do it, even from a wheel chair. It is best to remember the few simple rules and practise first on an experienced equine, rather than both lunger and lunged trying to learn together.

Most people who start lunging a horse from the beginning by themselves attach a second lunge line around the outside and around the horse's quarters, which leads to the hand of the teacher in the middle. The idea of this is that if he turns in (which first timers are likely to do), the outside line can be pulled. If you are beginner, this may be helpful, although it is an extra restraint, and all the lines may get in a muddle. I have never done this, rather I start a youngster alone with one line and ensure my body is behind his shoulder so I can drive him forwards all the time with the whip behind, and keep him on a small circle to begin with, which is much easier. Occasionally equines that have been handled too indulgently may be difficult but keeping them moving forward is the key.

If you and the horse are both learning, then get someone to lead him around the circle. Gradually the helper can leave go of the horse, and walk away to the *outside*, describing a larger circle, so that the horse, who will be inclined to follow, keeps out rather than turning in to the person in the centre. When he has grasped this concept, then the assistant can walk right away and the teacher in the middle keeps him going forwards and out, using body language, voice, gesture and the whip.

For the more experienced, just as for free schooling, it is not difficult to teach a youngster who has no previous experience to lunge within a few minutes without anyone helping by using the body position correctly. It may be helpful to summarise the most important considerations:

RULES TO HELP WITH LUNGING

(a) Start with a small circle. As the equine and the human become more confident, increase the size of the circle.

(b) Make sure that you and the whip are behind the horse. As soon as you are head to head with him he will stop and turn his quarters out, so keep at his shoulder or behind.

(c) Start by walking him around slightly ahead of you, with the whip behind. Do not worry about keeping still or describing a perfect circle at this stage. Gradually as he and you get the idea, you can move less, and he moves more and faster and the circle is formed.

(d) Always keep behind him with the whip in the hand which is behind. The other hand holds the lunge line, and this *must not be held so it can tighten around your hand*. If it is, and the horse charges off suddenly, you can lose a hand!

(e) As with free schooling, the position of the body is crucial; if you do not want him to approach, use an upright posture and look straight at him; if you want him to approach, use a collapsed posture and do not look him in the eye.

(f) Once you have mastered the art of keeping the equine in the desired gaits, getting him to do simple gait changes and asking him to come to you when required, it is then important to make lunging (or free schooling) more interesting by teaching him new movements or he may either become very lethargic and show no interest, or start to invent problems, leap about in order to invent interest for himself. There are more options for different movements with the free school as the lunge line gets in the way, but there are in both cases many different movements you can teach.

One way to make things a greater challenge for the equine student is to reduce the signals that you give until they are undetectable by another human observer. He can learn (by associative learning page 58) to respond to whatever consistent movement, gesture or word that you teach him. It is even possible to teach him to reverse his tendency to go away from an upright posture, but rather to come towards you!

The difficulty with lunging is that if you are not very experienced, and the horse is large and bumptious, he may leap and turn about, and you will get in a tangle with the line. If this happens and you cannot solve it or become scared, then the best thing is to get someone to help you get him started, or make up a small enclosure and start on the free school instead. Once he knows what is required, and realises he is not going to have a frightening time, he will be easy.

If the horse pulls or leans on the line (not uncommon), the best solution is to pull the line very hard briefly and then relax it. Every time he starts leaning, repeat this. Even individuals who have a long habit of leaning will, with this treatment, tend to stop it after a few lunge lessons.

An equine that has been free schooled will understand being lunged immediately, provided the body is used correctly, and *vice versa*.

(c) No restraint schooling method

Here the equine is unattached and not in an enclosed space. He is taught by gesture and voice to walk, trot or canter around the teacher. He can also learn to go in a direction indicated, to come when he is called, to change the rein, to *volte* (see page 125) and so on. Since the equine has a choice not to stay with the teacher, this is the method that shows the most mutual trust and communication, but it does need both the human and the equine to have some experience.

No restriction work is perhaps best used as the next stage after working on the free school. It is great fun to do, but you have to choose your time and place well.

The best solution often is to do a little of each, depending on the facilities. Our experience is that if you do not have a round pen or permanently enclosed space around 20 metres x 20 metres, it is easiest to start the naive equine on the lunge and when he has the concept of going around you, he will adapt this to the free school, even in a temporarily enclosed area, and then finally it will be possible to do this without any restraint or enclosure.

The challenge here is to ensure that he *does* want to stay with you, and to use much positive reinforcement. It is wise not to have other horses around as they will distract him. The equine learns the language: to go away, come or jump over jumps, just by being asked. This is a particularly challenging way of teaching, although some, particularly amateur owners, may get a long way with this.

We tend to combine no restraint schooling with free school and lunge work. It is useful and very good for improving the teaching of static movements (e.g. crossing the legs); not so easy with more active gait movements, but it can be done. After being free schooled and lunged, many horses or ponies will tend to circle around the person in the centre. If you go into their field with a long whip and ask them to go forward they may begin to do this. If they gallop off, then your first exercise should be to get them to come to you and gradually change this to walking and trotting around you. Many of our horses have not been taught this, but will when asked keep circling the person in the middle, sometimes with extra enthusiasm and gaiety I must admit!

An amusing exercise we have used when TV companies come to make films is to go out in the field, and then tell the horses to gallop off. One or two who understand start it off, and the rest take part. Soon the TV company has some fine footage of elegant Arabs swirling around in the field, occasionally coming swooping up to the camera, just for fun, sometimes, with cameraman and camera beating a hasty retreat because they do not know that the horses will gallop around, past, or up to them, but not knock them over (e.g. 'Captive Friends' TV movie, Channel 4, 1990).

Work on the ground, as an end in itself, does not require any other equipment. However, if work on the ground is being used as a preparation for riding, then equipment should be introduced to the equine. We will quickly run through some fairly well known and obvious ways of doing this without problems.

'Bitting'

There is much mystique about introducing the equine to a bit. Which bits to use is a hotly debated subject. It would seem logical to have him wear the bit that he will be ridden in when he comes to be ridden. This will allow him to become familiar with it. A bit with side pieces for a novice equine in order to prevent it sliding through his mouth is wise, but whether the simple snaffle is jointed on not, whether it is rubber or not may make little difference at this stage. The most important things are that:

(a) It does not pinch or hurt him, or he will quickly learn to avoid the bridle being put on, and this can develop into awkward habits such as throwing the head around.

(b) Ensure that he cannot put his tongue over the bit at the start. This happens when the bit is too low in the mouth.

He will try initially to dislodge the strange object in his mouth by opening his mouth, chewing and particularly moving the tongue to try to get it behind to push the bit out. If the bit is low in the mouth, the tongue can slip over the mouthpiece and is then uncomfortable and difficult to draw back. Equines can quickly develop a habit of having the tongue over the bit which may take some re-educating. Preventing them opening their mouths is one way of stopping this, so many people put on a cavesson with a tight noseband, or even a drop noseband to prevent it. But this is an extra restriction and unnecessary if you think about it. Better to make it uncomfortable for him to put his tongue over the bit. This can be done by having things dangling from the mouthpiece which encourage him to play with them on his tongue (these are called 'keys'), or by ensuring that the mouthpiece is high enough in his mouth for it to be very difficult to put the tongue over it. The bit may have to wrinkle the corners of the mouth considerably (depending on the length of the mouthpiece), so that he cannot draw his tongue back enough. Look in the mouth and see where the middle of the mouthpiece is lying. Often it is much lower than the side ring, even if the ring is wrinkling the side of the mouth, and this allows him to put his tongue over.

On the premise that you should have the minimum of equipment, you can argue that an equine should not be ridden in a bit at all. Certainly this is quite possible, equines can be educated so that they willingly do what is required, and perform all the movements in company or alone, even galloping around in unenclosed places without a bit. However, it is easier to teach if one starts by using a simple bit, and then takes it off.

Much depends on what you want to achieve with your horse. There is generally no problem at all teaching a young horse who has been well educated up to this point to be ridden alone in a headcollar, or even quietly with others, provided you are happy and relaxed riding without a bit. But if you wish to do dressage tests, for example, you will not be allowed to ride without one, and the same applies for most competitions. It is definitely more of a challenge to do a correct dressage test, run a race or jump a cross country course just with a headcollar, a halter, or even a rope around the neck. Few people can do this with their horses well, but perhaps it is something we should be encouraging, if we are trying to work towards greater harmony and communication between human and horse. It is generally believed that it is not possible to have the horse go 'correctly' in the classical school tradition without a bit: not so. Imam points this out, working his horses in a headcollar, and doing advanced movements, but the majority of people never even try.

Putting on the bridle
It is important from the start not to have a struggle to put the bit into the equine's mouth, and the headpiece over his ears. Remember, equines form habits quickly (page 52). If you have one struggle, it will happen again and again until it is difficult to change. There are simpler ways out of this:
(i) Have some food in your hand as you put the bit in. This will encourage him to open his mouth and then the bit can be slipped in, and a further food reward given.
(ii) Particularly with a larger horse the top of whose head is difficult to reach, undo one side of the bit so that you do not have to put it in and over the ears all

at once. Once the bit is in his mouth, hold it there with one hand while giving him something to eat so he drops his head, and put the headpiece around his ears and do it up.

Repeat putting the bridle on a couple of times and if it is a problem, continue until the right habit is established. There will only be a problem if you have started hurriedly and thoughtlessly.

Side reins

If you are going to introduce the youngster to a bit, then it is important not to make mistakes with the bitting; even more importantly, not to make mistakes with the use of the bit the first few times he is ridden. Unfortunately, the most common riding problem is related to the use of the hands. Riders use the bit as a 'command mechanism', even using the analogy of a steering wheel, rather than a 'conversational instrument' which allows an exchange of communication and development of co-operation between horse and rider. Quite advanced riders, who do converse through their hands, will still talk about 'pushing the right buttons', and 'applying the brakes' (that is pull on the mouth). But, as one of my teachers put it, 'it takes two to pull'. It is crucial to learn that if the equine resists or pulls against the bit, it is very important not to pull against him as this will increase his resistance because the pull hurts and he will try and rush away from it, gradually forming the habit of doing this rather than giving to the bit. Similarly if you give with your hands when he pulls seriously he will learn to do this, often putting his head down and using his neck as a lever. With side reins, he has to learn (with the constant tension on the side rein) that levering or resisting does no good, so he has to give to the rein. Once he has worked out the basic physics of this, as with learning to give to a rope when he is tied up, all he has to learn (in order to be a delightful easy ride and communicate with the rider through his mouth and their hands) is to give to a side rein pressure, and then he will give to the co-operative hand of the rider.

One of the problems with using the hands on a young horse is that, however skilled the rider is, the hands are not consistent. Consequently the horse may receive confusing messages, and, as we know, this is not conducive to quick learning. If the unpredictable hand continues, it is not unusual for him to give up trying to understand the intricacies of subtle communication with the rider through his mouth and her hands. Consequently he gives up responding to slight pressure, and is then called 'hard mouthed'! To avoid this problem, we normally fit side reins *with no elasticised parts,* between the saddle and the bit before the horse has any other contact through the rein. Initially the side reins are loose. Thus, the first message is that he cannot put his head down or up without the side reins restricting the movement. The first contact should be reasonably gentle, hence the long side reins to start with as the more reactive equine will panic when his mouth encounters the restriction and he may throw his head up, increasing the pressure, and even jump up in the air. Gradually over a period of a couple of days working for around 30 minutes a session, the side reins are shortened until they are about 3 cm longer than they would be to maintain his head in the perpendicular position when he is walking. The correct length of the side reins is to ensure that when trotting or cantering, his head is carried vertically to the ground. At the walk, it is slightly in front of the vertical. Shortening the side reins to the correct length must be done with tact and depends on the individual horse's ability to learn basic physics. Too fast and he will panic, too slow and he will establish the habit of holding his head in front of the vertical. He may take a while to understand the principle, 'Give to them and they give to you,' but he will. If there is excitement or panic, then just lengthen them until they only just contact his mouth when he raises or lowers his head too much.

The point is that the side reins are 100% consistent; when he stretches his neck to their limit, they prevent further stretch and give not at all. To avoid pressure on his mouth, therefore, he must teach himself to give with his head when he feels the tightening, and the pressure goes away. Once a youngster has learnt this, he will maintain a correct outline, and be able to balance and begin to shorten his body and use his hind legs more, in order to keep going forward. He has learnt to 'give to the bit'; the more tricky stage is to teach the human rider to 'give to the horse' with her hands!

So, although side reins are indeed an added restraint which we should not have, for a short while at the beginning of teaching the youngster to move forward, they can have a very important use which will then ensure that he and the rider have a better time for ever more. Although side reins reduce choices, they give him security when there are new things to be learnt (e.g. going to different frightening places). Running reins are another story (see page 161).

It is true that it is possible to educate him and ride him without using side reins, or indeed any tack, headcollar, bridle or saddle at all from the beginning. The main disadvantage of that is getting him to pay attention. Using side reins is a compromise, if you will; hopefully eventually you will be able to do without any restraints, if you wish.

Even a horse whose natural movement may be somewhat 'hollow backed', such as many Arabs for example, will rapidly learn to drop his head and relax his back from the beginning with side reins, and without trauma. In this way, the equine has 'bitted' himself, and all the human teacher, whether on the ground, driving or riding, has to do is recognise this.

Saddling

Before putting a saddle on a youngster, it is a good idea to have him used to the idea of things being put on his back – rugs, surcingle, etc. Then putting the saddle on will not be an important event. All that has to be done is for the saddle to be presented to him in front, so he can smell and touch it, and become slightly familiar. It will have been on other equines, so ensure that it smells of one he likes first. Presenting the colt with a saddle that has recently been on one of the stallions who attacks the colt will cause him, understandably, to draw away and become somewhat suspicious the first time or two.

After he has seen, touched and smelt it, it is gently placed over his back. If he jumps or shows any fear (head up, nostrils extended, faster breathing, higher heart rate, moving around), then this is done again and again until he stands quietly. Then the girth is put around his stomach and tightened enough to stop the saddle slipping. Again if he dislikes this, do it again and again until he does not mind it. When he does stands still, praise him. Generally, the equine who has been properly handled will not object to the saddle or girth, provided it is done carefully by observant and self-analytical people. Start leading him around with the stirrups up, but, as he gets used to it, the saddle flaps can be raised and lowered, and then flapped about, and the stirrups allowed down to swing around him until he pays no attention even though they touch his sides. Then he can be lunged with them down. It is also a good idea at some stage to put on a breast plate or a crupper to get him used to all sorts of the bits and pieces he may have to wear to keep the saddle in place in difficult terrain.

If he is to be driven, then, once he is accustomed to a riding saddle, the whole harness can be fitted. The crupper and the breeching are the pieces they usually find worrying.

Attention

It is important with all these processes neither to have too many things going on around him, nor too few. Make sure he is paying attention to each stage, as otherwise you may have trouble after a few uneventful occasions. The equine student suddenly pays attention for the first time and realises all sorts of things are being attached to him, and may surprise you by becoming scared. The human handler or rider can quite easily be lulled into a false state of security, and then the equine is described as 'unreliable'... only because no one had bothered to explain what was happening to him from the start and made him aware of it. Once he has had a scare, he has to relearn 'reversal learning', which is more difficult for him, and to teach.

Attention can also be distracted when an equine appears to be likely to be disturbed by one of these processes. I have found it useful to have some food in my hand, but not let him take it all at once, so he has to nuzzle away to get one grain of oat or a nut. This will take his attention off something unpleasant or frightening, so it should be used only when things have to be done. It is much better to just talk quietly to him which should relax him, and ensure that he is paying attention to what you are doing so that he learns about it and that it is not frightening, and repeat it and repeat it again if he is worried, ensuring that he is paying attention.

It is also very important to ensure the saddle does not slip forwards or backwards or around his tummy the first few times. Make sure that the buckles are easy to do up and undo so that there is no fussing about, particularly if you are slightly nervous. You can always pretend to fuss about with them while he must stay still, and yet know that you can get the saddle off or secure it quickly if you need to.

If the handling has been done well, it is possible to deck the equine out with a whole harness of riding tack without any objection or anxiety from him in around ten minutes. He then needs to take a little time to get used to the funny feelings, but continue with the golden rule of not letting him become frightened, as he can easily frighten himself.

> The colt, Luxor, wearing a saddle and a bridle for the first time, was being lunged and started trotting. The saddle flapped, and he began to canter; as he cantered the saddle flapped more on his back and he began to buck. Rather than let him continue working himself up into a panic, the best policy was to ask him to come in, or bring him in with the lunge line if he is too panicky to listen. We stopped him and calmed him down, then started again, leading him for a couple of steps only and praising him when he did not panic. In this way, he avoided learning that the equipment is scary; he also learnt that if things go wrong, it is best to stop and have them put right.
>
> The next day, we tacked him up again, and walked him on a short lunge line; then trotted, leading him, so if he became worried, the leader would just go back to a walk. Within three further sessions he was cantering around with the stirrups down and flapping without worries or bucks.

Secondary school

There are almost no limits to what can be taught to the horse from the ground. As we have mentioned, one of the research centre's main interests is the degree to which an equine (and various other species) can learn to comprehend language. Working from the ground opens up many vistas for experimenting with teaching the equine to listen and comprehend language, so the field is wide open for anyone to have a go.

Teaching using word commands only

As we have emphasised (chapter 4) there are distinct advantages to using the voice to communicate with equines. The most important is that it is our easiest method of communication. The question of how much language equines might be able to understand when they are taught is relevant to improving our relationships with them and their education.

Skills such as long reining, driving and liberty work with several horses or ponies – or any particular action – can be taught. The more the teacher and the equine improve, the better the communication.

> The Spanish riding school (and various other people) give displays of long reining in which the horse may do half pass, *piaffe*, *passage*, canter changes, *levade* and so on as the human trots along behind. Here the teacher has only two reins and uses her voice to ask the horse to do these various movements. She cannot be seen in any detail when she is running along directly behind the horse, and usually she does not rest her hands on his rump, so has no tactile communication with him other than through her hands on the reins to his mouth. Nor can she use any changes in her weight which is often used when riding. Yet the equine learns to do these advanced movements by interpreting

Katherine has been learning to work at liberty 4 horses, including 3 youngsters, and their mentor Shemal (on the right). She has just called them in, all have come in to face her, even though they are not in a straight line!

her hand movements and tensions on the reins and from word command.

The truth is that, although this looks impressive, teaching the equine advanced long reining movements like these is not particularly difficult, provided one has set up the 'way of learning' for both teacher and horse student. The voice is particularly important and the word command has to be learnt by association with other cues first. Of course the horse will not do it completely correctly the first time, but once he starts to respond he is praised, and then when it is repeated he must do it a little more correctly. If he learns the meaning of particular words then he is quite capable of doing the appropriate movement with the right word, and no other cues, but it takes a little time to gradually drop visual, touch and gesture cues.

There is no magic to this type of display, nor does it require years and years of practise for either horse or human. It involves some hard work and thought, but you can *all* have your horses doing all sorts of things to word commands within a few weeks.

The sorts of things we have taught some of our horses to do to word command include things like shaking the head, lifting the right or left front leg, yawning, nodding the head, pawing, kicking a ball, swishing his tail, lying down, kneeling, doing the Spanish walk, Spanish trot, *piaffe*, *levade*, and so on. There are other movements outlined in circus books and classical high school texts that can also be taught.

One of the major reasons for doing this teaching is not to impress other people with one's skill, but to ensure that the teacher spends time observing the student carefully and thoroughly so that teacher and student get to know each other better: they become a team.

It is not always clear who is learning most! Remember it is not just doing, it is always about improving and is never finished. One of the goals with these exercises is to have the equine performing the movement the way you would like it done (however this is. There is no 'right' and 'wrong' way, it is how you and your equine decide to do it) to just a word command. It really does not matter if this is a conventionally approved movement done in the conventionally approved style.

It is also possible to use visual rather than verbal cues. A very slight visual signal such as 'every time I blink you do (a), every time I move my left foot, you do (b) can be used, as some circus trainers have done in the past. If you teach well, provided it is enjoyable for both of you, it will help both you and your horse relate to each other better. This in turn will allow both of you to progress with other activities, as well as just enjoying each other's company more as individuals and personalities. Teaching and working with the equine from the ground is not just a useful tool, it is an end in itself.

The Animal Behavioural Consultancy at the research centre has found that a

Oberlix and me, Chris and Shemal having a 'walk in time' lesson. I am
shouting out the legs and rhythm and you can see they are both listening.

ten-minute a day teaching session from the ground has a beneficial effect on reducing or eliminating other behavioural problems an equine has. This is because many behavioural problems are related to the equine not having enough exercise or brain work and insufficient time with his handler/owner. Enforced short periods of time together involving teaching and learning which require paying attention to each other, careful observation and self analysis can be very helpful. They also help the human's confidence; what better way to show off to your friends and relatives?

This is not a recipe book – 'how to teach your horse to lie down' – it is a recipe book on how to think out how to do it yourself, by helping you to provide yourself with some of the 'tools of the trade'.

Working a group together

Working a group of horses or ponies together at liberty is fun and can be very impressive. It is sensible to teach each individual the movement by himself first and then put two together, then three, then four, and so on. There is no need for all the equines to be the same size or age. Liberty work is something different to do with your equines and human friends on a wet day, or when you are unable to ride away from the stable.

Equines have no trouble at all in learning and remembering routines (one reason why it is not advisable to do a dressage test too often or the horse will know it and predict all the movements). They can learn the choreography of a dance rapidly and relate particular movements to particular tunes or rhythms.

This can be developed into other types of amusement for humans and equines, for example what about a football match between a bunch of equines who have been taught to kick a ball, and the humans can join in too! There are many games of this type that can be involved particularly when there are several people and horses in the stable who are keen on developing the ideas.

Can equines be innovative and creative?

One of the areas that we enjoy a great deal (when working with equines that already have some experience and understanding about working from the ground) is to encourage them to be innovative and creative, that is, not *always* to do exactly what we want, but to put their own two pennyworth in, and develop something that we can then encourage and help develop with them. This may look very much like making fun of someone else, or exaggerating something they already do and developing it into another movement. If they start to get rather wild (which is possible!), then, provided they have already had some experience with working with the teacher, just like a bunch of noisy school kids, it is possible to call them back to order.

The role of rhythm and music

Much can be done with music and rhythms, as many teachers demonstrate; working horses daily with music can relax, calm, give pleasure and give directive rhythms to both human and equine. You can take this further. Rather than the music being a background which the human listens to and makes the horse respond to (which is almost always the case, in dressage to music competitions), why not teach the equine to listen to the rhythms and invent appropriate movements to particular rhythms and sounds? It takes them approximately four 10-minute sessions to begin to learn about responding to the rhythm of a piece of music when at liberty. Start with a metronome or clapping in time or calling out the rhythm of their own gait. Gradually speed up your calling a little, or change from a 4 x walk to a 2x trot or 3x canter. Encourage the equine with voice praise to change their own rhythm of gait to keep in time, and praise them when they have it right.

> Druimghigha Cariff, a pure-bred Arab stallion and one of our experimental subjects, had approximately three hours teaching, listening to rhythm first by having a metronome and the teachers clapping in time, then with the metronome set to a rhythmic beat of the music which was fairly close to his own rhythm. Within this time he became very able at adapting the particular gait, and the rhythm of the gait to the beat of the music when trotting at liberty in the free school.

It may be that equines are better at rhythms than we are; they have individual gaits and can pick out particular friends when they hear their gaits approaching. When we think they are not listening to the music, it may be that they are syncopating, doubling or halving the beat. There is much more to discover here.

One thing we have found out is that different types of music induce different emotions, as in humans. So far we have evidence that faster, lively music will enliven the horses, at least those with experience of music, and slow dreamy music slows them down, in fact they even stop and start eating. The loudness of the music doesn't seem to make any difference. Much remains to be discovered about this too.

The two unexpected problems we have encountered with teaching groundwork to equines are:

(i) It does not take long before one has run out of things to teach! Thought, ingenuity and innovation from the teacher is therefore required – and quite soon!
(ii) The other problem is to keep up with the learning of the equine! Maybe I am just a little slow (but I have seen that other humans have the same problem).

It is very important to keep introducing new and different things, otherwise they will have a 'been there, done that' attitude which will often result in them inventing other, perhaps undesirable things to do, in order to have some response from the teacher. Language can be a help here as we can always teach them more words and phrases. But they need to keep doing things and need change just as humans do when learning; language lessons have to be interspersed or combined with something a little more energetic.

REFERENCES

Anon. *L'equitation, le cheval et l'ethologie. Colloque du 18 Sept 1999 a l'ecole National d'Equitation.* Belin. Paris.

Horak, V. P. Draber, J. Hanak & S. Matolin. 'Fibre composition and tubulin localisation in muscle of Thoroughbred srinters and stayers', p 262-268. in *Equine Exercise Physiology 3*. ed. S. G. B. Persson, A. Lindholm & L. B. Jeffcott ICEEP press. Davis.

Imam, S. A. H. A. A. 1983. *Mis-en-Main without a bit*. Imam Hazaribagh.

Imam, S. A. H. A. A. 1987. *The Centaur. A critical analysis of horsemanship plus relevant equitant history*. Indian Heritage. Hazaribagh. Iwanowski, G. 1987. *You and Your Horse*. Shutter and Shooter. Jo'burg.

Kiley-Worthington, M. & H. D. Randle. 1997. 'Animal handling and Animal Educational Psychology. Symposium Comparative Psychology'. Montreal. & Eco Research Centre 012a

Parelli, P. 1999. 'Natural Horsemanship' in *l'Equitation, le cheval et l'ethologie*. Colloque du 18 Sept 1999 a l'ecole Nationa d'Equitation. 23-34. Belin. Paris, and Demonstration.

Roberts, M. 1992. *The man who listens to horses*. Hutchinson. London.

Wright, M. 1983. *The thinking horseman*. Edwards printing. Tamworth. N. S. W.

7

FIRST STEPS TO BEING RIDDEN

- Reducing fear is of prime importance.
- Go quietly and slowly from step to step.
- A helper who knows the horse and is relaxed with him is vital.

I have divided the lessons into phases; you can proceed through them at your own pace. There are no rules. You can teach him to respond to any aid you like, it does not have to be in the classical tradition: for example, you can teach him to turn, stop, go, circle, etc, just by using your voice, with no bridle at all, or by particular leg movements, rubbing different parts of his body, or even winking! Moira Williams taught her horse to go forward when she pressed him in front of the withers, and donkeys in Kenya very rarely have bridles or reins even when driven on main roads: they just respond to hand movements from their drivers. Tutu Imam in Bihar, India, a very knowledgeable gentleman about the history of equitation in India, an author and high school rider, never asks his horses to do things, but arranges the environment so they want to do what he would like. Using conventional leg and hand movements results in a solid stop, head up, nose wrinkled and ears diverted back! Yet *he* can get them to do all sorts of high school movements, including remain rounded and correct in outline without a bit or hackamore.

Shortly after the first contact of humans with equines, around 5,000 years ago, probably in the fertile crescent between the Tigris and Euphrates in the Middle East, people began to try and ride equines, and teach them to respond to signals made by the mounted person. There are two characteristics of equines that were and are particular challenges when working equines on the ground or riding:

(1) Equines are a fast running prey species whose major escape strategy is to try and outrun their predators or captures, and whose immediate response to unfamiliar, potentially frightening processes, is to get away quickly.

(2) Equines are larger and stronger than humans and consequently can use their strength and weight to avoid being handled or ridden.

These factors have been very important in conditioning the way humans handle equines and get them to carry humans on their backs. Over the centuries two different methods or training equines have arisen as a result:

(1) The physically restrictive and violent method
One of the methods which is, unfortunately, still used today in some places (e.g. Western cowboys in the US) is that based on physical restraint of the horse. This

is followed by terrifying him, when he can do nothing to escape; eventually he responds with a type of 'learnt helplessness' (chapter 2). The equine stops trying to do anything and is induced into a kind of abnormal lethargy and submission. We now know that this state is accompanied by various chemical changes in the brain. The idea behind this approach is to teach the equine 'who is boss', and thereafter always to be able to dominate him and ensure that he is terrified into obeying. The capture of mustangs in the USA, and their subsequent training along these lines has become ritualised into the present-day rodeo events. This approach has much in common with Spanish bullfights where an unequal duel to the death has been developed for a spectacle between young male humans and a bull. The bull becomes aggressive as a result of 'defensive threat' – aggressive fear, where he has no escape. The rodeo horse is also terrified and tries everything to escape. The cards are always weighted in favour of the human since he has various other people, ropes, yards and so on to help him when he might be losing the battle. Such an approach has become a ritualised test of strength, aggression and chauvinistic masculinity.

(2) The psychological approach

Because when the first equines were domesticated, there were not many facilities for forcibly restraining them such as ropes, fences and yards, the origin of domestication probably started with a very different approach. Young foals, whose mothers had been killed and eaten, were bought into the human households, fed and brought up with humans from an early age, usually by the women. This familiarity between foal and human was helpful in teaching the young equine; as a result he would voluntarily take part, without needing to be physically restrained or violently treated in any way. This approach is one that is at the base of much of the classical European equine tradition, although, alas, today not usually practised well.

The 'natural horsemen' or '*nouveaux maîtres*', who mainly originated in the US from a Western riding tradition, put their methods across as an innovation based on the psychological approach, the second of these two, but of course the approach is probably the oldest around for training and riding equines. Some of these people have in their turn become good performers in a type of modern circus and perform impressive feats, such as mounting a young thoroughbred in half an hour (Monty Roberts, in front of the Queen in 1998). This has been a great eye opener, particularly for those who have been in the Western riding tradition. But these 'natural horsemen' have not been able to escape their cultural backgrounds entirely and are at pains to emphasise the importance of 'dominating' the horse, of being the 'leader' and having a 'submissive' slave of a horse. They argue that since horses have evolved to organise their societies with 'dominance orders', to have and obey a leader is the natural thing for a horse to do.

The idea of 'dominance hierarchies' in horse societies is not correct, as we (and others) have shown (see *Equine Lore* chapter 6 for full discussion). Their relationships are much more subtle and complex, as are those of humans. Consequently, this idea of 'showing who is boss' and being a 'leader' of horses may not be the best, or the most 'natural' way of conducting a relationship with equines. It may be that recognising what we have in common and developing more complex social relationships will be more useful in further improving the education of the horse to be ridden; just as development of co-operation is helpful when teaching on the ground

On balance, though, the popular appeal of this ever-growing band of natural horsepeople has probably had a beneficial effect on the equine owning establishment who have been (and many still are) in the grip of an unquestioning tradition. Perhaps they will now at least begin to question their methods of teaching horses.

Backing

To reiterate the principles that need to be borne in mind:

(1) The important thing is to **reduce fear.** Fear is induced by the unfamiliar, or a previous unpleasant experience.

(2) Since equines are larger and stronger than humans, the most relaxed and pleasantest way to teach them is to obtain their **co-operation** rather than using restriction, force or domination.

(3) Equines, like all of us, prefer to live an easy, trauma-free life. Consequently they try to avoid confrontation, fear and trauma. But, they need to learn what is the easiest route to this end. They must comprehend what is required and what is not, and be shown how to achieve this.

(4) **Positive reinforcement,** avoidance of punishment and the minimum of restraint, rather than negative reinforcement and punishment, is an easier way for them to achieve these goals, that is to educate them well.

Bearing these four premises in mind, there are many ways in which an equine can be backed and learn about signals from the human rider. As always, once one has decided on where one is going, there are many routes to choose. Here I will briefly describe the way we have built up to do this, and its evolution as a result of the monitored results at the Druimghigha stud over the last thirty-five years. These may not be new techniques, but they may have a new emphasis.

The young equine has been educated from the ground, can be led, tied up, have blankets, headcollars, bridle and saddle put on and off, be handled all over and be familiar with having his feet inspected, trimmed and cleaned. He has been exposed to some basic language, say around twenty words including 'yes', ' no', 'come here', 'go away', 'stand', 'walk', ' trot', ' trot on' (extension), 'steady trot' (shorten stride), 'canter', 'steady', 'good boy/girl' &/or 'brave', 'left' and 'right', his/her name and that of those he lives with. These words will have been used carefully in association with appropriate gestures and postures of the teacher's body, but the student will respond appropriately to most of them without gestures. He will also have been free schooled and/or lunged, and probably have had side reins, so he has learnt to give to a constant pressure on the rein. For the first stages of backing, we usually continue with the side reins. They are an extra restraint, but this is countered by their consistency: they give when they are given to, they pull against the equine when he pulls. They are more consistent than

Waving hands about in the peripheral visual field of the horse; jumping about, hitting the saddle. Lilka is slightly tense here, as seen by her higher head, and chewing the bit, indicating slight worry and frustration.

A food reward, and she relaxes.

(Above, left) Foot *in the stirrup and out several times; she must stand still all the time, and be relaxed. Here she is again slightly tense, indicated by her ears and contraction of her neck, but not as much as before.* (Above, right) *Weight on, Chris holds the other stirrup to stop the saddle slipping and Vicki quietly and slowly places her weight on her, repeating this several times. Now Lilka is more relaxed, but paying attention with one ear around to the rider, and one to Chris.*

The next pictures show Lilka more relaxed, doing something she knows about, even though she is carrying someone which she has never done bfore. Vicki is on here, moving around in the saddle, standing up, sitting down, patting her, talking to her. Making her aware of her presence.

Walking along with Chris.

Lunging with Vicki on. She has the weight, but she is doing something she knows about in the way she has done it before, so she is relaxed and confident.

Now walking alone, but with Chris there telling her what to do: 'walk on, and keep out,' in this case, with his voice and body; again she is relaxed and confident.

even the best rider's hands, which is very important in these first phases of using the hand to communicate through the rein. Most importantly, they are familiar, and familiar things in new situations give some security. When the side reins are there, the horse has learnt to go forward in a familiar mode with cadence, balance and an even pace. Thus, he has learnt (by associative learning) that this is what the side reins require.

We have divided the stages of backing into several lessons, but it entirely depends on how things progress, and how the teacher likes to do things. Each of these stages could be a separate lesson, or sometimes the first few lessons can be compressed into one; the latter can be important for demonstrations or films. The important thing is to progress at the speed the teacher thinks is correct and both the student and the teacher are enjoying. No extra 'brownie points' for gritting your teeth and trying to do more!

Lesson 1
Stage 1 Repeat lunging or free schooling routine with the familiar equipment, so any bumptiousness and leaping will be dispensed with before you start a new lesson.
Stage 2 When he is going well and quietly, call him into the middle. Ask him to stand while one or two people place themselves at his side and begin to familiarise him with noises on the saddle (banging it), putting weight on it (pulling down in the stirrups both together and one or the other), and doing odd things in his peripheral visual field (leaping and waving their hands while standing parallel to his quarters). He must learn to stand still while all this is going on; when he does, and relaxes, he is praised and rewarded with a tit bit (positive reinforcement). The humans remain relaxed and continue to chat to him with quiet praise in the voice, while they to do these things. Getting onto his back without familiarising him with these experiences is foolish: of course he will jump, tense, put his head up and become scared as suddenly the weight is on one side as the person mounts, and then he has this creature on his back whom he can partially see, and is unbalanced.

If the equine has been well handled and accustomed to many exercises and movements, he will probably hardly budge when these antics are carried out. It is best if he stands without being held or with anyone at his head while two people bounce about around him before anyone gets on. In this way we are assured that he is familiar and confident with such goings on (see picture page 146).

It is at this stage that we begin a very important lesson which goes against his natural tendency to run: 'Stand still when things go wrong, and things will be put right. This will be less scary than the consequences of running away. ' This is a difficult but very important lesson, and it is surprising how frequently it is not taught. The reason it is not often taught is because most people do not believe that an equine can learn such a lesson. They maintain he will not be able to overcome his in-built tendency to run when things get frightening. However, there have been many people over the centuries who have managed to teach animals including equines to do this and have lived to tell the tale.

Oberlix, one of my mentors, a pure-bred Arab stallion bred at the Druimghigha Stud, had been taught to work the land when he was three, without blinkers. Since he was pulling dangerous equipment such as spike harrows, spring tyne harrows, and so on (see chapter 11) it was important that he learnt to stop when things went wrong, such as he put his leg over a trace, for example. Care had always been taken not to frighten him, and he became very relaxed with this work when he did it regularly. He was then put to a light two-wheeled vehicle, and accustomed to blinkers, and he pulled that around the lanes with no problem or fear. He continued to do some of this work all his life; when he was thirteen, we moved, and put him to an old traditional Mull Cart with very large wheels, so that the driver looks down on the horse, and, because we planned to drive down fairly busy roads, he was wearing blinkers. He was terrified. He stood shaking in the shafts, and when I asked him to walk forwards he squatted down and walked, trying to stop at every moment. He was so frightened that he was rapidly in a running sweat and still shivering. There was something seriously wrong, which we obviously had to put right: perhaps it was a series of frightening changes – wearing blinkers, the height of the cart and the new location, or a harness that was hurting somewhere. We stopped and took him out to search for the problem. What he did was stop, so we could put things right, rather than rushing off. If he had done so, he would have spilled the cart, the driver, crashed everything and terrified himself even more. Even though terrified, he had gritted his teeth, and controlled himself *not* to run. He had learnt to overcome such a strong natural tendency.

In fact it is not that difficult to teach most equines to do this because the positive reinforcement for so doing can be immediate: when he stops it is less frightening and, better still, what is frightening him is finally removed. But it is very important to sort out the problem and then continue with the lesson otherwise the equine will have learnt to stop and not to move again, something that many young ridden horses do learn and it is difficult to change. Equines and elephants can be taught not to run, when running would be to their disadvantage. They would go into battle and then stand there while slaughter went on around them. However, Hannibal's elephants, instead of standing there among the slaughter, turned and ran into their own side, destroying the foot soldiers! After this elephants were rarely used for war again, but horses continued to be right up into the World War II, when the Polish cavalry charged the German tanks. The cavalry dashed around close to the tanks, shooting the men in the tanks from the top. They were eventually annihilated by the superior war technology.

Stage 3 The next stage is to place a foot in the stirrup. The helper holds the horse's head with one hand and the other stirrup with the other (so that the saddle does not slide). Then quietly and gently the rider levers herself up and lies over the saddle. At this stage it is important to ensure that the horse is aware that the rider is there; if it is all done so quietly that he is a little tense while his attention is focused elsewhere, then when he does pay attention to what is happening, he may have a fright. The more he jumps and leaps the more he becomes scared, and the more he jumps ... wouldn't you? Eventually either the rider falls off, or he is restrained severely; either way, he has had a bad experience that he will not forget. The next time someone tries to get on, it will be the same or worse. So, if there is any sign of tension we continue to chat on to him – both the person on the ground and the rider rubbing and scratching him without any tension or fear. If either is scared don't go any further, stop and try again later, or have another person.

After a minute or two, the rider slides off, and the horse is lavishly rewarded, and told how brilliant he is; this is repeated several times. When all is very quiet, advance to the next stage.

Stage 4 The person mounting places herself over the saddle, and then quietly, without kicking the horse, raises the right leg over the saddle and sits in it, while the helper holds the opposite stirrup and the horse (picture page 146). When she is in the saddle, and the horse has stood still, then a food reward is given and praise is lavish.

It is important the horse realises someone is on top of him, so the rider chats to him and rubs him, in front and behind the saddle, she stands up and sits down in the saddle, swings her legs about, swings her body about. Anything that makes him tense is repeated again and again as he is praised and rubbed until he manages to cope with it without tension, and realises that there is someone on his back. Five minutes of standing with someone on top is more or less sufficient for the youngster for the first time, accompanied by lavish praise afterwards.

Food reward and praise can be used at any stage. It can be used to divert attention at tricky moments, but it must be given when the horse has managed not to be frightened of another slightly new exercise or movement from the rider. Using tit bits indiscriminately will debase the reward value and with it the motivation to pay attention and to learn.

Stage 4 The next stage is to ask the horse to walk forward a step or two, led by the familiar confident person on the ground. This is something he initially finds difficult as his balance is all queer with the large weight on his back. A similar experience for a human would be carrying a large rucksack. Put on a heavy rucksack and try and walk stepping over some rough terrain, or climbing some rocks. Every time one lifts a leg, the wretched thing falls over to the side, unbalancing one's progress; the looser it is, the more difficult.

The horse may be carrying around $1/4$ to $1/3$ of his weight, so he has to adjust his balance to be able to do this. Allow him time, repeat walking a few steps and then stop and praise him again and again (picture page 147). If all goes well, within another five minutes he will be walking, slightly stiltedly perhaps, with this large weight on his back, but calmly and with growing confidence around the ring. A still relaxed and well balanced rider is essential. Being tense or lurching around will make the problem worse for the horse. It is better not to try until you have found a rider who is balanced and relaxed.

One of the things that equines fear a great deal is falling over; any risk of this as a result of having his balance upset is bound to cause some fear.

It is very important at this point not to overload him with new experiences by the rider using her legs or hands, even with familiar commands from the person on the ground. The rider must remain quite still until the equine has mastered rebalancing. We find that thinking of the experiences of the youngster in these terms has greatly helped and eliminated any jumping or panicking.

That will do for this session. Around ten minutes of walking around is plenty for the first time up. The session can end with getting on and off a couple of times.

If we are demonstrating this method of backing, then we might, if all is going well, continue to work on the lunge or free school with the youngster and the rider, and even try a little trot in the first session, if it is necessary for the audience, but, generally, for the equine, this is enough for the first time.

An interesting point about equine learning, which many remark on, is that often after a break, the equine seems to progress faster than if one goes on and on in one session. It looks as if the period of rest or even sleep may be important in assessing and organising cognitive information. Sleep has recently been suggested to have this function in humans, and it is unlikely to be quite different in equines.

Lesson 2

Stage 5 The previous exercises should be repeated until the student equine shows no fear or wariness at any stage. Assuming that the previous lessons have gone well, progress to the next exercises can be made. These are:
(1) Lead the equine while he is being ridden in the trot
(2) Lunge him in the familiar way with the rider on top at the walk and the trot
(3) Teach him by association the meaning of leg and rein aids.
(1) Leading at the trot ridden. The problem for the equine here is again to be able to balance while the rider rises at the trot. It is advisable to start this being led from the ground so that if he becomes frightened, he has the leader there for security. It is important to have a rider who is able to balance well even when the stride may be irregular and not crash about on the youngster's back. It is also important to have done some rising and sitting while walking so that he is used to the different view he may have in his peripheral visual field, and the different feel on his back. If he had already learnt to balance the rider at the walk, this is usually no problem, but pick the place well and ensure that there are not going to be any surprising things happening while the lesson is going on so that the student will pay full attention, and not jump and frighten himself by the change in weight on his back. A few steps only to start with.
(2) Lunging at the trot. When he has the idea that all is well in the rising trot, and can be led around the lunge circle, then is the time for the leader to move away and the person in the middle to begin to lunge the horse in the normal way (picture page 148). Some horses do become anxious when they realise they are on their own going forwards with someone on their back. If he tenses up at all, then stop and let him relax and then try again for a few steps. When he can perform a whole ring at the walk, then a few steps at the trot (always accompanied by the familiar verbal and gestural commands) can be performed. After a few times, if all goes well, he can be trotted around half the circle, and perhaps the

whole circle. This may be a good place to end this lesson, but it is up to the teacher to decide. We normally do not ride a sitting trot until a little later, but some horses seem to feel more secure at a gentle sitting trot, so this again has to be played by ear.

It is important that, at this stage, the rider does nothing but sit quietly and lightly in balance on the horse. Sometimes this is difficult and when he slows or stops, one has consciously not to use one's legs. Remember, he has not had any introduction to the use of the leg; the more sensitive equine can become extremely worried by the use of the legs, so use them very carefully and use your voice as well. I have seen horses, relatively quiet until then, suddenly blow up because the rider has applied the legs in an unthinking way.

(3) *Learning the meaning of leg and hand aids*. When he is relaxed and going well and quietly at a walk and a trot, perhaps even doing a lengthening and shortening of the trot to word command, on the lunge, then the next stage is for the rider to begin to teach him about hand and leg aids. The golden rule that he is going to learn in this lesson is, 'Go away from the leg or legs, and go towards the hand aid.' All the more advanced work is based on these golden rules, and how to perform every movement can be worked out from this. This then is perhaps one of the most important moments in riding education. For the rider it is the first beginning of the establishment of the art of riding and communicating with your new mount. If the aids are used clumsily, and no effort is made to teach these straightforward rules, the clumsy rider ends up with a clumsy equine. The moral of this story is that at this point it is crucial to have a rider who has some serious knowledge of how to ride in balance but also in a sensitive and feeling way. These people are relatively rare, alas, but if you know what you are looking for, and the rider will really listen, it is not too difficult to correct the rider at the same time as looking after how the horse is learning. The leg aids are probably the ones to start with, as the first concern is to ensure that the equine goes forward. The French school of equitation has only 2 rules: '*Droit et en avance*' (straight and forward).

The more one learns about equitation, the more one appreciates how difficult these are!

The equine student learns to associate leg movements and the tightening or loosening of the reins with the word commands that he already knows from the person on the ground. The first step then is that both of the rider's legs are gently moved back a fraction and applied to the side at the same time as the person lunging asks the equine to move forward, by moving a step towards his rear, and raising his arm or the whip behind him (this is something the horse should be familiar with without a rider). When he moves forward, he is praised. This is repeated several times, with the lunger giving fewer signals, and the rider asking verbally and gently applying her legs. If the horse does not respond, then a little more from the ground-person is required, rather than stronger pressure from the rider. It is the concept of 'move away from the leg' that you are trying to instil, not an automatic response to a stimulus. It is remarkable how quickly most young equines who have been given this type of education will understand. It normally takes little more than five attempts with a little aid from the ground-person before he has absorbed the message. It is wise sometimes to give him a little time to work it out before assuming he has not understood. A mistake often made at this stage is to continue to use the legs harder and harder when there is no response, which can frighten the horse, or to continue using them every step to try and get him to walk forward easily. This gradually reduces the effectiveness of the leg, and one can end up with a horse 'dead to the leg'. Much better is to realise how important it is that the horse understands the concepts and *use the minimum aid* right from the start so he becomes more tuned into the rider; the rider, in turn, will have to become more tuned in to the horse – that is, develop what is called 'equestrian tact', being sensitive with the aids.

The next thing is for him to learn to go towards the rein. Here it is better, we find, to start with using one rein at a time to suggest bending his head into the centre and asking him to go that way, accompanied by the ground-person encouraging this movement with her body. A slight feel of the left rein is accompanied by the words 'turn left' and the ground-person moving to the left, or using whatever gesture she has previously used to get the student to go to the left (e.g. moving slightly behind with a right arm lifted, or, if a whip is used, lifting the whip and extending it behind him). The equine learns rapidly to associate the known signs with the new sign, that is, the rein. Make sure that he turns his head and neck in; if he resists the rein, then reduce the contact and ask gently by increasing the pressure and then letting go every second or so. If he still has side reins on (which is advisable for the reasons given above), he will not be able to turn his head very much to one side, but if he just begins to give to the rein on the required side, that will do. If you have trouble and he resists the rein, just try and get him to move his head a little this way and that at the halt. The use of the voice is again extremely useful here as he already knows the meaning of these simple commands and will associate them with the new signals within a couple of trials if it is done carefully. Three or four repeats, and he will have an idea of what is required.

When he is responding to the word command and aid of the rider, then exercises turning to the centre and walking across, changing the rein, *volte* (a tight circle in one direction), initially accompanied by the ground-person but then alone, can be performed. Halting is also important: the pressure is slightly increased on both the reins, and the rider's back is tightened slightly as she verbally asks for a halt. It is crucial at this stage that when there is a response to the rein it is immediately relaxed so that its action mirrors that of the side rein which gives when the horse gives.

Lesson 3

Stage 6 The side reins are still attached to help with security, but also ensure the attention of the horse. In this lesson the horse and rider begin to move without the aid of the ground-person, with the rider making sure that she uses her voice to help back up her rein and leg aids, but if the horse does not understand, rather than increasing the strength of the aids, the ground-person steps in to help. It is as this stage that we teach the turn on the forehand, a good exercise demonstrating clearly going away from the leg (the leg is back and applied on the opposite side

Shezam investigates by touching and smelling whether this wet area is a bog –
and Robyn lets him.

from the way you wish the quarters to swing; the other leg remains on the girth, but if he begins to go backwards, it is gently applied). The rein is used on the side to which you wish him to turn (towards the hand), and the other rein just held firmly to stop him walking forward. It is important to take it very slowly, step by step, so he has every opportunity of understanding what is being asked, and working out how to do it, and being praised at every correct step. Then if the forward walk is going well, a very small *volte* is asked for, using the rein and leg aids to ensure the bend in the body around the circle, and finally a slow walk (of course the rhythm may not be constant at this stage) will be asked for and perhaps the beginnings of a pirouette (the smallest possible circle turning on the hind legs), but only to help him understand the concepts of 'towards the hand and away from the leg.' More and longer trots are often appropriate here, to break up the lesson with a little more active work, serpentines, turns down the centre and any number of figures you like to invent in the enclosed, familiar environment.

Lesson 4
Stage 7 This is a trip to the great outdoors with an older horse who is well educated and whom the equine student knows and respects. The older horse leads to start with, particularly if it involves going on roads, or past strange objects. A good idea is to go around a route that the youngster has already been on in his pre-riding days. If you are worried at all, then the best thing is to put him on a lead line from the rider of the older horse. Gradually, if things go well and he remains

*Shezam is now confident to take the lead through a wet, but not boggy place,
after being allowed to investigate it.*

quiet but interested, the youngster may be able to come up alongside and even
take the lead for a little while (see above). It is very important to let him stop,
look and approach strange objects, or places. It may take ten minutes of standing
waiting, but this is what you are there for.

Think carefully where you go, for this first ride – not on a major road with
large vehicles, unless he has already had much experience of this. If you get to a
difficult place and the rider becomes slightly nervous, it is important to get off
and lead him, and relax yourself. If you become tense, he will respond strongly,
and things can easily go wrong. If all goes well, then go through different terrain,
water, muddy places, up steep hills, down steep hills, over rocks, in woods and
under trees, but don't rush it, and use plenty of voice to praise and encourage
him. Choose your situation for first canters carefully: a slight uphill with plenty
of space in front. A lane or a track with hedges or fences is a good place for a first
canter; keep going after he has got the gist of it so he has enough time to get
himself balanced and happy. The rider should stand out of the saddle initially but
in balance. Any sign of a buck must be sorted by:

(i) seeing that the saddle and all equipment is not irritating

(ii) the rider is in balance, and not all over the place

(iii) a gentle feel of the rein so that any sign of putting his head down to buck can
be corrected

(iii) keeping going so that he is puffing and blowing and has to use his energy to
keep up, rather than jumping about.

If you are anxious, do not canter for a while, but continue to work from the trot for another few weeks. A long enclosed uphill towards the end of a long ride is the best place to start the canter, and, once this is going well, and you can ask him to take off into a canter when you like on slight uphills, you can practise it in the manege, and gradually reduce the size of the circle.

Over-feeding before backing can be a problem. *It is wise not to give any hard feed to a young horse you are backing for at least two weeks before you start.* If he is losing weight, then your fodder strategy is wrong, or there is something seriously wrong with him: consult your vet or a good nutritionist. Horses have evolved to live on grass, hay and other such fodder crops, they really do not need hard food unless they are working very hard. We do not give ours any hard feed until they are doing at least two hours' hard work every day, which must involve a serious sweat and usually more than 40 kilometres (25 miles).

Go at the pace and to the places *you* feel confident with, and he will be confident. Remember, you don't lose any brownie points by getting off if you really don't like the look of some thing or suspect that things may become unpleasant or uncomfortable. The most important thing is that both of you have a good time and feel happy and relaxed all the time ... not just at the end when the whole thing is over! This is the way to build confidence in your mount and him in you so that eventually you will be able to go anywhere or do anything together without any anxiety.

Lesson 5

Stage 8 This is back in the school (see picture on following page) or schooling out and about. Now the side reins are done away with, and the horse practises all the work he has been doing in the school. He must begin to go around the corners with his head bent in the direction of movement, and taking a longer stride with the outside legs than the inside ones, so from the beginning he learns to bend correctly around the circle rather than resist and poke his head to the outside. To help with this bending, he can start 'work on three tracks' (see page 177 and following): things like 'shoulder in', 'renvers' and 'travers' and the beginnings of a 'leg yield'. There is little difficulty about these movements provided (a) the rider uses the basic principle of away from the leg and towards the hand, and (b) she really knows what she is trying to achieve, and has not been overawed by technical language which means nothing.

We have had most of our young horses doing a quite reasonable shoulder in and travers by lesson 5 and some before this, just because of applying these simple principles of learning we have outlined.

Stage 9 If it is not too wet and slippery, a ridden canter around the school or an enclosed area can be begun this stage. The horse can begin to understand the concept of leading with one leg or the other at a canter and the aids that go with this right from this stage. This prevents habits being established such as 'always lead with the inside leg' which are difficult to change when, for example, one wants a counter canter (leading with the outside leg). He will already have some idea about this from the free school or lunge work that he has done, now he should associate the particular aids with taking off on one leg or the other.

Shezam back to school - he is doing a lovely trot but the rider (me) has low fixed hands - not good!

Bends, transitions, extensions and well cadenced, even paces must be practised, together with plenty of voice and praise when things are right, and a 'no' when they are wrong.

Don't underestimate what your youngster can learn, but be sure to be consistent and then the right habits will be formed and stay. This requires a certain amount of self-discipline, but it is really worth it, one has a horse that is interested, willing to learn, lovely to ride, and delighted to please, so one is delighted to please him.

One of the mistakes made in much classical riding is to underestimate how much the horse can understand; everything must be repeated and repeated, never progressing to interesting things but riding wretched circles endlessly – so he often becomes bored. What matters for both of you is that it is **fun,** and that the horse and human are learning to learn, and learning to teach each other. Never be frightened to teach something new to your horse, but, remember, there may be down sides of this. Teaching a horse to shake hands for example, can encourage him to throw his legs forward to try to get a reward of some sort and knock old people or children over. The job is to teach him *when to do it*, and *when not to do it*, as well as *how.*

Summary

• Do not get into a panic or emotional state during these first lessons of being ridden. Both horse and rider must enjoy riding or being ridden from the beginning, and have the foundation of wanting to do more.

• If you are not entirely clear what you want your horse to learn, or how you are going to teach him, then leave that and do something you *are* clear about.

• Horses can be educated by quite different routes, so choose your own, decide yourself how you and your horse will behave together, and work towards your ideal. You can achieve it with hard work and thought, and so can your horse.

• Some people like their horses to fuss and leap about, whereas to another such things are frightening or annoying; it is up to you to choose and then educate your horse so that he will come near behaving as you would like, while at the same time, of course, giving him room to develop his own individuality and put himself into your relationship. Think of it as a marriage where there is no point in bossing if you want things done, but every reason to put forward what you would like done in perhaps a somewhat indirect way until it seems to become the idea of the partner.

REFERENCES

Anon. *L'equitation, le cheval et l'ethologie. Colloque du 18 Sept 1999 a l'ecole National d'Equitation*. Belin. Paris.

Fillis,J. 1969 *Breaking and Riding*. trans M. H. Heyes. J. A. Allen London

Gueriniere, F. R. de la. (1733) 1994. *The School of Horsemanship*. trans T. Boucher. J. A. Allen London.

Imam, S. A. H. A. A. 1983. *Mis-en-Main without a bit*. Imam Hazaribagh.

Imam, S. A. H. A. A. 1987. *The Centaur. A critical analysis of horsemanship plus relevant equitant history*. Indian Heritage. Hazaribagh.

Kiley-Worthington, M. & H. D. Randle. 1997. 'Animals handling and Animal Educational Psychology. Symposium Comparative Psychology'. Montreal. & *Eco Research Centre* 012a

Rees, L. 1991. *Riding: The True Techniques*. Stanley Paul.

Skinner, B. F. 1938. *The Behavior of Organisms; an Experimental Analysis*. Appleton-Century-Crots. New York.

Swift, S. 1996. *Centred Riding*. J. A. Allen.

Wanlass, M. 1987. *Ride with your mind. A right brain approach to riding*. Methuen. London.

Xenophon, 350BC. (1972) *The art of horsemanship*. J. A. Allen. London.

8

MORE ADVANCED RIDING AND TEACHING

- Riding for its own sake, as a pleasurable experience for both horse and rider
- The three most important things to achieve are: **balance, relaxation** and **rhythm**
- Good riding is not about domination but about co-operation
- The less restrictive the tack, the better; the final goal being to ride without tack

The reason why Skinner and the other early behaviourists put animals into laboratory situations to study their learning was that in this way they could cut down the variables and learn more about how learning worked. The problem with this approach, of course, is that the real world is not like that. Learning and teaching in the real world is subject to an enormous number of variables and changes which the subject has to contend with and adapt to. This is particularly obvious when educating equines to be a delight to ride, which is the reason for 'schooling' them.

When a human is riding an equine, in addition to all the usual environmental variables, there are two beings involved: the horse and the rider. Both are interacting with the world and each other. The temperature, weather, situation, what is going on around and the surface will be affecting both the horse and the rider. How the two are interacting will affect whether the horse is learning and the rider teaching or learning herself. The rider will already have ideas about horses, how to ride them, and probably about this horse in particular. This may or may not be helpful. In addition, her tact, balance and physical riding skills as well as her mental approach and her personality will vary. The horse will also have different past experiences, skills and abilities, mental attitudes and personality. The good teacher, whether the rider or someone teaching the rider from the ground, must take all of these factors into account and try and gently suggest how to manage them in order for the horse/rider unity to be harmonious. One of the most important things here is to ensure that both the equine and the rider are having fun. This does not mean that hard work does not take place from time to time, just that there must be a sense of enjoyment in the movements and a sense of the job well done and achievement.

When riding, as opposed to working the equine from the ground, there is another factor that makes life more difficult, and this is balance. Communication has to be by feelings and weight changes and involves an understanding of rhythms. If things go wrong, the cause could be the rider.

Regrettably, the horse is often blamed first; try to resist this urge, and reassess why things are not going well. Often you can rectify the situation by changing your behaviour. All too often unhelpful and unnecessary physical restraints are applied

• drop or grackle nosebands tied tight under the chin – to prevent him opening his mouth

• martingales – to stop him moving his head up or down

• running reins – to hold his head in a particular position

• bits including jointed, curbs, curb chains, side pieces of different lengths, bits that slide up in the mouth to sort of gag the horse, such as 'gag snaffles' – to achieve all these things by causing discomfort

• hackamores which put great pressure on the nose rather than in the mouth

• whips and spurs – to drive him forward

It is taken for granted (even by those who should know better, that is, some of the top dressage trainers) that the horse *must* have a drop noseband which forces his mouth tight shut and applies pressure to his nose, under his chin and head should he try to open it. Less able riders go further and instead of learning how to communicate better through their hands, restrict and restrain the horse. Ultimately, there is no reason for using any such gadgets if the aim is to have a harmonious co-operative relationship with the equine. If there is a need for them, the rider should try to work out ways to avoid their necessity. The problem is where to draw the line. We have thought much about this, and justify using only the following tack:

• Simple snaffle bridle with no noseband. Bit can be rubber mullein, jointed metal Phillis, Fulmer with side pieces (to stop youngster pulling it through the mouth), a thick but comfortable mouthpiece.

• Non-slip rein of rubber, baler twine, plaited non-slip leather or rope.

That is all that is really necessary, but we do, for our own comfort, usually ride in a saddle for long distances.

• Saddle. This should cause no restriction to the equine, provided it fits properly and does not rub. To ensure over the long and fast periods we ride that this does not happen, we normally fit the saddle to the rider, then pad it up underneath with blankets and numnahs and so far we have never had a seriously sore back. Ensure that the saddle is not rubbing on the backbone of the horse.

• Breast plate around the neck to the saddle, nor around the shoulders (we find this less restrictive, but this is not important) – to stop the saddle slipping back

• Girths that are not too tight and rub. We usually use string ones and have soft covers on them for long rides.

The more restrictions that the horse has, the less good the rider. We should all aim to be able to ride our horses across the moor, asking for any gait, or performing other movements as we or the horse desire, and in the company of other horses with no equipment on at all: that is the ultimate in the art of riding. Most of us do not achieve this, and certainly not with any horse, although some will do it (as indeed we do from time to time) as a demonstration. But, just because we cannot play Beethoven's violin concerto like Oistrakh, does not mean we should not learn the violin. What we must be aware of is we need to get better, and not cause any suffering to the other member of our duo, the horse. We must not lose sight of the aim of riding – the voluntary working together of a horse and a human who is on top of him. Yes, most of us use some form of bridle, some more restrictive than others, and saddle (not necessarily restrictive but helpful for balance).

If advanced jumping 'professionals' have to have martingales, drop nosebands as a matter of course for jumping the jumps they jump (100% had these in advanced jumping competition at the Royal Devon Show in Exeter, 2000) and some of them (50% at the same show) have to have running reins, then the Animal Liberationists are quite right in questioning whether horses should be doing such competitions, or even ridden at all. Such gadgets should be far more widely banned, particularly in competitions. The horse-riding fraternity should seriously understand what a serious welfare problem this is. They should be aware of the importance of understanding these as a result of the recent success of the anti-hunting fraternity! There are serious arguments here, it is not bigoted silliness; horses are suffering unnecessarily from humans who have insufficient skills and understanding.

Of course there is a safety argument in some cases for using different bits and gadgets when riding outside a confined area on equines that have already acquired bad habits; but their use should always be a means to an end, a means to give confidence to the rider. The rider should then gradually reduce their use rather than becoming reliant on them.

On top of the use of unhelpful restrictive tack (good only for the saddle maker!), for some curious reason, it has become establishment practice that when riding the voice should not be used. This is particularly unhelpful as
(1) The equine has already learnt to respond to particular voice commands at least when he has been worked from the ground, and
(2) The voice is the main method of communication for humans, and the one they find easiest to use. Consequently, it is more likely to be used consistently which will make understanding much easier for the equine who may otherwise be seriously confused by erratic hand, leg or weight aids.

It must be remembered that, when ridden, the horse's communication is disadvantaged since he cannot use his expertise in reading visual signals, but rather he has to learn to interpret inconsistent tactile signals from the human, and if the human does not talk, he cannot even be helped by his recently acquired understanding of voice!

No wonder there is a mythology that it takes years and years to teach a horse more advanced movements, and that most people, even those vaguely interested in the 'art' of riding, will only ever manage to ride circles and be able to 'control' the gaits and have an obedient horse.

But first, to understand differences in the approaches to teaching the equine to be ridden we need to know something about the dominant theories behind riding in order to achieve the different goals that riders have. There seem to be three major different goals people have had through history for riding equines and these have given rise to rather different methods of training.

Look at the restraints on this Grade A show jumper in the warm up ring. The horse – by bad riding – has learnt not to respond to the rein and leg: so running reins, martingales, deep noseband, spurs and a stick are used. It is extraordinary that the horse jumps at all. That he has difficulty is also illustrated by all the boots to 'protect' his legs. The rider has 'lost his head' indeed.

(1) Riding equines for practical goals

Included here is the use of equines for ridden transport, for fighting wars, or for looking after other animals. Here, there has been no emphasis in entering into any complex relationship with the equine, or even considering him other than in order to be able better to achieve the goal. So, as far as the riding goes, all one has to do is stick on, control the pace, and ensure that the job is done. Some would put much of modern competitive riding, racing or show jumping in this category: these are activities mainly done professionally to win money, make a living or in order to be part of a particular human 'team'. They are not done *primarily* to enjoy the company of equines.

Having said this, however, some of the most sophisticated ideas on how to ride have come from this type of riding. The whole of the European Classical Equitation school was developed in order to train the cavalry, so that they could be more effective fighters in war, and stay on their horses.

An interesting aside here comes from Imam in India, who, having studied the ancient Indian cavalry, maintains that the origins of the European classical schools of equitation are the Indian cavalry several centuries before Christ where over 300,000 men and their horses would be sent into battle. They traditionally often fought ridden elephants. Consequently, many of the advanced movements, such as the airs above the ground (for example the *levade*, *palisade* and *capriole*), Imam suggests, were developed and taught first in order for horsemen to fight elephant riders effectively (page 193). In these movements, the rider is lifted up to be able to spear the man on an elephant. Imam suggests that these ideas and practices moved west (with some of the horses and people) through eastern Europe, or the Middle East to Spain, where they became part of our Western European equestrian tradition, and continue today in the Spanish Riding School in Vienna, the Cadre Noire in France, Spanish High School and Neapolitan schools of riding.

Another school of riding that developed as a result of riding horses to get around is the Western riding tradition. The horses were used to help the humans get around the prairies and to look after their grazing livestock.

Again, the main thing was to stick on; the Western saddle is almost impossible to fall out of, and holds you in the correct position to keep in balance. The curb, which was widely used throughout Spain, became part of the US Western riding tradition to ensure that even the most novice of riders could stop their horse, because it can cause severe pain. New movements were developed, useful when working cattle. These movements involve cutting out particular animals, or sliding and turning very quickly, rushing forward and stopping and turning. As a result, modern Western equitation arose which involves different movements and riding from the European/Asian tradition.

The West was a tough place and encouraged a competitive and chauvinistic attitude to the world in general and horses in particular. They carried this over into their relationship with their horses demonstrated in the modern rodeo. Man had to conquer 'the wild'. This philosophy is also unfortunately used even today in the training of the Western cowboy's horse.

Most modern 'natural horsemen' come from this tradition. What they are doing (which has achieved great public appeal) is suggesting that overcoming the equine by fear and violence is unnecessary. They are beginning to take on board some of the ideas and techniques that for centuries have been traditionally taught by good teachers in the European riding tradition.

(2) Riding for fun

One of the most important riding traditions has come from the British history of hunting. When hunting, the whole idea is to stay on the horse whatever happens, jump anything that comes in the way, never mind how, and to go as fast as possible … within the limits of the game-rules, which were learnt by tradition; knowledge of which identifies one as a member of the group.

At the end of the day one was either injured, dead or delighted with having achieved such feats of endurance and daring. I have nothing but admiration for these people's risk-taking feats. It was, and maybe still is, not unusual for old ladies over 65 to go hunting 3-4 days a week, side saddle at that, jumping almost anything that came in their paths, having no idea what was the other side of the hedge. They and their horses were certainly fit. The Pony Club, the British Horse Society and all its recent spin-offs, the International League for the Protection of the Horse and various other equine training and welfare organisations, arose

Imire Safari park and farm in Zimbabwe where the cattle men ride horses to move the cattle around to various areas, one of the most important reasons for the Western cowboy tradition. Here however they ride without the gear and restraints of the Western riding tradition. Horses are still used in many parts of the world for moving cattle about.

because of hunting and were (and probably still are) run by people who hunt. It was assumed that this was the whole point of having a horse and riding. It was also assumed that everyone *must* want to do it.

This fosters a riding attitude dominated by daring, speed, risk-taking and feats of fitness. Consideration for the horse, or what might be a good or bad idea from his point of view, is not part of the tradition. One well known authority admitted to me that the horse is equivalent to a slave, while the owner likes to see herself as a benevolent master who 'knows what is good' for the somewhat mentally defective animal.

The type of riding that this approach encourages is one where above all the equine must be obedient, stop and go when told at the speed required; if the rider cannot manage to control the horse, then more gadgets are applied – the horse is a tool again. Although I am sure many riders became fond of their mounts, they were means to achieving the risk-taking, hearty, social goal. So strong are these traditions that discussion of any of their premises are banned. Examinees in the BHS qualifications as instructors fail their examinations if they start to discuss issues concerning the horse's welfare, how he is taught, his mental attributes or necessary changes in husbandry or training practices.

Riding in this tradition is somewhat like climbing the Eiger (which the British were also good at): risk-taking, physical fitness and skill in being able to stay on never mind what happens. Certainly courage and risk-taking can be admired, but this kind of riding misses what to me are the central values of riding.

(3) Riding for its own sake

Riding as an end in itself – the 'art' of riding – evolved out of the necessity to ride in Europe, begun probably with some of the aristocratic Indians or Chinese several hundred years before Christ. However, one of the ancient Greek exponents was Xenophon in the 3rd century BC. It then continued to evolve throughout mainland Europe, practised by rich aristocrats throughout the next 2,000 years.

Movements were further developed (by what are now called the Masters of the Classical School of Equitation) and slightly different approaches to both the teaching of the horse and riding became dogma. It is worth remembering that many of these people earned their livings by performances, often in the circus. For some 1,000 years in Europe circuses have been at the forefront of animal teaching, particularly equine art and entertainment. There have been good and bad equine trainers through history in circuses, but even today there is much to be learnt from some circus horse trainers, even though they are a dying race. They have been practising more sophisticated 'Monty Roberts' type work for the last 500 years!

The central reason of riding here is because one is interested in it and it gives pleasure. With this approach, there is a necessity to develop a greater awareness of the horse and his needs and desires, at least when being ridden. Thoughtfulness about how to ride, improve communication with the horse and consequently how to teach the horse are central. But unfortunately, such riding and training techniques have become dogmatic; there are slight regional differences in methods and movements of teaching, which are endlessly squabbled over.

But there are some useful ideas and techniques that can be extracted from these approaches to riding and teaching equines. The best of the art of riding comes from the European school. This is illustrated by the fact that someone seriously trained in that school can ride like all the others and do well, but that is not true of those who have learnt to ride in the Western school or the British gallop about/risk take school. Unfortunately bad teaching abounds, which discourages novices from the established schools and sends them to the new master, the 'natural horsemen' who often have no understanding of the sophistication of these other schools.

There is much overlap between these three types of riding, and today almost everyone would consider that they are doing a bit of all three. There are also many other schools of riding throughout the world, but in general, I would argue, that they all fall predominantly into one of these three groups.

The distinction between the 'sport' and 'art' of riding rests with the two individuals, the horse and the rider. Not every horse nor every rider is interested in the 'art' of riding or being ridden. We will concentrate on the 'art' because by definition it involves the intricate relationship between horse and rider.

Over the years I have been worrying about how to achieve this better, and have read, listened and learned from humans and horses. I hope I can make some useful suggestions and also suggest that it is not difficult if you stand by who you are and why you want to ride to short cut the mythology of how difficult it is and how long it takes. It is not necessary for either the horse or the rider to be a particular shape, size, weight or age: everyone can get there, and quite quickly if they work at it. If you don't get there, it is because it is not a high enough priority for you, and you are not prepared to make the efforts and sacrifices required. Motivation and hard work, laced with self-examination and positive thinking will get you there. You don't have to be picked for a team, win the Olympic medal or become a household name among the horse-owning public. You can do it too, that is, develop and enlarge your communication with your horse from his back in order to enjoy each other more, whoever you are.

It is important to bear in mind that there are always many roads to Rome. The following ideas have been distilled from looking at many different types of riding, and trying to combine the parts of each that appear to help towards these goals. The 'Western riding' or the 'natural horseman' approach, at its best, is similar to the best masters of the European school. Unfortunately, bad teaching is all too common. Often teachers in the classical school have lost touch with its central message – to develop harmonious and delightful oneness between horse and rider. There are some modern writers in this tradition, whom I have found helpful (listed at the end of the chapter), though some make statements about equines which are destructive of a co-operative relationship and discourage efforts to better understand the ridden horse ('remember he has the brawn, you the brain', the rider must 'show who is leader'. Pojansky's book *My horses, my teachers* is a better guide. I will try to distil some of the most important and useful ideas.

The art of riding is to have the feeling that at one moment the two of you will dance a minuet, at another you can together both jump over the moon, or out-gallop and out-jump others around, or relax sleepily in the sun together. It has to be based, not on domination of the horse by the human, but on co-operation between the two. It helps to think of your relationship with your horse like a relationship with a partner. Give and take: 'You want to do this, fine, and then I would like to do that, OK?' is a good attitude. The same principles of respect, support and above all affection, enjoyment and pleasure in each other's company apply to your relationship with your horse. The sky is the limit of what this can achieve; perhaps few of us have perfect relationships with human or animal, but at least, if we can self-analyse, recognise when we made mistakes or become angry or frustrated and why, we can learn, if we want to.

So, the best approach in the first place is ensure that at least to start with, **the whole experience is pleasurable for the horse.** Of course not everything he is asked to do at all times will be enjoyable, any more than it is for any of us who are trying to learn and get things right, but one has to work towards the goal of encouraging him that, even though putting up with particular processes and events or learning a particular movement is difficult and sometimes frightening or frustrating, it is worth it for the end goal. From the equine's point of view, the end goal may in the first place be to know what to do and how to do it in order to reduce fear, aggravation and uncertainty. But when this lesson is learnt, the ridden

Chris rides a dressage test on Oryx with nothing on his head. He is going to turn left at the end of the school – note Chris's right leg back and Oryx looking in that direction. He is certainly going forward with enthusiasm.

horse can be encouraged to work for pleasure. Pleasure can come in many forms: it can come from knowing what to do, and doing it well in order to be praised. This gives pleasure because it causes a similar emotional reaction from the rider. But in order for the horse to value this, he must of course have some positive emotional relationship with the rider. . . he must care if he pleases her.

Then he may have pleasure actually doing some of the things he is asked to do for their own sake, such as visiting new places, galloping with others, or just pleasurable sensations in his body from exercise and movement of particular types. He learns that jumping the jumps, galloping around the field, or performing a particular movement, gives pleasure to himself physically, but also psychologically as he has given pleasure to the rider which, because of his emotional relationship with her, matters. If this is to be the case, it must be demonstrated by the rider, the horse must be praised so that he knows when he has pleased.

The easiest way to start to make whatever riding you are doing enjoyable to the horse is to perform something that he wants to do, and praise him with your voice. Soon he will be performing a movement in order to obtain your praise. Patting and touching can also be rewards, but if this is the case they must be used consistently for this aim (not as an apology by the rider when she feels she let the horse down).

The next phase is to try and construct a situation where he is likely to *want to do* whatever it is, having established that he knows *what to do* and *how to do it* (or at least start to do it). Praise him when he does it and then reduce the praise until he only gets the praise when he does the movement more completely or with more energy or with a more exaggerated style. Initially the aids may have to be somewhat exaggerated, but as he grasps the concepts implicit in these, they are reduced until the two of you appear to do it without anything but just common feeling or telepathy.

Other things are important in order for the equine to enjoy being ridden. One of the first lessons in learning to ride well is **balance**. Without balance there is no way in which a rider can ride in any sort of sophisticated way. For work on the flat, as many books have pointed out, to be in balance there must be a straight line between the shoulder the hip and the heel so that the centre of gravity of horse and rider are in the same place when he is not ridden. Failing to ride in balance, with the weight too far back or forward will ensure that the horse runs to keep up or slows to let the rider keep up. It is difficult to overemphasise the importance of the rider's balance to an equine, who has a great fear of falling and who specialises in speed of movement and an ability to keep in balance.

Run around and jump over logs with a floppy heavy rucksack on your back. This is what it is like to carry a rider who is out of balance. Look at other riders around you and see whether they stay 'in balance' (that is, keeping their legs in line with their bodies even when doing different gaits or movements.

Stand up in your stirrups as you walk, trot and canter, and see if you can stay there without holding onto the reins, or anything else. Practise this with a neck strap or by grabbing the mane; eventually you will be able to balance on flat and rough terrain. It is vital that you do not balance yourself (as very many do) by holding on to the reins.

Correcting the balance by gripping with the legs is not helpful if one wants to develop what is called an 'independent seat': being able to retain your balance while being completely relaxed and doing different things with one's hands and legs. So riding bareback is not a good way to start, as it encourages one to grip. A better exercise is to ride in a nice secure saddle, without stirrups and without reins, while sitting still and relaxed and learning not to control the horse, but just stay with him wherever he goes and at whatever pace.

Exercise 1. If you have a friend who will lunge the horse while you are riding and keep telling you when you are no longer relaxed, it helps a great deal. The horse should have side reins, the rider a saddle but no stirrups or reins. Start walking around and making sure you are in the correct balanced relaxed position. To do this it is helpful to have some images:

(a) Think of a sack of sand being poured in through a hole in your head, and gradually falling down to your heels so that your heels are being pushed downwards by gravity, not forced down by yourself.

(b) Shut your eyes and think about the little man in the clouds above who has control over you as a marionette, the strings running down to your shoulders and the top of your head, every now and then he lifts you off the saddle, so you imagine your light contact with the saddle; you are relaxed, and sitting tall.

When all is well, proceed at the trot and continue to relax without slouching in the saddle and moving with the horse.

Exercise 2. Now back to the walk and call out the four time rhythm of the walk, starting with one of the front legs which you can see, and ask your friend to confirm this. Usually people start by doing this with only the front legs, so make sure you include the hind legs. Then start calling it out with one of the hind legs, and then just the hind legs until you have the feel in your bones of the rhythm of the hind legs.

Do this at two-time trot as well, and when this is going well, into the three-time canter. If you lose your balance to start with, do not tighten your legs to hold on, grab the saddle, relax your legs and back and just get the feel of being balanced. It is a pleasant sensation, and it becomes quite clear that the quieter and more relaxed you are, the more even the horse's stride will become, and the more relaxed he will be. As your balance is established you will gradually be able to leave go with one hand and then the other until you, briefly to start with, have that perfect balance feel as you and your horse canter around. It is possible for someone to have the beginnings of that sensation in their first lesson, although it may take a little more time before someone who has habits of gripping and rising out of the saddle manages to correct these and feel relaxed into the horse. Don't give up!

Keep going back to the images to ensure that you remain relaxed and in balance, and ask your friend to call out if your legs go too far back or forward, or your shoulders tip in front or behind.

One thing that often happens is that one's shoulders stiffen up, and although it is easier to get the lower back to absorb the bumps at the trot, the shoulders do not go along with this. It is very important to have relaxed shoulders as otherwise your arms, and then hands, may not be relaxed.

Exercise 3. At a trot, concentrate on your shoulders and get them to move up and down even in an exaggerated way to start with, in the trot stride, so that they go up almost to touch your ears and then down again. Keep this up for a few rounds and try it in the different paces.

You become more aware of your shoulders, and more able to relax them when you need to. After a while, you will be able to say to your self 'shoulders floppy' and they will move up and down in rhythm by themselves. Then you can say to your self 'shoulders relax' when ever you need to.

Another useful shoulder exercise is to move just one of them around and around, backwards and forwards, keeping your arms more or less in the same place. Then both together. This is a good exercise before you start serious flat work every day.

The next series of exercises is to help you develop an independent balanced seat so that when you move one part of your body, the other part does not move. It is the sort of exercise one practises when rubbing your stomach with one hand while patting your head with the other, but geared to keeping your relaxed position in balance while moving different parts of your body. First your arms and the top part of your body:

Exercise 4. Lift one arm keeping the other one as if you were holding the reins, and circle the lifted arm, stretching out as far as possible in all directions, trying to touch the sides of the manege, the clouds, and the floor as it goes around. The other hand and arm must remain still, or move slightly in rhythm with the walk. Then the other arm, then both at once, always remaining in the balanced relaxed position and still, except for the moving arm.

Exercise 5. Hold up both arms sideways, making sure they are really horizontal, and, as you reach out, circle from the waist to the left as far as you can, looking around too so that you see around at least 360° as you walk and then trot around the school. Then to the inside, and repeat several times before relaxing your arms down to be held again in the correct position around 10 cm above the pummel of the saddle.

Exercise 6. At a walk, and then eventually at a trot if you can, bend the top part of the body forwards and let it lie with your head relaxed one side of the horse's withers and neck. Keep your legs in the correct position. Then up again, without leg movement, and repeat. It will take a little time before you manage to relax in the downward position, but this exercise is extremely useful when you are riding out and passing under trees and bushes, have to duck, but do not want to have your leg close on the horse which will make him leap forward at a crucial moment when you do not want him to.

Exercise 7. Halt, and first make sure that your mount will not be worried by this, so have someone hold his head the first time or two, and then lie back flat on his back, then sit up and go forward and relax, then again. As you bring yourself back and forwards, make sure that your legs from the knee down move very little if at all. This is a good stretching exercise too, and makes your stomach muscles work.

While you are doing these exercises, you must not move from the pelvis downwards, so your legs remain in the same position all the time; they become 'independent' of the movements of the top part of your body. Ask your friend to tell you when your legs move backwards or forwards, and make a note of how it feels when you have it right. Take it slowly and you will get it. You can invent other exercises to do too, hands and arms forward and up, then swing them as far back as they can go, for example, and so on; there are also many other books with different exercises that you can try. There are also exercises for the lower part of your body, moving your legs without your arms or hands, or your weight changing in the saddle.

Exercise 8. Keeping your upper body relaxed and in balance, swing your legs from the knee downwards, forwards and backwards, together, then one forward, the other back, then rotating your ankles while you do it, every now and then correcting your position to make sure you are still in balance, and visualising the sand pressing down your heels.

Exercise 9. Bring your pelvis forward a little and raise the whole length of your legs off the saddle sideways so that you are balancing on the points of your pelvic bone; hold this for a second or two, then correct your position. Make sure your hands remain still in the correct position while you do this, although the top part of your body may go backwards a little.

There are many exercises you can invent to better establish your balance, and you can of course familiarise yourself and the horse with strange movements like going 'around the world' by throwing one leg over then the next and so on until you have been right around the horse; a half dismount is another Pony Club favourite. Here sit sideways, then roll over onto your tummy and then place your leg back over to be back in the saddle. The more of these types of movements are done quietly and gently so that the equine becomes accustomed to them, the better, as he will find them less strange and potentially frightening at a later date. Slide off over the tail, creep between his legs, and so on, talking to him all the time so he knows you are there; do not take silly risks, think carefully where you do these movement and what is going on around, and praise him well when he stands still.

The other most important thing to understand about riding is that it is fitting in, absorbing and becoming conscious of the horse's gait rhythms. The two-legged human has to be aware of the four legs underneath her which move in different ways at different gaits; she must become so aware of the position of all these legs at any one time that it is automatic. First a rider must become extremely aware of the rhythms of gaits, which are in the same rhythm for every equine, but the movement is different for each individual. When the rider is aware what the horse is doing with all his legs at any one time, then it becomes possible to teach the horse to do different things with his legs.

Exercise 10. Asking the horse to take a larger step with one leg will be much more effective if you apply your own leg just as his leg is about to leave the ground than if you apply it after his leg has been returned to the ground.

Exercise 11. When you have more or less grasped where each leg is at any time by feeling and without having to think about it, which will come with practice, then walk with a friend on her horse and see if you can keep your horses in time, both lift left front leg, then right front leg (page 140 and 188).

As you wish to teach slightly more complicated movements, such as taking off on particular legs in the canter, or work on three tracks, it becomes increasingly important to have a sort of automatic knowledge of rhythm to be able to apply the leg at just the right time, in fact this is the most important secret for teaching advanced movements and airs above the ground.

Beginning to become one with the horse when riding is all about **feelings,** and becoming more aware of being with another mammalian being but one that has slightly different world view from oneself. It is not just about imposing our world view on the equine, and trying to dominate him of have him respond in a stimulus-response type unthinking fashion. Thinking about what you are doing in a concentrated linear type of way, trying harder and harder, often obscures the horse's world more, and superimposes one's own. The result, when riding in particular, is a stilted, although may be obedient performance of the horse/human duo, but it lacks the 'art' and the joy implicit in a co-operative performance, even though this may be less technically 'correct'.

There are many exercises one can do in order to try and achieve balance, rhythm and feel from the horse. The horse is your teacher, remember, so cue into him when ever you can.

Exercise 12. A useful exercise we often practise is to ask the rider to give a running commentary on what she is picking up from the horse. This often helps her to concentrate more on doing this afterwards. Some have much trouble with this to start with. The sort of thing you might notice would be 'he is feeling tense', more advanced, 'he feels like he is having difficulty on this corner', 'he wants to do something else now'.

Almost every horse can be ridden in an enclosed space without reins and stirrups quietly in order for these exercises to be practised, whatever his experiences previously, provided it is done quietly, tactfully and everyone is relaxed. The important thing is that the rider feels comfortable and relaxed. Without relaxation there is no way in which she will (i) be able to become one with her horse or (ii) not disturb him so he becomes more worried or excited. Even if you are not listening and feeling him, be assured he is listening to and feeling you!

Exercise 13. A simple exercise for the hand is to ask the horse to bend his head right around to touch your foot, first one side, and then the other, without moving the rest of his body. When you have enough subtlety in your hand movements to achieve this, then try asking him to hold his head in to the circle or out of the circle a little at least while walking, trotting and then cantering around in the manege. The next phase is then see if you can move his nose in while his ears stay where they are, so he is turning his head and not bending his neck.

Exercise 14. Another exercise is to tie the reins in a knot and ride him around, first at a walk, then a trot, then a canter. Then circling, turning, twisting, serpentines, *voltes* (small circles and continuation on the same rein), changes of the rein, whatever you like, using only your legs and weight. The more you do this, the better both of you will become. Then lengthening and shortening the stride, changing gaits, jumping or whatever you want to do. Remember, use your voice as well, it will help both of you greatly (picture page 168).

Exercise 15. Take the reins and experiment with a friend who holds the other end until you are holding them taut, but putting on the very least possible pressure before they slacken. When you have this feeling, get on your horse and try keeping them like that. Do movements you like to do, using the very minimum rein to stop it flapping, again don't be shy to use your voice to help.

There are many more exercises you can make up along these lines, I am sure. Develop two for yourself that will help you relax, balance, understand rhythm and have the greatest conversation through your hand. Remember the reins (and the legs) are conversational pieces, not command mechanisms.

Try teaching the 'that' and then the 'how' using very slight movements of the hands or legs in different positions following the basic premise 'towards the hand and away from the leg. If the horse only does what is required a very little, be sure to praise him, and then repeat with the same amount of pressure of aid, even if it takes longer to obtain what you are after. In the end he will have learnt it faster and be receptive and anxious to learn more. Usually, the horse will be logical in his response, but frequently the rider is not in how she asks.

There are many exercises that have been developed to help riders achieve these central aims in riding, and no need to go into these in detail, any really good teacher will be able to help, or a read of some of the equitation classics will help. There is nothing like a little yoga, Alexandra technique, or other ways of encouraging you to think differently about the world to help here because what you are trying as a rider to do is to cue into the horse's world and at the same time you are, so to say, 'in his hands', more so than when on the ground or with any other work with horses. Perhaps this is one reason why riding, and riding well, is what almost everyone who is interested in horses really wants to do most.

REFERENCES
Anon. *L'equitation, le cheval et l'ethologie. Colloque du 18 Sept 1999 a l'ecole National d'Equitation*. Belin. Paris.
Burger, U. 1959. *The way to perfect horsemanship*. J. A. Allen. London.
Gueriniere, F. R. de la. (1733) 1994. *The School of Horsemanship*. trans T. Boucher. J. A. Allen London.
Imam, S. A. H. A. A. 1987. *The Centaur. A critical analysis of horsemanship plus relevant equitant history*. Indian Heritage. Hazaribagh.
Rees, L. 1991. *Riding: The True Techniques*. Stanley Paul.
Swift, S. 1996. *Centred Riding*. J. A. Allen. London.
Wanlass, M. 1987. *Ride with your mind. A right brain approach to riding*. Methuen. London.
Williams, M 1960. *Adventures unbridled*. Methuen. London.
Xenophon, 350BC. (1972) *The art of horsemanship*. J. A. Allen. London.

9

THE ART OF HORSEPERSONSHIP

• More advanced movements

The art of horsepersonship is what most of us who are interested in equines (how they behave, who they are, how to teach them, drive and ride horses) aspire to, although not everyone makes it. However, in my travelling around giving workshops, I have been surprised how one finds the art of horsepersonship occurring in unexpected places: an amateur perhaps who has worked away with her equine and achieved an extraordinary level of communication and intricacy of co-operative relationship. The art of horspersonship is not restricted to the professionals and the equestrian centres of the world (although there may be artists there as well as anywhere else). Whether you wish to take part in dressage competitions, circus acts, displays, quadrilles or dances or have an intricate and harmonious relationship with your equine or teach him something different, there is no reason why you cannot have a go. But to pursue this art, it is first imperative to:

(1) Understand how the equine learns (see chapter 2)

(2) Master balance, rhythm, relaxation and a flexible hand when riding or driving (see chapter 8)

(3) Understand the basic premise: the equine goes towards a hand and away from a leg aid.

It is not likely to be easy or necessarily impressive, but once you have mastered these three skills, then you can build on them.

Here we will discuss a few common more advanced movements and things to teach that some are either confused about, frightened of trying, or have no idea how to approach. These are:

(1) Work on 3/4 tracks (shoulder in, renvers, travers, leg yield and half pass, at different paces)

(2) Canter leading on the leg asked for, counter canter and flying changes

(3) Collection and pirouettes

(4) *Piaffe*

(5) Standing on things and other odd movements

(6) The Spanish walk and Spanish trot, *passage, levade*

There are many other things you can teach your horse; once you have practised these basics, you will be able to work out how to teach him whatever you wish. It is possible to teach your horse to do almost all these movements in some form or another by restrictions and gadgets, domination, and/or inducing fear, but this

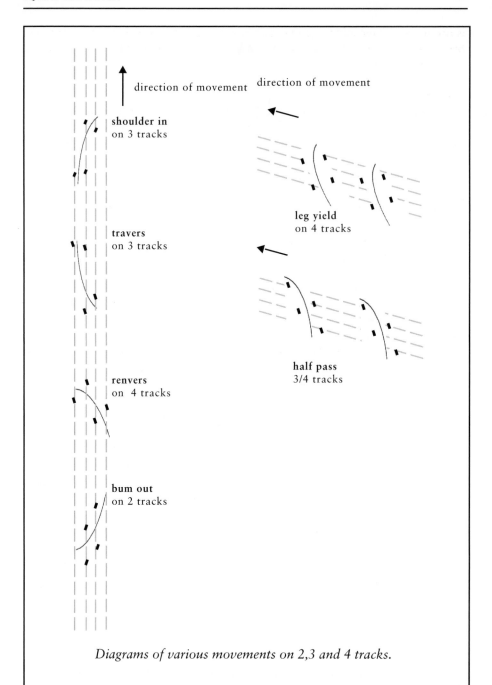

direction of movement   direction of movement

shoulder in
on 3 tracks

travers
on 3 tracks

renvers
on 4 tracks

bum out
on 2 tracks

leg yield
on 4 tracks

half pass
3/4 tracks

Diagrams of various movements on 2,3 and 4 tracks.

is not the art of teaching equines'. It is not difficult to see whether the horse has been co-operatively educated or dominated and forced to do what is asked if you have learnt to observe well.

(1) Work on 2/3/4 tracks

In the traditional schools, most of the movements we will describe should be performed with the horse making 3 tracks, but, provided you have asked for it, there is no reason why this should not be taken further so that the horse, when asked, moves on 2 tracks sideways, the front end making one track and the rear feet making the other, or 3, that is, obliquely so that the leading front leg makes one track, the remaining front leg steps in the same line as the first hind leg, and the last hind leg makes a separate track. If progressing sideways, at a smaller angle, the equine can progress on 4 tracks.

It is also possible for the equine to progress on one track only, crossing the feet over so that each foot is in the same line as the last one. Walking over a narrow plank is an example – it is difficult.

A **shoulder in** (**on 3 tracks**) is going at an angle to the straight line of about 30° with the front legs leading the way and crossing over, the head bent away from the direction of movement, the inside hind leg in line with the outside front leg, and the outside hind leg making its own outer track.

A **leg yield** means going sideways, so both the front and the hind legs cross over each other, although the hind legs may be a little behind the front. The head is again pointing in the direction from which the horse has moved.

A **travers** (**on 3 tracks**) is bringing his quarters in, but having him look (and bend in so far as he is bending) in the direction of movement, and it is a little more difficult than a shoulder in. Easier is the **renvers** (**on 4 tracks**), which is shoulders out, bending and looking away from the direction of movement. The fourth one is **bum out**, and looking in the direction of the movement.

Out of these movements comes the '**leg yield**' from the shoulder in where the horse is looking away from the direction of movement but moving more sideways rather than forward, and the 'half pass' which comes out of the travers, where the horse is looking in the direction of movement, but progressing sideways.

All these movements (with the exception of walking on one track, where the horse must just be very straight) involve a bend. The problem for the horse is that it is difficult for him to bend his back; he can hardly do this at all, unlike a dog or a cat who has a backbone that moves a great deal sideways (look at a dog wagging his tail) as well as arching and rounding (look at how a dog or a cat gallops forward, straightening and rounding his back). It is quite easy to ask the horse to bend his head to one side or the other, in fact this is a useful exercise to ensure he is listening and giving to the bit, and also to educate the hand, but to follow this by bending his back inwards or outwards is much more difficult. Equines rarely do manage to bend their backs, it just looks as if they are; they are keeping themselves in line with the slight bend of the neck to one side or the other. So the idea is to change the angle so that the equine is progressing on 2, 3 or 4 tracks, depending on which you choose. It is very simple of course, as the equine will go towards the hand and away from the leg, so all one has to do to, say, progress down the side of the school in a shoulder in where he is looking away from the direction of movement, to the inside, is to use the inside hand, the outside leg behind the girth, the inside leg on the girth, to encourage the middle of the back to move outwards, and the outside leg behind the girth to stop the quarters going out too much. Then bring the forehand off the track to the inside and encourage him by pushing with the inside leg, to cross over his front legs. If he crosses his hind legs as well he will be on 4 tracks, or if he is moving at a greater angle to the straight side, 2 tracks, it is up to you. What you don't particularly want is his head bending inside without his body changing its angle. So it is really just like riding a circle and ensuring that the horse is bending, or appears to be bending around the circle, by looking in and keeping his body in the line of curve of his neck.

Using the leg next to the girth strongly helps to ensure the appropriate bend progressing down the straight line, but when it comes to moving sideways, it is the outside leg which becomes more active to push the horse over away from the leg, and the hands gently adjust the position and angle as required. In half passes, equines find it difficult to keep their front and hind ends parallel.

The best way of practising these movements is, first, to make sure that you are very clear which aids you must use for each one. With practice they come almost automatically, but it is easier to start on a horse who knows what to do so you can find out if you are asking correctly for the movement. There are many variations on these movements and no reason why you should not have a go: they do not have to be done in the way the dressage fraternity insists.

Teaching the 'concept'

A new approach that we have found effective, and which is not often pursued systematically, is to introduce the concept of what is required to the horse. In chapter 2 we discussed 'learning that' and 'learning how'. Because we now know that equines can also form concepts, it is worth seeing if we can improve their learning by teaching them the concepts, rather than just have them responding to aids that they have learnt. Once they have understood the concept, the 'that', then we can progress to teaching them how we want it done, the 'how'.

Oberlix was being very slack about progressing sideways in a half pass; although he was keeping the bend, his hind end was left well behind and I was having trouble getting him to move sideways. I wondered if he had any idea what he was supposed to be doing, so decided to teach him the concept of 'go sideways and keep your body nearly parallel'. To do this, we did not worry about the bend, but I just asked him to go sideways along the rail in what is called a 'full pass' at a walk to start with, and used the word 'sideways'. After a time or two, he grasped this, and with only slight aids began to walk sideways along the rail on two tracks. We then tried a full pass across the school, and this he understood. So the next thing was to ask him to bend his head in the direction of movement, and to go forward as well as sideways, not letting his quarters drop behind.

With a little help from the legs and hand aids, he had little trouble and our half pass had much improved. He had grasped the concept of the 'half pass', it was not just responding to this and that aid any more, it was 'going sideways and forwards, bending in the direction of the rein and with a nearly parallel body'.

After this success, it occurred to me that although going towards the hand and away from the leg was all very well for elementary type riding, it might be better, when asking the horse to do rather more complex things, to teach him the concept of the movement. This must involve learning to do the central core of the movement, that is 'learning that' (page 67), and when he has grasped that, 'learning how', exactly how you want it done, in this case with the head bent slightly towards the direction of movement. It also involves praising the horse well when he gets it right. Many horses if they are asked to do this and that in this and that way all at once, which is usually the case since they are not taught the concept of the movement but just to respond to the leg and hand, can get into quite a panic when things get complicated. This is probably why it takes so long to teach an equine to do many of these movements and compete at Prix St George dressage for example. The person has to ask them to repeat it many times, so that the horse gradually learns this requirement of the movement, the head position, then the quarters position, and then the sideways part and so on. But if you teach them the concept first: 'going sideways' or 'going down the school at an angle' and they understand that, then is very much easier and quicker for them to learn how you want it done. This is again illustrated by Oberlix.

Once I had understood the importance of Oberlix understanding the concept of the movement, I set about teaching all the movements required for the next level of dressage test by teaching him 'that' first, then exactly 'how' we wanted it done. We started competing in affiliated British dressage at medium level in November, and set ourselves the aim that when we had achieved at least half marks (50% +), a pass, not marvellous, but at least adequate, we would go up to the next level. There were not many competitions near us, but each time we competed we went up a grade, so by March we were taking part in Prix St George, by July Intermediare. Then I had to go abroad, had an accident and so on, so we have yet to do Grand Prix, but it was surprising and impressive that we managed to move up through Medium, Advanced Medium, Advanced, Prix St George and then Intemediare in 6 months having only competed previously in a couple of Elementary tests!

Oberlix is a pure-bred Arab with a natural way of going that is not conducive to conventional dressage, that is with a high head and tail carriage and almost concave back ('hollow backed' it is called), even when he is rushing around loose in the fields. Of course he can learn to go in the way required. This well known characteristic of Arabs does mean that many judges are somewhat biased against them doing dressage, perhaps because they often do the tests before they have learnt how they are expected to move. We always did the test 'hors de combat'

Oberlix doing a renvers or shoulder out in a head collar; note the bend against the direction of movement and the three tracks.

which means that one is doing it for the sake of doing it, not to win or be placed in a competition, and this allowed us to concentrate more on our progress and learning. After all, you can win a competition because everyone else on that day was very bad, so winning tells you nothing about your progress!

The discipline of practising the movement and getting it as the judges (or you) want it, and then doing the tests, is very real. I would encourage many more people to take part in dressage in this way, it is surprising how much you learn and how much better your riding can become; I am now hooked. The aim was that Oberlix should take part in International Level Long Distance and International Level Dressage in one year, which he did. We did not win but we did well in both, with above average performance. How many other international level dressage or long distance horses can claim this I wonder?

Teaching the concept of what is required is something that can be more widely used when educating equines, and something we now use very widely.

(2) Canter leading with a particular leg, counter canter and flying changes
To take off on the left lead, for example, the aids are again based on those for going around the bend to the left, so the left hand (inside), left leg on the girth (inside leg on the girth) and the outside leg behind the girth (right leg behind).

A horse will find it easier to take off and balance with the inside leg leading to start with, so start to teach him to take off on the leg asked for on a circle, even quite a small one so that he is more likely to want to do this, and praise him when he does it. Gradually the circle becomes larger, and the bend less and less until you can ask for the left or right lead on a straight line. If there are mistakes, you tell him 'no', try again and then return to the circle if he cannot get it. When he gets it right you praise him. I like my horses to take off on the leg I ask for when we are riding out and about, and gradually I will make it more difficult, so that once he has understood the concept of left or right lead and the aids associated with them (also the voice saying 'canter left or canter right'), we progress to asking for a left lead on a slight right bend, or staying on the left lead around a right bend. Usually they favour leading with one leg over the other, so we start with the easy one, and progress gradually to the more difficult one. Once it is working reasonably well outside, we come into the school and ask first of all on the straight side of the school for the counter canter, and gradually continue this until he can canter a 10 metre circle in a counter canter, but make sure the horse is well balanced and even in the canter first. This is where rhythm comes in; ask for the canter when you have brought the horse back to a cadenced even slowish trot just as the outside front leg and inside hind come to the ground in the trot, so that he takes off into the canter with the inside front leg, and *vice versa* for a counter canter. This becomes automatic after a while, particularly if you have done the exercises described in chapter 8.

Once he is understanding that he must listen to the aids and the voice before taking off into the canter and consequently leads with either leg when asked, it is not difficult to keep him in a counter canter as he canters around even a quite small circle; remember, keep him bent slightly to the outside and continue to reinforce those bending aids (outside hand, outside leg on the girth, inside leg behind the girth).

In the nature of things, one develops habits, and one leg or hand will tend to become dominant when asking for a canter. I use the inside leg more than the outside one, but other people do the opposite, as long as your horse understands you, and you can adapt your aids when you ride a different horse by finding out how he reads you, there is no problem with what aids you give at all.

Flying changes are easiest started outside also. Ask for an outside lead coming up to a corner, then as you turn the corner, change the aids to the other lead, that is use your inside hand a little, inside leg on the girth and outside leg behind it. Repeat several times while saying, 'change' loudly and clearly as you give the aids, and when he does change, even if it is only in front, tell him how marvellous he is. In the school, you can start by cantering across the school and turning to the side he is not leading on as you arrive at the edge; it is easier though to canter him straight at the bar, then come straight to a walk, and as you turn ask for the correct different lead. Do this several times, and then try without the break to walk. You will have to experiment and make sure your timing is good, outside and inside, until you begin to get the feel of it. Then it is simple, first a flying change on a straight line, making sure now that he changes behind at the same time. If he does not, tell him off and try again.

When beginning to teach Shemal the flying change, she could not grasp the idea easily; we did many changes through a walk, but she found it difficult without a walk step and got into a panic. After repeating it for a couple of days, and praising her as much as possible to stop her getting worried, she finally changed on the straight line, but in front only. I praised her no end, and then it was easily done, but only in front. I told her about behind, and as I gave the aid, I touched her on the quarters very gently with a whip to remind her; she bucked, but came down on the changed leg. So the next few days were spent enthusiastically changing with enormous bucks! There was a danger of her believing that was what was required, so the next thing was to reduce the aids, and just ask with the voice, and keep going at quite a pace (it seems much easier to do flying changes fast to start with), and finally she managed one without a buck, all praise, and so we set up a new habit, and she can do about four 2 time changes with panache now, although one time changes are still not clear!

Once you have both managed a single flying change, it is only a question of staying on a straight line and asking for another after 10 strides, then 5, then 4, and then another perhaps if that goes well. Gradually the 4 times, 3 times and 2times changes will become quite easy. I like to count out loud to help the horse (and myself), but it takes a little practice to get the timing right and if the timing is wrong it will not be easy for either of you.

The 1 times changes are the most difficult, of course. Oberlix and I are developing them by doing 2, 2 times, then one 1 times, return to 2 times, then another 1 times. A few successes here where the horse is seriously listening to you, and you are getting the timing right (not easy), then you are all set to string them together, but make sure the hind legs are also changing, this is the challenge. I also like to do changes around the school so that it is not always done on a straight line, a 2 times skipping around the ring is impressive and not that difficult once you can both do 2 times changes.

(3) Collection and pirouettes

The beginnings of collection have already been established in the half halt and shorter strided walk, trot and canter. The horse shortens his body, taking shorter strides (but in the same rhythm if possible), becoming lighter in hand holding himself up more in front. He appears to put more weight on his hind end (although weight tests to date show this is not really the case) and bends his hind legs more so his head is quite early higher, but still vertical to the ground.

I find it easier to introduce the concept of collectionr, so when the horse comes into a more collected state for a pace or two, he is praised; remember well what aids you gave to achieve this. Although there are general rules for the aids, as we have emphasised, nevertheless, each horse and rider are different, and each must search out the best way of communicating. The good rider's job is to quickly find the best way for that particular horse by trying a variety of approaches; some require stronger hand aids, but many object to this, and need very light simple movements, such as an elevation of the hand. Some respond to strong leg aids, others almost none, some just weight changes some just the voice. If it does not happen, remember, it is never the horse's fault, it is the rider's, she has not managed to convey the message, and needs to try something else. When the horse has the general concept of collection, then it is important to make sure he is doing it right in 'self carriage' - that is, holding himself rounded and 'correct' with a slack rein. Collection is naturally shown very often by excited and restrained horses, they want to go forward but are prevented (usually by the rein), but instead of leaping about, in the manege, this energy is controlled, and channelled into the movement that you are doing, whether this is a walk, a trot, a canter, or even further to the *piaffe* (trot on the spot).

One thing that is common is that the dressage horse becomes bored with the same old stuff every day, and lacks impulsion, or is very difficult to enthuse; he is loath to put energy into the work, and particularly the collection which becomes an 'oh, good, a slow trot at last' rather than a very energetic demonstration of how much he would like to go forward. I find a good way of obtaining a collection to start with, rather than boring them with daily exercises of half halts, and then having to enthuse them with a stick, is to construct a situation where the horse will become somewhat excited, and wish to go forward to see a friend passing, or when a group of horses meet to go off on a ride or whatever. That is a good time to practise collection; ask for a collected trot instead of just a jog, ask him to put energy into what you want rather than being a nuisance. At this time, he has the energy, it is just a question of channelling it, and having the will is one of the major problems horses have with flat work, after a while! The other important thing to make it all worthwhile for him is to ensure you praise him when he gets it right, even if this is only for an instant, and give him a tit bit if necessary. Much of this collection can be done in hand as well. Once he has grasped the concept in hand, it is just an association of the word or the aids you have used on the ground with those when you are riding.

Shemal had done very little flat work, other than that explained in chapter 8, but I was in Cambridge for the year, and the riding out was full of traffic so I decided to concentrate on her more advanced flat work. Collection was one of the first things. She easily panics if she thinks she is not doing the right thing, or is unsure of it. So I asked her to go forward, then checked her, and repeated this, and soon she was jogging along, beginning to worry and her energy rising. All I had to do was to channel that energy into getting her to lift her legs higher in the trot while not going faster forward, and lo and behold, we had a really nice collected trot!

The collected walk is more difficult than the trot, and tends to fall into a slow unenergetic 'ok, we are about to stop' type of pace. So the next move is to try and collect the walk but energize it, and shorten the stride so that the hind feet do not overstep the imprint made by the front (which they should at a normal or extended walk). The problem is often that as soon the horse is energized, he starts to trot. So the walk pirouette comes in useful here. He must walk along in a collected walk, you then ask him to stop moving forward, but keep the four-time rhythm of the walk and in particular the hind legs lifting and being put down while he turns around, first 90° and then 180°. Be careful he does not swivel on his hind legs; if he does, make sure he walks a small circle, and do not try and make this smaller until he has grasped the idea of keeping walking, or it will quickly become a habit that is difficult to change. Go back and forth across the school doing pirouettes both sides, and praising him when he gets it right, and telling him 'no' when he (and you) make a mess. Gradually, if nothing else, you will end up with

Shemal doing a canter flying change – she is not entirely happy about it, although trying hard. Swishing tail and grinding her teeth!

a much better collected walk, and he will have the concept of the pirouette. Make sure when you are riding out to ask for the correct performance of a turn. Do not just let him wander around or you will establish habits that are more difficult to change, at least not until you are sure that he has understood when you are asking for a particular movement, and when you are not.

The collected canter then needs work. It takes time of course before the youngster can balance well at a slow canter on the small circle, as we have mentioned (chapter 6). So the first thing is to try and keep the horse cantering, but bring the canter back, imagine you are cantering on the spot, and gradually you will manage one or two strides.

The pirouette often helps also to collect the canter.

Exercise 1. Canter as collected as possible straight to the edge barrier of the manege, then when you are very close turn a 90°.

Exercise 2. A few of these, then do a 180° turn while still cantering and repeat it when you reach the other side of the manege. After about four goes, he will have grasped the concept of cantering around in a very small circle, and keep cantering. Then it is a question of making the very small circle of the hind legs even smaller, keeping the bend, and keeping cantering. If you lose the canter, allow him to enlarge the circle a little. Once he has understood that he must keep cantering and keep more or less on the same spot, he will himself solve the problem by jumping around in the canter pirouette, which is always at a slower rhythm than the normal canter. In fact he may do some quite elaborate jumps up with his front end, but don't worry, just keep quietly helping him understand.

The added advantage of these exercises is that all you will have to do to obtain a collected canter is make him expect that he might have to do a pirouette in a little while, and he will bring himself back, but then you explain that that is fine, but just keep going straight forward, and both of you will have solved the collected canter at least without hauling or leg bashing, whips and restraints.

Exercise 3. After using the barrier of the manege to help, try asking him for a canter pirouette anywhere in the manege, and praise him when he gets it a little better than before.

The aids for the pirouette are obvious, it is just a very tight bend, so inside leg on the girth, outside leg behind, inside hand to obtain the bend, and outside hand to prevent him going forward too much.

(4) Piaffe

The *piaffe* is an elevated trot on the spot with a slow rhythm, in collection, showing the energy and enthusiasm of the horse, but without moving forward. As explained above, it arrives out of collection. It is relatively easy to teach, once you have generated some energy somehow, preferably by enthusing the horse to try harder by praise.

> Shemal, with her rather panicky personality, learnt the *piaffe* very quickly; in around three sessions she was doing a very presentable one for at least four strides. This was achieved by simply riding her first in collection, then asking her not to go forward, but keeping her energy bubbling. She naturally started to trot on the spot, then a touch with the legs further back to ask her to lift her hind feet up higher, and lo and behold, the piaffe begins to emerge! Oryx, by contrast, a laid back character, found this daft. Why keep trotting on the spot

Oberlix learning the 'how' of piaffe.

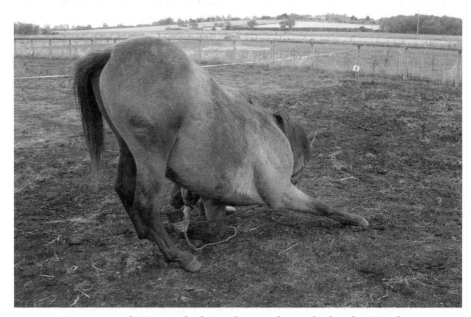

Luxor aged 18 months lying down when asked to by Marthe.

for goodness sake? So we taught him to keep going forward in a trot, but to elevate the hind legs more, and then gradually come back so that he hardly goes forward at all.

There have been many books written on the *piaffe*, but it really is a matter of common sense. If the horse becomes too worried and starts leaping around, you have overdone it; go back to something simple and easy and praise him for doing this, before returning again quietly and with less aids. To distinguish it from a collected trot, I use my legs alternately; as the left front leg leaves the ground, I use my right leg, and *vice versa*. If your timing is bad here, don't worry, the horse will put it right once he understands what it is you want.

It is more difficult to teach to the less enthusiastic. Oberlix is very laid back in the manege, much too laid back, and we can usually only do about ten minutes before he gets so bored that it is all not worth while. Yes, I could hound him in to it for longer by serious use of spurs and whip, but I want him to do it because he wants to, so I have to work out ways of interesting him in what he is learning. One way is when he gets things right and is praised, or even is given a tit bit, so I started the *piaffe* with him from the ground, and when I raised my whip behind or touched his quarters with it in rhythm and asked him to *piaffe*, he was to start doing it; provided you trot along beside, gradually reducing his forward movement (and this can be in a headcollar, it really does not need a curb bit as many of the 'grand masters' say is imperative), then he starts to piaffe. One stride, and he is praised and given a tit bit. Now all I have to do is say, '*piaffee*' and raise my hand when I am on the ground, and he will do it for me. When I am riding, he remains rather un-energetic, I must admit, but that is my next problem, how to enthuse him more. He is much better in competitions, or displays, where he knows he is being watched!

(5) Standing on things and other odd movements
Standing on a pedestal or a rock
If the horse has already learnt to imitate, the easiest thing here is to lift one of your feet onto the pedestal or rock, and ask him to do the same thing; when he does, reward lavishly. Once one leg is on the object, then it is not difficult to ask the horse to move forward and lift himself up on this leg, then place the other down. This may be something that is not particularly useful, you would think, but actually it is surprising how often it has been useful to have our horses easily step up onto things, so one can look over perhaps, or get over objects and so on. It is all part of getting the horse used to doing a variety of things, easily and without concern. You can also do the other way around, stand up on something, and ask the horse to step down just with his front legs and hold it like that.

Be careful that whatever you are asking him to stand on from the start will bear his weight, and he will not slip: one fall, and it will take a long time to gain his confidence again with doing this, and maybe with other things too.

Kicking a ball
The difficulty for an equine is to kick the ball forwards rather than send it backwards by lifting the leg and pawing. Both Shemal and Oberlix both learnt to do this in our teaching experiments, and they will now both follow the ball and continue to kick it forwards. The next phase is a football match, which I think might get a little fast and furious, but we may try. This exercise, like most of the movements in this chapter, is just as worthwhile to do as to teach him some advanced dressage movement.

Learning to lie down
Many people want a recipe to get their horses to lie down, as it is impressive, and requires a lot of confidence in the teacher. Lying down is something that can be done for display, but is also useful, for example, when the horse is in need of particular veterinary attention to a leg, or for someone who cannot mount otherwise, or even to be able to hide from someone.

The most important things here are:
(1) To ensure there is plenty of room when you are teaching him to start with, so that he will not be stuck or bump his behind.
(2) A good soft surface, not slippery or hard.
(3) A familiar place, with familiar people to give him confidence.

We usually start in the middle of the manege, and then as he becomes more

First lesson in lifting the same leg together for the Spanish walk – Chris on Shemal and Marthe on Oberlix in their Cambridge University quarters. Rather too much leg and hand aid being used by both of us.

experienced, ask for a lie down in the stable, and gradually in less familiar places. When lying down, horses are very vulnerable, and it is important that they have confidence in you before they will lie down, so do not try it until you have performed many of these other exercises and feel able to do almost anything with your horse without being upset.

The phases we use are:

(1) Accustom the equine to being stroked and even lie with him when he is lying down in his stable or out at grass, so he first learns that he can be handled normally when lying down. He will get up to start with, but a feed in a bucket while he lies is a good incentive to stay there.

(2) As he stands quietly in a large soft area, without distractions from other equines, hold one of the front legs up, and gradually pull it backwards until he bows down onto the other knee. If he leaps around, do it again and again until he does not. Sometimes we tie the leg up to a surcingle (but not if the horse is likely to panic) only because it can take 10 minutes or so before he discovers that lying is the best solution.

(3) When he is bending down onto his other knee and has his weight right back, a gentle rub of the withers followed by a slight push may be enough for him to topple down.

(4) Give him a food reward. Before he gets up himself, ask him to get up.

(5) The next phase, when he has full confidence in lying on his sternum, is to gently roll him out flat when he is lying and reward him again profusely. Then he learns 'lie' and 'lie flat'.

Unless you have time, patience and are not frightened if the horse leaps about a little, don't try to teach him this or it will develop into a panicky unpleasant lesson doing neither of you any good. It is much best to start when the horse is young and he is supple and falls and lies down and gets up much more frequently than an adult.

Go anywhere and do anything

Sometimes it is useful if your horse will climb steps, stand on odd things, clamber over cliffs and creep through things.

> About eighteen years ago we had a glorious holiday in May riding in the Highlands of Scotland from Mull to Wester Ross with some friends. At one point, the Forestry Commission officer had told us that the gate was not locked through a piece of forest we had to cross but when we arrived, high up in the moors, some 28 miles from the centre, we found that it was. There was a deer fence either side of the gate some 8 feet high, with wire netting at the bottom and plain wire above. We realised that we could not go back that night, and that our friend was waiting for us in a valley below with our small son Jake, so we had to go though. With a little coaxing, we managed to stretch the wires sufficiently wide at around 3 feet high for a horse's head to get though, and a human to ease himself through. Aisha, being the smallest, was asked to put her head through and then to jump over the bottom wires as her head was held by the top wires. She had hardly a moment's hesitation, and then was quickly

Obie levade.

Oberlix doing a levade in a head collar only. His hocks are nicely bent, but his head a little high. I am unfortunately looking down, too stiff and hands too low.

followed by Cariff, a young stallion at the time, and Shiraz. The bigger horses had a bit more of a tussle, but were game for anything. When we got down to the valley, we found our friend and small Jake had been hiding in a telephone box for the last three hours, driven there by the midges.

Our young horses usually have such experiences with others who are knowledgeable, as we adventure about the world, so we tend to take it all for granted. It is somewhat of a shock when out with other people to find their horses cannot go there or do this or that. Usually though it is the people who won't try, not the horse! If you want to, it is possible to teach almost any horse to go anywhere and do almost anything quietly and calmly.

Exercise 1. Start asking your equine to stand on something small and solid, a step for example. One leg and then the other, when you are on the ground. Then something higher but wide, and so on, until he has confidence in standing on all sorts of things. As usual, be careful he does not slide or fall off or you will have to start all over again.

Exercise 2. Going under washing lines is another one. Gradually lower the line until he has to squat down as he goes under, and eventually almost has to do the conga. Be warned here: he may try it on fences, particularly electric ones when they are not switched on.

Exercise 3. Clambering up very steep places, or walking along narrow paths on the edge of cliffs are other things you can practise. With others who know, to start with. Sometimes the horse's attention wanders, so make sure they are thinking of what they are doing. If you have the heebie jeebies, get off and lead him, or shut your eyes.

There are many more exercises you can think up, I am sure; the point is to make sure you use all the opportunities in your area. There are now competitions for doing these sort of obstacle races, which might encourage you, if you are competition-minded. Le Trek is one, and various gymkhana games others, but you can teach your horse much more than these competitions require, if you want.

(6) The Spanish walk and trot
Learning 'that'
(1) The horse/pony/donkey already knows to lift his leg when asked. He has been taught this in a schedule of exercises: (a) lift your leg left or right when I touch it and ask you from the ground,(b) lift your leg when I ask you by using the rein on that side and the opposite leg and my voice, (c) lift your leg on the appropriate side in sequence when I ask you with very slight aids on the rein on that side, and keep going forward.
(2) So, first he does the Spanish walk lifting his front legs every stride to get into thinking and doing this action.
(3) He is asked to trot, and then the aids for Spanish walk, including the touching of the leg to be lifted with a whip, the voice and the rein and leg aids are used.
(4) He does one leg lift but stops as he does it. He has the 'that', now he has to learn the 'how'.

Learning 'how'
(1) He understands what he is supposed to do: lift his front legs in sequence when asked, but keeping in a trot; doing this requires some serious changes in tempo of all four legs, and is not easy. So the next exercise is to teach him to lift only one of his legs when asked as he trots along and keeps trotting, every 4th stride or so to start with. This requires some serious timing of the aids, give them just before he lifts that leg, and ask him with the voice as well of course. Eventually he will remain trotting and be able to lift that one leg every stride.
(2) Now the same with the other leg. Probably he will find one much easier than the other.
(3) Ask him to trot and then lift one leg, and then the other; do this sequence of two lifts for a few days and then
(4) Continue the lifting for a longer sequence until, eventually, he can keep it up for a 50 metre length. The exercises can be done anywhere, out for a ride, in a field, wherever, but always ensure that both of you manage to finish having done something positive, even if that means going back to an easier stage.

There will be a moment when he 'gets it', and suddenly manages to do several lifts. Don't worry about how high or anything else at this stage, this can come later. Oberlix took around three weeks to get the general drift, doing some of these exercises nearly every day for around 5-10 minutes only, with plenty of 'yes' and 'no' which he understands, 'lift' 'right' 'left' and of course 'well done' 'good boy', 'hurrah' and so on with plenty of expression.

Shemal has recently been learning this too. She has entered her 'washer woman' stage, where she understands the 'that' but the 'how' is still a bit of a mystery and

Oberlix doing a passage *up a mountain track; note the lift of the hind leg as well as the front.*

so she enthusiastically throws first one and then the other front leg up and down and then leaps about a bit, as though she is pounding her washing in the sink! Keeping the sequence for more than two is still difficult, but it will come with practise in the next week.

The *passage*

The *passage* is a lovely suspended trot, related to the Spanish trot, but the hind legs must lift much higher than normal, just like the front legs, and the front legs do not have to be stretched out straight as is often required in the Spanish trot. I find it easiest to teach by first teaching the horse the Spanish walk and the *piaffe*. So start in the Spanish walk, then *piaffe* and then Spanish trot while going forward out of the *piaffe*. The horse will then probably end up doing a step or two of *passage*, for which he should be effusively praised.

Keeping it up for more paces is the next step. Try five steps one day, then ten and so on until you can keep it going for 50 metres or so. Then do circles and other movements in *passage*. Once he has the general idea, it is not difficult to do this, but it is also tempting to be sloppy and let him drop back into an ordinary trot before you have asked. If you allow this, soon you will have a habit on your hands that needs to be changed. Once you both have the *passage*, it can be done going forward in a swinging, suspended pace, which is required for the Grand Prix dressage tests, but can also be performed with a shorter stride, even turning into the *piaffe*, so it becomes a very useful dance step, everyone likes to see it. Each horse does it a little differently, and I like to encourage this, unless I am aiming to take part in dressage competitions, in which case it has to be done in a particular style.

The *levade*

The *levade* is a rear with the hind legs very bent, and held in this crouched position for some seconds. It is important not to begin to teach your horse to do a *levade* until you are quite sure that he will not generalise and try and do it (or its cousin, the rear) at any odd time, particularly when he gets excited or frustrated. It is one of the later movements we teach.

> I learnt this the hard way by watching my sister teach her Somali cross Arab pony to rear when we were children in Kenya. After Gazelle had more or less understood what was required, whenever things got tight, she would rear, and these became higher and higher as time went on.
> I have had several horses, whose rearing has become a major problem, brought to me as a behavioural consultant. Once rearing has become an established habit, it requires a commitment to re-learning, and rewarding non-rearing.
> Over the years, I have bought three thoroughbreds cheap because they reared. This was when I was young and inexperienced, but it was a hard lesson, because it needed a great deal of commitment and often nerve to teach them not to.

So be quite sure your horse will not take to rearing before you teach him a *levade*.
(1) Have the horse *piaffe* either in hand or when ridden, whichever you like. Then continue to encourage him to shorten his body and not to move forward, but continue energetically. Sooner or later he will jump up a little with both front legs while still keeping his hind legs bent. Reward him. I taught Oberlix by placing the whip under his girth to encourage him to go away from the whip, and asked him to 'jump' while doing a *piaffe* with me on the ground. This is the 'that' phase, which he quickly understood. But then it has to be controlled to the 'how', which does not mean a high rear, but rather a squat holding of the position. This I am doing by simply telling him 'yes' when he gets it a little better and 'no' when his hind legs stretch. The difficult thing for him is to balance for a few seconds, presumably because he has not yet got his hind legs under him enough. So at the moment it is not a bad *levade*, sometimes at least, but he cannot hold it for long. However we only do it when he has been doing other flat work.

Remember that the high school horses that do these 'airs above the ground' never do anything else. So the problem of doing a *levade* or a rear at inconvenient

times when out and about does not arise often. With 'no's however, so far Oberlix and I have managed to ensure that he makes a distinction between when asked and when he feels excited. But we have had fifteen years together!

There are many other things that you can teach your horse, not just high school movements. Would you like him to get his water bucket, for example, for you to fill up? Not to muck in the box. To urinate when you ask him? To yawn when asked? (see picture)

Equines may not ever design moon rockets but they are surprisingly quick and able at learning. Nobody knows what the limits are to what they can learn. Questions concerning whether or not they are conscious, and if so conscious of what, quickly emerge. They are certainly aware of things and the world around them, but are they able to reflect on themselves and their own doings? These are the questions we are now researching through teaching them in a one-to-one relationship. The more you teach your horse, the more fun it is, whether you ride or not.

REFERENCES

Anon. *L'equitation, le cheval et l'ethologie. Colloque du 18 Sept 1999 a l'ecole National d'Equitation.* Belin. Paris.

Burger, U. 1959. *The way to perfect horsemanship.* J. A. Allen. London.

Fillis,J. 1969 *Breaking and Riding.* trans M. H. Heyes. J. A. Allen London

Gueriniere, F. R. de la. (1733) 1994. *The School of Horsemanship.* trans T. Boucher. J. A. Allen London.

Imam, S. A. H. A. A. 1987. *The Centaur. A critical analysis of horsemanship plus relevant equitant history.* Indian Heritage. Hazaribagh.

Oliveira, N. 1976. *Reflections on Equestrian Art.* J. A. Allen.

10

Equine Physiological and Psychological Fitness

- How to assess fitness
- How to increase fitness
- Feeding while training
- Stimulating the mind

In the last couple of decades there has been much research emphasis on both human and equine exercise physiology, and much has been discovered. No one yet has seriously considering the importance of psychological 'fitness' which has become a major factor in the training of Olympic sports people, although every trainer 'knows what is best for each horse'. Somehow such subjective opinions have not begun to be examined to date. The majority of researchers conclude that there is no quick fix, just as in humans, but they do point out some general rules.

The first thing here is that the equine must be kept in an environment where his physical, emotional, social and cognitive or intellectual needs are fulfilled, and the shocking truth is that there are more horses showing evidence of distress in racing stables than any other form of equine husbandry, including travelling with gypsies, in circuses, and working donkeys in the third world!

There are many things that can and should be done to improve the quality and length of life of the racehorse as we have emphasised previously (e.g. *Equine Welfare*). Here, however, we will in the first place outline some current ideas on equine exercise physiology, and then consider the importance of the equine's psychological preparation to win races.

Increasing body fitness in equines

When taking part in a Levi jeans sponsored event, the 'Ride and Tie' in the '70s, a US veterinarian gave us a talk on fitness in the horse. He divided this into **mechanical fitness** (getting the body, limbs and feet, including all the necessary muscles, tendons, ligaments and joints supple and able to put up with the strains and stresses of uneven terrain, speed and carrying weight without strains and lameness), and **physiological fitness**: developing the functioning of the systems in the body (e.g. the cardiovascular system, digestive tract, renal system, etc.) to be able to cope with speed and distances without fatigue. The third one must be **psychological fitness.**

The first thing that is worth knowing, is that it is not possible to tell how fit a horse is just by looking at him. Of course if he is hopping around on three legs, grossly overweight, or almost dead from malnourishment, one can say 'he is not fit' but when people make judgements standing in the collecting ring watching future competitors they are making judgements which may have no bearing on either the actual facts or the performance of the horse. This was bought home to me by my horses.

> We had a group of students who badly wanted to compete in an introductory 25 mile (40 km) long distance competitive trail ride in 1980, but even then they were popular, and the ride was full. So we decided to run our own with our own horses and students, just for everyone to get an idea on how such a competitive ride worked, and how to assess the body fitness of each horse, how the vetting procedure worked, how to ride the ride, and what effects different riders' speeds had on the fitness of the horses. We had three horses in training for 50 mile (80 km) races at the time, and thought they were reasonably fit, but we did not have enough 'fit' horses in fitness training, so all the equine residents who could be ridden were commandeered, at least to start, although they would be closely monitored. One of those was Druimghigha Aisha Evans, an Anglo Arab x Welsh mountain pony, 13.2 hh, aged 6, (see picture page 198). She had been doing nothing but giving a couple of lessons a week all summer. She was fat, not well muscled, and looked a typically unfit pony. We monitored her over the ride where she was keeping up with the fit horses, and she seemed fine. At the end her heart recovery rate was quicker and lower after 15 minutes than the fit horses (38 bpm compared to 40 & 42 bpm). This was a great surprise and resulted in our bringing her into training the following year, and eventually her winning the Scottish Endurance Championship, and the best condition award in the Endurance Horse & Pony Society Summer Solstice (100 miles/160 km in one day). We would never have known she had this potential without monitoring her heart rate before she was fit. Aged 26, and fat, her muscular development obscured, she still surprises me with her recovery heart rates, even when compared to the horses whom we have bred and trained for two further generations in endurance racing!

What is curious is that those who are training their horses for short races, for cross country, jumping and so on do not monitor their horses fitness in any objective way. Many of them do not know even how to take a heart rate!

Of course it takes months, sometimes years, before the horse is seriously mechanically and physiologically fit, and sometimes one gets it wrong and overdoes it, missing the event because s/he is not quite right, but sometimes one gets it right too! The pleasure is in the doing and learning about how to do it, and what mistakes to avoid next time.

If you want the youngster to grow up with a well developed solid structured body to be able to be a good athlete, it is important to ensure that he is given plenty of exercise. Horses even out in a field cover around 25 miles per day. In a feral state, fulfilling what their bodies have evolved to cope with, they cover 31-44 miles in 24 hours. All his muscles and joints have been designed to move almost constantly; keeping him in enforced immobility is asking for problems.

We start ensuring sufficient exercise in our foals. When they are healthy and doing well at around 6 weeks old, they will start to go out for rides with their mothers (see picture on page 113). Of course they must not do too much work, but this can gradually increase, and the results are that the youngsters grow up with well developed bones and muscles, a greater knowledge of the world in general as well as an increase in their mechanical, physiological and psychological fitness and live longer.

I remember another talk given at a seminar I was at once where a researcher working on lameness mentioned that no horse was entirely even; it is a question of making a judgement on where the line will be drawn to say that that horse is lame. Everyone who is serious about having fit horses becomes aware of unevenness.

Stride length affects how quickly the equine becomes tired. However, this must be off set against other mechanical advantages, for example ponies with short legs and less weight to carry have shorter strides, but this, certainly in the case of Aisha, has never made any difference to her becoming tired before anyone else. Many horses will use a particularly long stride when they are not tired, but as they tire, this becomes shorter, with less suspension. Short strides are supposed to put more strain on the legs and stride frequency increases on hard surfaces. Perhaps more important from the point of view of riding horses in endurance is that equines with short strides are much more tiring for the rider. When the rider becomes stiff and sore, and out of balance, it puts extra strains and stresses on various parts of the horse which are unaccustomed to this. Long strided Arabs may have been selected for endurance because they are more comfortable for the riders, not because the Arab is any better at endurance than the thoroughbred, or naturally fitter, which we know they are not. Stride length seems to make much less difference to rider's comfort at higher speeds; short strided canters are not as difficult to ride for hours at a time than short strided trots. The western quarter horses, Mongolian ponies and many others whose humans more or less live on their backs, often have short strides, but are usually ridden at a canter rather than a trot.

Since Arabs now have a name for doing well in endurance, most of the people who want to take endurance seriously buy an Arab horse. Consequently most of those who know something about getting horses fit have Arabs, so it is hardly surprising that they do well, but to date there is no serious evidence that thoroughbreds could not do as well given the same training from birth. Arabs can rarely run as fast as thoroughbreds, though, their legs are that much shorter.

It is also often believed that jumping puts enormous strain on particularly the front legs of the horses. However, it has been found that the strain on the front legs when landing over an admittedly small obstacle (0. 8m) was no greater than

Aisha Evans, aged 17, ridden by Lynn, about to be presented with the 'Best Condition' prize at the International Summer Solstice 100 mile (160 km) ride at Ludlow (after 30 minutes after competing at 7.5 mph (12 km/hr) average heart rate was 42 bpm).

that put on the hardest working leg at the canter, that is the non leading fore leg and the leading hind leg. What puts greater stress on the legs are the changes in stride length before or after the jump, so the stylish jumping where the horse and rider float around the arena at the same speed is not only pleasanter to watch, but also causes less mechanical strain.

Physiological fitness

This involves the improvement of how bits of the body, mainly internal organs, function as a result of exercise. The most important here is the cardio-vascular system which can operate to improve the flow of blood with oxygen to all parts of the body, and consequently ensure that all the systems in the body, but particularly the muscles, can go on functioning properly although they may be working very hard for long periods. Much has been learnt over the last few years. By monitoring the dehydration and heart recovery rate (now believed to reflect any upset in the body) it is possible to measure how physiologically fit the horse is, and whether he may be becoming exhausted.

It is well known that muscles will develop with use, and the trick is to develop them without overdoing it. For muscles, heart and lung development, hills are helpful. Gradually longer, steeper hills can be introduced to the training schedule.

Heavy going on sandy beaches or ploughed land, trotting in water in rivers and the sea and doing hard slow work on the land can also achieve high levels of fitness. High speeds, although they may help with cardio-vascular fitness, can put excessive mechanical strain on the horse. The best plan, even when training flat-racing horses, would seem to be to rarely gallop at speed, and spend much more time ensuring that the horse is seriously puffing for long periods of time.

It has generally been believed that thoroughbreds have more type 2 fibres: ('fast twitch' sprinter type) in their muscles, and Arabs more type 1 ('slow twitch' endurance type fibres) but it has been found that, although there was some genetic basis for this distinction, the effects of experience can overshadow this. In other words again it is the lifetime experiences that affect even the structure of the muscles.

Another difference in training strategy which is common is that since sprinters must retain their speeds (and even increase them at the finish) over relatively short distances, they must develop their anaerobic respiration, which means that they develop an oxygen debt and become able to continue to work with this. Endurance horses, who must keep going longer at slower speeds, must develop aerobic respiration, and keep going with an oxygen debt for hours at a time. Consequently thoroughbreds for the race track are galloped almost daily at high speeds, whereas endurance horses are taken out for hours and hours at slow speeds.

But the most important thing probably is for the horse to be able to switch from anaerobic to aerobic respiration and *vice versa* easily. Anaerobic respiration is less commonly used, and is impossible to sustain very long (without the accumulation of lactic acids), but to win, fit horses who are going to compete in almost any event should be able easily to switch in and out of anaerobic respiration. Consequently training strategies should involve working the horses in both aerobic and anaerobic respiration (but not galloping at maximum speeds which will put them at risk mechanically). Interval training involves getting the horse into anaerobic respiration for a time and then having a recovery interval at a slower pace. The idea is that during the recovery period the horse will return to aerobic respiration, and then work hard again in anaerobic.

For the rider, a rough distinction between aerobic and anaerobic respiration can be assessed by checking if the rate of respiration is faster or slower than the rhythm of the pace. If it is slower or the same, then the respiration is aerobic, if faster, anaerobic.

One of the problems associated with cardio-vascular fitness, and particularly anaerobic respiration, is the accumulation of lactic acid in the muscles which results in fatigue, stiffness, cramp and sometimes azoturia. Monitoring heart rate recovery rates (see below) gives a guide here. When a horse has been fit, a decrease in exercise can increase the lactic acid, so if your horse has had a rest for a week or two before a major exertion, he is more likely to tie up or become stiff and sore in his muscles than if he is having regular hard work up to the event. For a fit horse, exercise should slowly be reduced, not suddenly stopped, after an event.

Dehydration can be monitored quickly by pinching the skin on the neck and

Trot downhill: Shezam, the youngster, and Robyn lead around the rocks.

timing its recovery to lie flat again. This should be less than a second if there is no problem. If it takes a couple of seconds then this is an early warning of slight dehydration. Offering water at frequent intervals is very important, but equines are fussy about what water they drink, so it is important to ensure that either he knows and likes the water that you are offering, or he has experience of drinking water from various troughs and streams in many locations. The problem with this is that much water that is found in streams nowadays is polluted by agricultural chemicals or human sewage. Some people habitually put electrolytes (salts that are lost by over heating and sweating) into the drinking water when getting horses fit for racing or endurance. This would not seem to be a very sensible strategy in the long run as the equine should be able to adjust his electrolyte balances himself and not depend on having them fed at particular levels. His body must become able to make the correct adjustments on a daily basis, although when he is asked to do much more than normal or under the stress and strain of competition, it is advisable to give him electrolytes to ensure against exhaustion.

Heart recovery rate is now generally considered to be the best indicator of whether he is fit to continue. The resting rate of a horse of around 15-16 hh varies greatly, from 26 beats per minute to 44 or so. The heart recovery rate is assessed with a stethoscope at a standard time after returning from work, or by having a heart monitor fixed to the horse, and monitoring the heart rates with different work, as well as the recovery rate. If the heart rate is not back to resting rate after 30 minutes, he is not as fit as he could be to do the work he has done. If it is over 60 beats per minute, then he has done too much and is beginning to show signs of exhaustion. There is a limit to how fit each individual will get, but it is by no means clear that thoroughbred race horses or eventers are near their maximum fitness when they perform, since they have not been carefully monitored. We keep records of the fitness training of each horse to assess their heart recovery rates. This is helpful to develop an appropriate schedule of training for each individual.

It is generally considered that wild animals are physiologically fit, but recent evidence from, for example, red deer, elephants and zebra indicate that they are by no means as fit as one might think. The elephants we monitored pulling a relatively light trailer after around 15 minutes of walking had very high respiration rates. We had to stop and let them rest every 10 minutes. A couple of fit equines could have pulled the same weight easier and quicker and without showing evidence of dehydration or exhaustion, even though the load would have been a

Physiological fitness. The vet taking the heart rate with a stethoscope at a championship ride in South Island, New Zealand, where the temperature was 40° C.

Gaining 'ecological knowledge' in a winter endurance training session on Dartmoor. Shemal followed by young Oryx.

very much larger percentage of their body weight! Zebras are renowned for becoming tired very quickly when they have been trained to be ridden or driven; perhaps this is because, as yet, that they have not had the same sort of fitness training that is given to equines.

On the other hand, the fitness of regularly working donkeys is extraordinary although it has not been carefully monitored to my knowledge. They are able to pull huge loads, several times their body weights, for prolonged periods of time, and continue doing such work daily, often for years while living on cardboard, or whatever vegetable waste they can scrounge. They seem to be extraordinarily physiologically efficient animals. By contrast, when they do nothing, donkeys are very prone to laminitis. At the Donkey Sanctuary in the UK, where the donkeys live mainly at pasture, a very high percentage of them suffer from laminitis (personal communication: chief veterinary officer at the Donkey Sanctuary, UK). This indicates that perhaps as a result of a long history of domestication and exploitation, these equines have adapted to working very hard, and, curiously, suffer if they are not living a rather tough life.

As equines become fitter, their resting heart rate usually declines, although this may take a few years but the differences in resting heart rate in youngsters of the same age can be considerable.

Omen, one of our 3-year-old geldings, had a resting heart rate of 28bpm, while Sher Khan, Shirack and Shergar, other 3-year-old geldings, with the same father but a different mother who had done the same work, had resting heart rates of 46 and 48bpm which is more usual at this age.

Shirac and Sher Khan went on to do advanced endurance riding, and after 3 years of fitness training, their resting heart rates were in the late 30s.

Oberlix and Shemal's resting heart rates when they were 2 years old were 48bpm, but after 5 years of fitness and doing all sorts of work, Oberlix's is now 32. Shemal, his daughter, who has done 3 years of fitness training, now has a resting rate of 32 to 36.

It is important to take the resting rate frequently when the horses are in an environment in which they are familiar. The psychological effects on heart rate are very obvious; the resting rate changes dramatically when there are environmental changes such as when another horse approaches, when he hears a noise or when he sees a friend.

Aisha Evans completed a 50 mile (80km) Competitive Trail Ride with a pulse monitor on one occasion. The pulse monitor remained on her over the 30 minute period after the ride. Her heart rate was leaping and dropping from 32 to 78bpm depending on who came by, what was going on, where her friends were. She finally was monitored by the veterinarian over a one minute period with a stethoscope at 39 bpm.

It can be quite difficult to ensure that you present the stallion to the vet at the right time and very easy to get it wrong!

Once Druimghigha Oberlix and I almost put up a record speed at a 50 mile (80km) endurance race. Afterwards, we presented to the veterinary judges to ensure that the heart rate was lower then 64bpm. Just as the vet began to monitor his heart rate, the mare we had been riding with all day finished having her heart monitored, and walked off. His heart jumped from being 56bmp (monitored the minute before presentation) to 70! It has to be below 64, so we were disqualified. It was our fault for not taking into account that the mare he liked was likely to walk off before he was finished. We know his heart rate had recovered because we then walked over to do a trot up test, where the heart rate is monitored again, and it was down to 54bpm, but it was too late by then, we were already eliminated!

Monitoring the heart rate is a useful way of identifying any sickness and emotional response to different or new activities. Thus if the horse is standing resting in the stable, provided his friend has not just been taken away or any other change made, and his heart rate is over 60bpm, then he is sick or in pain, and it is wise if you cannot identify the problem to call the veterinarian.

If an individual is worried or anxious, he may not show overt behavioural signs

Mechanical and physiological fitness training: Shemal and Oberlix arriving at the top of Cosdon at a smart trot all the way in the ice and amongst the rocks.

of this, but it can be detected in his heart rate. Just like people, some horses are extrovert and show what they are feeling, whereas others will show much less of this, and one may believe that they are quite relaxed when in fact they are seething inside.

> Crysthannah Royal, a pure-bred Arab mare whom we had bought as a two - year -old, was always passive and quiet when at endurance rides or other strange places, and we always assumed that she was just laid back, compared to some of the others who would mess around, at least when they were new to the game. However one day I took her heart rate as we were waiting and she was quietly standing waiting to start, only to find that it was substantially higher than one of the youngsters who was messing around anxiously near her (60bpm compared to 52bpm).

Feeding for fitness

I am constantly surprised by how little many people know about nutrition. It is important to know what are the main important constituents of different foods, and their functions so that you can choose the right amount of fibre, energy and protein for your equine, depending on what he does.

If you are confused about what and how to feed, read a book. One thing I would caution people about is, without any prior knowledge, to jump into the hands of an 'alternative medicine' person. Although some of them do know the basics of nutrition, some do not, so I suggest you first ask your vet and learn something about the fundamental principles so that you can make up your own mind what might be best for your equine. Most vets are now becoming interested in 'preventative veterinary care' rather than just curing diseases, so s/he should be helpful.

For those who need a kick start, we will very briefly outline some important things to know before you can begin to make judgements about feeding your equines for the level of fitness you require.

One thing that is certain is that equines generally do not need and cannot utilise more than around 10% of proteins in their diets since they are herbivores who are evolved to digest cellulose (the rather indigestible fibrous walls of the plant cells). Feeding high levels of protein changes the metabolism of nitrogen in the body (all proteins contain nitrogen) both at rest and during exercise. It also can cause a retention of urea and consequently an increased need for water.

Electrolytes are also fashionably fed to horses to help get them fit. Again, it would seem unnecessary, and in some cases possibly unwise to force-feed minerals by having them fixed in the compound food, or given as an extra supplement.

Surely, what we ought to be aiming at is having horses fit enough to do the competition they have done without giving of extra chemicals or artificial foods.

In 2000 I was asked by the Soil Association to outline what the organic standards should be for horses, so people are beginning to think about this. The best thing is to buy only organically registered foodstuffs for your horses if you wish them to win races and have long healthy lives.

Fashions and quick fixes often emerge in equine nutrition.

The psychology of the sport horse

This is an area which has to date received little careful thought. The central problem is: how does one motivate the equine to perform at his best each day during training in order to get fitter? This problem is not only confronted in training, but also in the competition where one hears of many horses in jumping, combined training, dressage, endurance or racing who have 'gone sour' and will not try, or even perform at all at what they may have been good at.

With humans this problem can be overcome by ensuring that the trainee keeps his goal in mind: training for next week's race, or winning the medal at the Olympics, being picked for a team and so on. Such goals can help to retain the motivation to try very hard in daily training, even putting up with pain, or boring exercises of one sort and another. Generally we do not have an option to present some future goal of this type to the equine, so their continued motivation can become very difficult, particularly when the training requires months or years, and even the event may not be very exciting; for example endurance rides can go on for many hours (up to 24 hours for a 100 mile/160km race is allowed).

Druimghigha Omeya (Oberlix's mother) was a very elegant pure-bred Arab, and was reasonably fast and extremely good at long distance. She started doing the odd ride when she was 6, and then continued doing longer rides most years (except when she was having foals which was around every 5th year), doing the 100 mile(160km) summer solstice when she was 13, finishing 7th and with a heart rate after 30 mins of 48bpm, so she was not physically exhausted. After this, although she had been doing all these other things as well, she would go on strike where there was a hill to climb on a longish ride. She would just stop and refuse to go up the hill. It would seem that the cause for this was too many long distance competitions, that is over 50 miles (80km) and the necessary training. This despite the fact that she was never vetted out for not being fit enough, and she never did more than 2 rides of 50 miles or more per year. We tried everything we could think of to encourage her and overcome this, but she was over 14 by then, and we settled to doing only up to 25 mile(40km) rides after that, which she did with enthusiasm.

This problem has to be confronted in every equine discipline, but because long distance goes on for so long, and requires so much energy and prolonged work, lack of motivation is particularly common in experienced long distance horses. It is rare to see a horse, who is physiologically and mechanically fit enough to continue, going forward willingly and enthusiastically between around 62 to 80 miles (100 to 130km) in a 100 mile (160km) one-day race. They are physically fit to do it, but not mentally. After 80 miles(130km) or so, they may recognise that they are on the way home, and perk up again, but the middle part of the competition can be very heavy going for horse and rider. The riders are careful not to show that they are having to push their mounts on, when being watched, and will deny having to do this, but being honest, and having trained and ridden many horses in these sorts of rides, ridden with and watched many others, the vast majority of experienced horses do not want to continue after around 50 to 85 miles(80-140km). There appear to be two main reasons for this:
(a) They are hungry, having, despite the crew's efforts at the holding points, not had time to eat properly for maybe 5-8 hours.
(b) They are bored; they have been going along a route for many hours. Often the same route is done twice, so they may even know it.
Generally, the more competitions over 50 miles(80km) in a day the equine does, the more likely he is to want to stop at least around 18 to 25 miles(30-40km) from the end, although this does of course depend on the speed, the company, how he is ridden and his general physical fitness.

As a result, we need to ask ourselves if we should stop running such long races. Another possibility is to have a more varied course, with more frequent food stops. The challenge is how to train our equines so that they do want to continue to complete the course enthusiastically, without having to be pushed along.

The general problems that most stale horses have are rather different from the endurance horses: for example

(a) They had an unpleasant experience and are frightened/wary of having to do the same thing again. This could have been an accident, but it can equally be a rider losing his temper and hitting the horse, or the horse having to perform a movement that hurts.

(b) They have done it all so often that they are bored and tired of doing it.

If the cause has been an accident this can often be easily identified, and sorted out by a reversal learning schedule (Chapter 3) where the event must always be carried out with pleasurable and rewarding experiences.

Boredom is much more difficult to overcome. The first rule is do not do the same thing every day. Do not take him in the arena every day to practise more. If you do, then make sure you do at least some different and interesting new things as well as practising the old ones. Take him out and about, jumping little things or doing some dressage movements in an open clearing or around some gorse bushes, using what is encountered along the way, however imperfect the conditions. After all this is what 'dressage', or 'cross country' means: training to be a good ride in any conditions. Do some galloping and fun things. If you cannot do this because you are frightened of him and he has not learnt how to behave out and about, then this is part of his, and your, education. It is more important for the long-term quality of both the equine's and the human's life than going to the competition.

One of the best ways of relaxing the horse and rider as well as having a lovely time together and chatting to other humans, seeing different countryside and so on, is to take your dressage or jumping horse on a few long distance rides. An 18-25 mile(30-40km) ride at around 5 miles an hour is a good start. Both rider and horse will relax, learn that rushing around and being excited all the time is not necessary or particularly pleasant, and will have the opportunity of learning more about each other. The rider can also ride on a loose rein and allow the horse to make his own decisions much of the time, safely. If your dressage or racehorse cannot be taken out because he behaves badly, or you are frightened of him injuring himself, then you must ask the question if dressage is worth the paper it is written on, or the racehorse fit to race.

Long distance events, where others have done all the hard work in organising, finding and marking the route, are often much more relaxed and friendly than other equestrian competitions. Indeed you do not even have to compete against anyone, just monitor your horse's fitness.

But what of the long distance horse who becomes bored when doing very long rides? We have had to confront this problem with several of our international long distance horses we have bred and educated. It is less in the event that they may be fed up, but in the training. Consequently do a little of everything, and a lot of some. Working on the land, harrowing, spreading muck and helping make the hay is a good start. Pulling a light vehicle is a good way of acquiring some mechanical fitness of the legs without a weight on them, giving some riding lessons, going on treks and camps, doing dressage and dance, jumping, racing, liberty work, and lessons to help them understand language are all things one horse can do, and do well. In this way rotate what they do daily so that there is less chance of them becoming fed up with one thing. If one of them does, then we must think about what we have been doing with them and give them a break from that.

> Druimghigha Shiraz was the heaviest mare we had when we lived on Mull and she was having to give lessons and take beginners on treks in the hills all summer. She therefore usually had to carry the large men. One day with a large journalist on board having a lesson before going out onto the hill, she lay down in the school. I thought she might have colic, and told the rider to get off, and kept her under observation tied up by the school. But she seemed fine. After taking her heart rate and finding it her normal resting rate (around 38 bpm), I asked a light girl to get on her… but she lay down again! Thinking about this it became clear that she had worked extremely hard carrying heavy weights that summer and was fed up with it (we investigated every part of her body to see if she was in pain, but there was no sign of this). She seemed to be demonstrating that enough was enough, even going to the extreme of lying down (something that llamas and cattle may do quite frequently when they do not want to work more, but rarely equines) to avoid having to continue.

We retired her from teaching for a year, she had a foal and then came back to teaching, but we were careful not to give her heavy people too often. She continued to teach, and be ridden and driven, work and do long distance until she died at 28. Just as with humans, horses need changes, and if they have this, they can often return to their original work and skill with renewed vigour and pleasure.

> Cariff, one of our Arab stallions, also taught himself to lie down when he was working on the land and had had enough, particularly at around lunch time!

Of course there are some ways to encourage and motivate the equines, but it needs to be thought about from the beginning of the training of the horse for a particular discipline, which must always be interesting and exciting for the horses involved.

We do not have the time, money or motivation to go to too many competitions, but like to take off with our horses for a week or two riding around in some beautiful area for a holiday for us and our equines, while also improving their and our fitness.

Since we have run ecological farms for the last 35 years, where the experimental herd of horses live, we always have much farm work to do. One of the obvious ways of ensuring that our equines have new and different things to do is to teach them to do some of the work on the land, to help them become fit. In 1974 we started teaching our Arab horses to help us on the farm. Since then we have had much experience with how to teach them, what to do and what not to do, and what work is helpful and suitable for them to do. The following chapter briefly discusses the roles of both travelling with equines and working with them in agriculture and how this can improve their physiological and psychological fitness, and be fun.

Summary

• A grasp of basic physiology and behaviour is useful

• A stethoscope is also useful

• Fitness is either (1) mechanical (muscles, ligaments, tendons, etc), (2) physiological (lungs and heart) or (3) psychological - wanting to do it. This is becoming increasingly important.

• An understanding of nutrition is important. Feeding organic products is the safest way of avoiding toxins and environmental pollutants

• You can develop your own training strategies – but monitoring fitness is advised

REFERENCES

Barney, E. B. , B. Landjerit & R. Wolter. 1991. 'Shock vibration during the hoof impact on different track survaces'. p97-106 in *Equine Exercise Physiology* 3. ed S. G. B. Persson, A. Lindholm & L. B. Jeffcott. ICEEP publ Davis.

Buckingham, S. H. W. & L. B. Jeffcott. 1991. 'Skeletal effects of long term submaximal exercise programme on standard-bred yearlings', in *Equine Exercise Physiology 3*. p411-418. ed. S. G. B. Persson, A. Lindholm & L. B. Jeffcott. ICEEP publ. Davis.

Budiansky, S. 1996. 'Don't bet on faster horses', *New Scientist*. 10th August. p 29-31Butler, P. J. ,A. J. Woakes, L. S. Anderson, K. Smale,C. A. Roberts &D. H. Snow. 1991. 'The effect of cessation of training on caridorespiratory variables during exercise', in *Equine Exercise Physiology 3*. p71-76. ed. S. G. B. Persson. A. Lindholm & L. B. Jeffcott. ICEEP publ Davis.

Dawson, F. L. M. S. 1984. 'Equine Reproduction' in *Horse Management*. ed: Hickman. J. p 1-54. Acedemic Press. London.

Harris, R. C. ,D. J Marlin & D. H. Snow. 'Lactate kinetics, plasma ammonia and performance following repeated bouts of maximal exercise' p173-178 in *Equine Exercise Physiology 3*. ed. S. G. P. Persson, A. Lindholm & L. B. Jeffcott. ICEEP publ. Davis.

Lawrence, M. 1980. *Flyers and Stayers. The book of the greatest rides*. Harrap. London.

Merkens, H. W, H. C. Schamhardt, G. J. V van Osch & J. van Bogert. 1990. 'Ground reaction force analysis of Dutch Warmblood Horses at canter and jumping', p 128-135. in *Equine Exercise Physiology*. ed. S. G. B. Persson, A. Lindhom & L. B. Jeffcott. ICEEP Publ, Davis California.

Miller-Graber, P. , L. Lawrence,J. Foremen, K. Bump, M. Fisher & E. Kurz. 'Effect of dietary protein level on nitrogen metabolites in exercised Quarter horses', p 305-314. in *Equine Exercise Physiology*. edit. Persson. S. G. B, A. Lindholm & L. B. Jeffcott. ICEEP publ Davis California.

Petersson, H. K. H. F. Hintz, H. F. Schryer & G. F. Combs. Jr. 1991. ' The effect of vitimin E on mebrane integrity during submaximal exercise', in *Equine Exercise Physiology 3*. ed: S. G. B. Persson, A. Lindholm & L. B. Jeffcott. ICEEP publ. Uppsala.

Schott, H. C, D. R. Hodgson, W. M. Bayly & P. D. Gollnick. 'Renal responses to high intensity exercise' p 361-367, in *Equine Exercise Physiology 3*. ed. S. G. B. Persson, A. Lindholm & L. B. Jeffcott. ICEEP publ. Davis.

Wickler, S. J. & W. Troy. 1991. 'Blood volume, lactate and cortisol in exercising Arabian equitation horses'p 397-401. in *Equine Exercise Physiology. 3*. ed. S. G. B. Persson, A. Lindhol & L.B. Jeffcott. ICEEP publ. Davis.

11

Co-operative Lifestyle:
Education for Travelling and
Harness Work

- Planning a trip with equines
- Transport and associated problems
- Securing horses overnight
- Training for harness
- Teaching to be driven

The most rewarding things when travelling for long distances over weeks with equines or working with them for hours are the unity between human and equine that results, the overall education of both equine and human, time to enjoy the environment and begin, perhaps, to think a little like the equine in the awareness of it. It is the best way of getting to know your horse, thoroughly recommended for any old or young, horse, pony, mule, donkey, large, small, quiet, nervous. It also helps with access to the countryside. By using tracks one is helping to keep open existing access for animal powered vehicles, ridden equines as well as bicyclists and walkers. Only in this way will our children and grandchildren be able to have such experiences of travelling with their equines, learning with them and absorbing the natural world that we are still lucky enough to be able to enjoy.

There are a host of travellers today who have had adventures riding or driving equines in far flung places around the world. Although there is passing reference to the relationship they develop with their equines during these rides or drives, it is more often the landscape and the human interactions and relationships along the way that take pride of place in their reports. I am sure some of these travellers develop interesting and profound relationships with their equines (how could one not when isolated often for days on end with them?). But, as a general rule, they do not dwell on these.

There is no need to ride to Timbuktu, you can have 'outlandish adventures' with your equine anywhere. The advantage of travelling or working together is that you are together, not for the duration of a weekend, or an hour during a competition, but for days, sometimes weeks or months. This experience inevitably results in a recognition of mutual reliance. This chapter is to encourage the growing number of people wanting to have that 'quality time' learning with and from their equine. It does not have to be particularly complicated or difficult; the more you do, the easier it becomes. Some of the greatest highlights of my understanding and enjoyment of equines has been when working or travelling with them.

There are times, as with humans, that the company annoys or infuriates, but if the equine has been regarded as a partner, rather than just a tool, it is the good times and the fun of it all that is recalled. There are several important considerations.

Access to the countryside
The first requirement of course is access to the countryside by being allowed to ride or drive over open areas – paths or bridleways. There are organisations dedicated to preserving and expanding the network of bridleways, and it is vital that all who use these pathways support and help these organisations. The first step here is to look at a map and make sure that you know all the options in your local area, and then use them. You can even help maintain them by organising working parties with horses, dogs, bicycles and walkers. Most riders in the UK are extremely unadventurous when it comes to exploring new routes, or even being able to read a map (!), and they stick to a path that they know, rarely trying different routes. The result is that many bridleways are not used, and consequently gradually loose the right of way they carry which further restricts access.

I was amazed when riding around in Dorset on the downs, how many bridle ways there were, but also how many were unused and almost impassable. We also found a squad of council workers clearing a bridleway who said that we were the only people they had seen on the bridleway for a week!

Even if you do not enjoy riding in the countryside, preferring to stay in your riding school manege or jumping area, if you wish to educate your equine well, and have a relaxed and pleasant time together, then hacking out in as many different places as possible is by far the best and most pleasant way for your youngster to learn about the world, and how to cope with everything in it. Bear in mind that if he has lived all his life in a couple of paddocks, he has very little experience of the great world; no wonder he sometimes freaks out at new things, so would you if you had only the experiences he has had. So enlarge his experiences, and take him everywhere you can in all sorts of conditions. Even if you do not like the countryside, he does, and it is an ideal way for him to learn and relax with you. He may also teach you a thing or two about the countryside if you bother to listen!

Where one goes, how far and fast, and what one carries vary enormously depending on the individuals, both equine and human, and the other companions, such as dogs or children. It is important that the expedition is fun for all.

Planning a trip
(i) Make appropriate plans for the equines that are coming. The vast majority of all equines will become easier, quieter, more tolerant, better company and generally more fun as the expedition progresses, however much their owner or rider starts of with a long list of things their horse can or cannot, will or will not do.

The social dynamics of the equine group are as important as that of the human group. If a stallion, as well as mares, is to be on the expedition, then unless the mares are intended to get pregnant, it will be necessary to have some contraceptives (ask your vet). If the group consists of stallions, mares and geldings, then they must be used to riding together without trouble, and it will be necessary to plan how they are to spend the nights so that the stallions do not do damage to each other or the geldings. Perhaps the most difficult combination is two stallions and a mare, but even this group can be educated to cope and get on, but it requires preparation (picture page 214). Failure to understand the equine social dynamics may result in you finding that the horses have disappeared when you get up in the morning; or, worse, someone has been injured.

The temperature, the terrain, the size and fitness of the humans and the equines must be taken into account in planning the distances travelled. A Dartmoor pony that has been out on the hill all winter will not find sub-zero temperatures in an expedition to say, Lapland in December, too distressing, but an Arab who has been in a stable and rugged up all winter will be another matter. It is not by any means true that ponies cannot go so far or fast as larger equines. Allowances must be made for youngsters (and children) who will not be either as physically

The basic equipment we fit into saddle bags. (1) Saddle and numnah(used for rider to sleep on); (2) waterproof warm coat for rider; (3) horse food; (4) bread, cheese, wine, etc; (5) video camera; (6) electric coral unit; (7) red cross bag; (8) light tent; (9) light sleeping bag; (10) hobbles; (11) skeleton grooming kit and bandage; (12) book and map; (13) farrier's basic equipment and spare pair of fitted shoes; (14) bit with clips on that can be clipped onto headcollar when required; (15) human clothes; (16)cooking stove and eating equipment; (17) optional spaniel. Total weight with rider no more than 100 kg.

or mental fit as older experienced equines (or humans), of whatever breed and sex.

To avoid problems, the fitness of all the equines taking part should be carefully monitored before and throughout the expedition, so that preparatory plans can be drawn up and the possibility of adapting them *en route* arranged to fit in with all the participants' abilities and desires. Monitoring fitness also helps the riders to understand their mounts better, and take more interest in them (details in chapter 10).

The vast majority of equines are very adaptable, so will be able to cope well in a great range of conditions, both mentally and physically, but they may need time to learn to do this. A thoroughbred from a racing stable who has hardly ever eaten grass, and has been accustomed to large feeds of grain twice a day, will need a couple of weeks' running out on grass with other equines before he has learnt about what to eat and how to find it. He will be able to do this, like the others, if he is allowed time and facilities to adapt.

The equines are often more able and quicker to adapt than the humans! If one of the most important aims of the expedition is to explore the fun that can be had living with equines and developing relationships with them, then time can be put aside for problem solving and interacting with the equines. Some people like to do exercises from the ground, learning to teach simple movements to word command and so on. New ones to help the participants have a better understanding and experience of equines can also be designed.

Exercise 1. After making up the corral or leaving the horses loose in a paddock for the night, everyone sits down and, without talking, observes the group for five minutes, and then discusses what they have seen.

The next day, take one individual and record on a note pad who he approaches, stays near, ignores, touches and shows an interest in, or avoids, withdraws from, or attacks. The social life of equines is not governed by dominance hierarchies, and if you take the time, you will find that every individual spends more time being nice to others than avoiding or being nasty (see chapter 6 *Equine Lore* for further details here). In fact they can show us a way of co-operating and behaving to foster the group sticking together instead of splitting it up. This is a good exercise if the human group you are travelling with is not 'gelling' very well!

Exercise 2. (a) Send people and their horses to different places with a job to do, so that they are alone with their horse, (e.g. to gather and collect firewood, to get hold of some food for humans or horses, to investigate a possible camping site not far away).

(b) Joint daily sessions teaching the equines to respond to particular word commands, and to begin to comprehend language can be beneficial in helping the human and equines learn about each other (chapter 3 & 4), help the inexperienced to fit in and with other problems.

The expedition can be arranged to cater for different people and equines with different experiences and tastes. We will start with expeditions with equines that involve transporting them.

Learning to cope with each other on expeditions. Two stallions, Oberlix and Oryx, and a mare, Shemal (on left) go out for an early training ride in the snow at La Combe, France.

Transporting equines by road, rail or boat

There are times, particularly in industrialised countries, when transporting equines by road or rail is a great deal pleasanter than journeying with them on their own feet. Transporting equines by road has become a whole industry in itself and is well covered in the literature. A careful consideration of the 'general rules of teaching and educating' (page 67) and understanding how learning works (chapter 3) should point out where the teacher has gone wrong when she has had problems, and help her to put it right. We will briefly point out some of the reasons for some problems.

Loading. Refusing to load is the most common problem. One of the major reasons for this is that the equine has been taught not to load by the use of force, and had a fright. As a result his fear is increased, he has learnt *not* to load. The more this continues, the stronger the habit of stopping and not loading becomes, and the more difficult it will be to change.

The main reason for the original use of force, further restraints of the horse and the resulting excitement and fear on the part of the horse, is often **lack of planning**. People do not allow enough time for the horse to become more familiar with the situation so that he will not be frightened, perhaps because they are late, or they want to get home fast after the competition. Consequently, the handlers are tired, nervous, or irritated and resort to restraint and violence when the horse only needs time. Remember, though, one mistake can cost many more hours of time later. Forcing animals into vehicles is often a false time economy!

Naïve horses who have not had a fright loading, or been pushed or forced are usually easy to load provided they have been well handled and taught to lead and be tied up first. It is relatively easy to load wild horses provided the ramp is not too steep, the entrance wide and the run up to the truck well fenced. It is the re-education of equines that have taught their owners they 'do not load' or had a fright or bad experience in some way when loading or travelling that is the problem. There are a great number of these.

Re-educating horses to travel in a vehicle
Over the years I have had many horses with different problems presented to me. The most important thing is not just to get the horse in (often done by using questionable techniques by people who give exhibitions) but
(a) to understand what the horse's problem is
(b) to bear in mind who the people are who have the horse
(c) to design a system that will be helpful to those particular people so that even when I am not there, they will be able to continue re-educating their horse, and, hopefully, not have the same problem with the next one.

At nearly every workshop I give, one of the horses will have been brought along because he has learnt not to load. Horses use a variety of strategies to avoid having to enter. The most common problem is that they will not go into the vehicle, but there are some who will load, but then set about deconstructing the vehicle,
(a) **Deconstructors** (kicking, leaping around and generally breaking up the box). These are best dealt with by having a very strong box or trailer to start with, and making sure you have someone ready to drive off as soon as the horse is in. If there is a safe place to stand, it is better to have someone with the horse, and whenever he is quiet and good, he is praised and given something to eat in the vehicle, whenever he starts kicking out, he is ticked off. In the case of a confirmed kicker, it may be important to select a rather wiggly road with ups and downs so that he has to concentrate on standing up and cannot start kicking or leaping without risking a fall. It needs some serious thought about what experiences he has had in order to understand why he is doing it. Gradually, as the horse improves, the time standing still in the vehicle before moving can be increased.

Others may not want to risk this approach, but rather just load him, keep him in for a minute or two while feeding him and then praise him if he has not kicked, and take him out. This can be repeated and repeated with slightly longer times spend standing in the box until it is acceptable to the horse, then go on a gentle drive for a few minutes only. It is important not to take him out before he is calm and standing still, otherwise he is rewarded for deconstruction. Another approach is 'no food except in the box' for a few weeks.

(b) **Will not walk in**. Here are some general rules to help with loading which have been developed as a result of understanding something about equine minds (see *Equine Lore*):

GENERAL RULES FOR LOADING AN EQUINE INTO A TRAILER OR TRUCK

(1) Make sure both you and your assistants have **sufficient time** before you start, and stick to it until the finish. Then do it again.

(2) Place the vehicle so that the equine cannot walk around it. One side of the ramp against the fence, the other with a hurdle, gate, hedge or whatever you have.

(3) Load him in and out several times at home when you have time, and feed him in the transporter.

(4) If a strange equine, or other animal has been in the transporter before, ensure it is washed out, and then place some of the faeces and/or urine of the animal to be loaded, (or that of a friend or sexual partner) on the top of the ramp and in the box. He must feel that he is entering a familiar smelling place.

(5) Ensure that it is light inside so he is not walking into a dark unknown area. Either open the door at the front if there is one, or fix up a light.

(6) For the first time either take out partitions or push them to the side so he is not walking into a narrow enclosed place.

(7) Make sure the floor is not **slippery**. The best floors are paint on rubber which do not slip even when wet, and are easy to apply and clean. Straw may be a familiar aid to start with but should not be used for travelling as it does not help with preventing slip. There must be anti slip bars on the floor if there is not rubber. Fear as a result of having slipped is one of the common reasons why horses will not load easily thereafter.

(8) If possible, load an experienced easy loading equine (who the subject knows and likes) before one who is naive, or a difficult loader. If there is a front unload door, then walk the experienced horse through, followed by the less experienced one several times before keeping them in and securing them in their places. If loading after an experienced horse into a trailer, ensure that both the handler and the horse have sufficient room to walk into the stall. This can be difficult with a trailer, consequently it may be easier to load the naive horse into a wide, light trailer without another there. In which case, bring the familiar horse around to the front so the horse loading can see him and will be walking towards him / her.

(9) Praise the equine for moving forwards and give a little food reward every time he takes a step up the ramp. Prevent a naive horse from stopping at the foot of the ramp by having an assistant behind with a whip that is raised if he starts to falter and use plenty of reassuring voice.

(10) When he is in, give him a generous tit bit, and tie him up. Stay with him talking to him while someone else quietly raises the back door.

(11) Ensure he has something to do to take his mind off an unfamiliar situation when he is in the transporter, and if possible, he can see and touch another equine he knows and likes. A hay net, or a small feed is a good way to start.

(12) If the equine has learnt not to load, as a result of having a fright, then it is

just a question of waiting on the ramp with the horse or pony asking him/her to come towards you, until he does eventually move into the vehicle. He must not be allowed to wander about or eat anything until he moves forwards, gradually up the ramp. If the equine has not been loaded before, but has been well handled and educated so far (chapters 4,5,6) then, if all is constructed right, it will not take long before he walks up the ramp. On the other hand, if he has had bad experiences or been taught not to load, it may take several hours. Unless he has been severally traumatised (and even in this case this approach will probably work) he will eventually go in, so *do not give up* but take your sandwiches, coffee and a book with you.

13) When he enters, praise and make a fuss of him, give him a small feed, and leave him in the box for 30 minutes or so, while you stay talking, brushing, fussing him before unloading him. Some horses are anxious after they have loaded. We prefer to keep the vehicle still until their anxiety has dissipated, which may be after several trials walking in, staying in for a while and walking out.

14) Lack of patience, irritation and annoyance, fear and aggression on the part of any of the handlers or helpers will prevent the equine entering, so take a book and send anyone without the patience off to make a meal, while waiting.

15) Take him for a short drive. **When driving take great care the first few times.** A glass of water filled to within 2 cm of the brim standing on the dashboard should not spill. If he learns that the journey is unbalancing and frightening because of bad driving or a slippery floor, loading will be difficult next time.

16) Use your initiative, and 'conditional anthropomorphism' (How would I behave in that situations, given his experiences?) and time, and all will be well with any horse in the end. Then repeat and repeat loading until it becomes a matter of course and the correct habits are formed.

The most important ingredient is patience. Make sure the box is in a sensible place and the horse cannot walk around the ramp then stop the horse wandering or eating, make him just stand still. Put a little pressure on the lead line until he comes forward towards you and puts his foot on the ramp, then praise him, and do the same again until he has taken a couple of steps on the ramp, then, with plenty of time, he will eventually walk in. Make sure the ramp is not steep by placing the box on a slight downhill, and that it is not too low or dark. Generally even the most traumatised individuals will walk in within a couple of hours, provided you have placed the box correctly. The same is then repeated every day, and he is only fed his food in the trailer. If he pulls back and pulls you out, start again, but this time put slightly less pressure on the lead line.

Another technique is to leave the trailer or truck in the field in a sensible place (see 1 above) and place his hay only in it, so he has to enter to get it. Make sure he knows it is there, and it is best if there is another horse with him who will go in and eat the hay. Of course there must be enough room for both of them, and don't expect him to walk in to a narrow partition to start with. He only has his hard food in the vehicle too, so he goes without unless he enters. Generally again in a few days, he will be walking in without a problem in order to have his food.

Some horses learn that by putting their heads down and pulling hard, or rearing up and pulling, they can get away from the handler and the vehicle. He has learnt, and taught the humans with him, that he does not load. If he is frightened, he still has to learn that he cannot get away, but more care on how it is done will have to be exercised, less pressure rather than more and plenty of time.

If he is violent, even when given plenty of time and not forced from the rear, then one of two approaches might be used. The first is to use a severe bit, or a halter or bitless bridle that hurts when he pulls back (there are several on the market). He will pull to try and get away from you, but then realise it hurts, and, unable to get away, after perhaps rearing or leaping a little, he will get the message and may walk in, after which he is lavishly praised and given food and tit bits. The disadvantage of this technique is that he may learn that when the particular equipment is put on, he must go in, but when it is not, he can pull away and not load.

Another approach is to tie a longer strong lead line to something in the vehicle which cannot break, make sure his halter will not break by putting two or three on and tying the lead line around all three. When he comes up to the vehicle in the normal way, wrap the end of the lead line around the strong breast bar so when he pulls back, he pulls against this, which does not give, rather than against a person who has in the past given in. He will leap, rear and cavort around but it is important to remain quiet in the box holding the end of the line which is wrapped around the breast bar. Eventually, he will give up pulling against the rope, and after half an hour or so, maybe less, he will probably lead in quietly. He should have learnt to tie up and stand when tied before you do this (page 110), so he has grasped the principle that when attached to a fixed object, pulling against it is uncomfortable and can be scary, whereas walking towards it is much more pleasant. Be careful using this technique that nothing breaks and he gets away, and that he does not get tangled up in the rope, or get it tangled around a part of the box. Use this technique only as a last resort, or because you are sure that the horses has learnt that his handlers are not strong and experienced, and that therefore he can always pull and get away rather than going where he is asked. Having a horse leaping about is best avoided but if he has really formed the habit of not loading and leaping about instead when asked, then it is necessary to change this. The important thing is that he re-learns not to leap about. If you get him in without him having the experience that when attached to an inanimate object he cannot get away, there may well be a time in the future when he does again pull as he has not learnt not to.

(c) **Will not walk out backwards.** Some horses have trouble backing out of the van or trailer. If he is loth to back out, make sure that there is someone behind him to push his quarters so that he does not bump them, or fall off the side of the ramp with one leg. For each slight step back, you praise him and push him a little more. It helps if he has already learnt to go back when asked. He should not rush, or he may hurt himself, so try and keep him quietly backing by stopping him with a tit bit mid way.

Raise the ramp to the same level as the floor by placing it on a bank for example so that when he gets to the end of the ramp, he will not have a drop or big step to take. Make sure it is supported on something that will not give way, and push him back so he does not have to back downhill. If he still persists, do not feed him in the trailer or give him any water or hay for a few hours, and he will eventually back out, he is not a complete idiot nor a robot!

It is very easy, by giving the horse more of a fright, to teach him that loading is even worse than he thought it was, so be very careful with more forceful ways, but there are occasions when they may be necessary. The important thing is to first of all understand why the horse is cautious, frightened, or has just learnt not to go in, and develop your own strategy, take time and then repeat it again and again before you go off to any event where there will be other pressures and problems that have to be confronted as well.

I have seen exhibitions by Roberts, and various other 'natural horsemen' loading horses reputed to be difficult by putting on severe nosebands which tighten fast when the equine pulls back. It seems to happen by magic, and the audience rushes off to buy the noseband. But neither Monty Roberts nor any of the others bother to discuss what the cause of the problems is in the first place. If the owners/trainers do not think about this, the same problem will happen again with another horse, and nothing is achieved. When doing such demonstrations, it is imperative to discuss with the owner what it is that they have done, how they can put it right, and avoid the same problem occurring again, although the solution may not be popular with everyone.

I was asked to work with an over 16hh heavy Hanoverian cross horse who would not load at a workshop in France. The rather inexperienced naïve owners were at their wits' ends because, as it soon transpired, the horse had learnt to pull back when his front legs were on the ramp and rear up, getting right away from the rather diminutive lady owner. We spent 45 minutes trying to get him in without exciting him in any way, and praising him for moving forwards, but as soon as he reached the top of the ramp, he pulled away and I could not hold him. Raising a stick behind him simply made him kick out aggressively, which was another indicator that he was not frightened, but had learnt to pull away and not go in. I explained to the group and the owner that what had happened was that he had learnt this way of behaving. To re-teach him, we had to stop him pulling away. The way of doing this was to have him wear two strong headcollars so they would not break even if he put much pressure on, and have a long lead rein which as soon as he might want to leap away was passed twice around the strong breast bar so he could not pull back. At first he pulled back severally and leaped about. Then at the end of the rope, having leapt about a while, he eventually stood still and we praised him. We let him do this a few times; he was large and leaped about quite a lot. Then after leaving him standing at the end of the rope for a while, I quietly went up to him and asked him to follow me into the trailer; he followed straight in. Despite the fact that I had taken much time explaining what I was doing and why, there was one member of the watching group who thought this was cruel and not the way to proceed with this horse and his owners. Now I have no doubt that if we had spent all day on this horse and not proceeded to working with the others that had come to be helped, we could eventually have had the horse walk in, but as soon as he went home to his owners, the problem would just recur and they were unable to hold him. As it turned out, after 30 minutes in the van, he was unloaded, and that evening walked straight in when the owners went to load him alone, and now two months later, he loads by himself! So for *that horse in that set of conditions and with those owners,* it was the correct thing to do. The woman who objected would not discuss it, nor did she stay to witness the success of the owners later in the day!

The good thing about her stand, however, was that it raised many issues that should be discussed and considered very carefully. For example,
(1) when do you use force when an equine does not load?
(2) and what sort of force?
There are times when for the long-term good of the horse and his owners, it is necessary to change his behaviour and teach him something different. This may require some firm handling. The alternative, in the end, is often the knacker's yard, only because the people were too soft and he learnt to do the wrong thing. But you must decide where this line is to be drawn. All we can do is give some guidelines.

The crucial thing is to understand the cause of the equine being difficult to load and then to develop a strategy that is possible for you individually to use to correct this. As a last resort, you can always ask someone who helps others professionally, but her job will be the same: (a) to understand the cause of the problem and (b) work out a way to solve it that will really help you, the owner, thereafter. What may help some will not help others, as the above example shows. **There really is no magic.**

Design of vehicle
Most people are of the opinion that it is exhausting for equines (and other animals) to spend time in the transporter. This is even reflected in the European law which states that the equine must not be travelling for more than 8 hour stretches at a time. It is true, of course, that very long journeys are exhausting for human and horse, but more important very often than the actually time of the journey is the route that is taken and the design of the transporter. Many manufacturers are taking advantage of owners' interests in designing the trailer or truck to reduce stress in the horses, but serious research on some of the design features for the horse's benefit (which have become selling points) has rarely been conducted. We have designed and made three different vehicles for horse transport over the years, while considering carefully the horse's needs and our own, and have looked at different people's ideas. We will briefly discuss what to date we have found out.
 (i) The first thing is the **orientation** of the horse for travelling. It is normal to travel the horse facing the engine, in a trailer or truck usually without windows, often with a floor that is not guaranteed not to slip when it is wet, and sometimes to give them much room. But there is some evidence to show that equines travel least well facing the engine. It is said to be easier for them to travel with the

quarters facing the engine. This is because the horse with his quarters to the front can swing them and change his weight distribution easily without unbalancing. Swinging on his front legs, which carry more weight, and with his head and neck protruding forwards is more difficult without losing balance, and it is to the front that the weight is thrown in road transport (e.g. with slowing or braking). The problem is that if horses are travelled quarters to the engine, the weight distribution is changed, and the position of the axle has to be changed. This change in design has not caught on, although by paying a great deal more than usual, you can buy such a trailer.

If equines are travelled loose and therefore able to make choices in the direction in which they choose to face, they usually take up positions diagonally across the vehicle if they can. This is easier to organise in trucks (although not trailers unless they are very big) and many are now designed to carry equines in this way. One of the advantages is that more horses can often be fitted into the space if they are oblique. But, in smaller trailers or small trucks, there is usually not this option. We have tried travelling equines both ways, and are not convinced that head to the engine is more tiring for them (see heart rates below). Much depends on other factors as well.

A recent invention is for the 'head to the engine' trailer to be wider at the base. The idea is that the equine will be able to spread his legs more and retain his balance better. Whether equines actually do learn to do this, or whether this is important, requires further verification; so far we have no evidence, although we do have evidence that other factors are extremely important.

(ii) Being **supported by partitions** or bars around the body seems to help the equine relax and balance since he can lean on the supports to regain his balance. Well packed with side bars and breast bars, they can travel quite comfortably facing the engine even though this is not their orientation of choice when loose. We have taken heart rates when travelling out horses this way. On motorways they are usually at resting rate, even after long drives of 7-8 hours and with large trucks and much noise travelling past. Much seems also to depend on what the horse is used to.

> Baksheesh had travelled for some eight years in our trucks with his head obliquely forwards. We crashed it going to the Highlands (without him in it), and had to borrow a trailer where he had to face the engine to attend the Arab Horse Society Marathon on Exmoor. He travelled very badly in this, leaning on the partition all the way, and even scrabbling with his legs as he leaned. On the way back, however, having won the marathon (!) he travelled quite calmly. So, as with most things, change was difficult, but the second time he had adapted to it.

(iii) Another important thing to consider in the design is **whether or not the equine should be able to see out of the windows.** It is normal not to have windows they can see out of. This is rather a peculiar feature I always think for an animal that is so visually aware. It is not a design to increase the traveller's confidence. If they can see out, then they can at least see familiar things, and are less likely to

A small truck where the horses look forwards out of the windscreen, and have windows to look out of sideways. Shindi and two-week-old Shenandoah ready to travel to France.

find the journey so distressing, provided of course they feel safe. In addition, if they can see where they are going, by being able to look forward, then they may be able to adjust their weight to the left and right hand corners that are coming up.

The importance of being able to see out and sub-consciously adjust balance can be tested by standing up in a trailer without holding on when you cannot see where you are going, compared to one where you can. It is very much easier to balance in the latter.

In the last two vehicles we have designed and made, we have fitted windows through which the horses can see out sideways as they stand obliquely; and in the latest, they face the engine and can see straight out of the windscreen forwards. Although the space is small, even naive equines appear to find this way of travel relatively easy. But this may also be because of the closeness to the human handlers who can talk to them and reassure them if necessary (picture above).

(iv)Perhaps one of the most important features in any transporter is **a floor that is not slippery.** Bedding when it is wet usually becomes slippery. A paint-on rubber floor prevents slip. We have used it in the last two vehicles we have made with success. It also protects the floor from rotting which is useful.

(v) The **isolation of the humans from the travelling equines** is common. The problem is to make it safe for the humans, but allow them to be near, particularly to reassure the young horse. One way of being able to do this is to have a walk way from the cab to the area with the equines in it, or to have a luton above the cab with an opening back to face the horses so that humans can travel safely and see and be seen by the equines. This allows constant monitoring and quick action to sort out a problem if necessary. It also allows the humans to point out features of interest to the equine passengers, and increase the interest of a journey that may be long and tedious. The third way, which we are now using, is to have no complete partition between the horses and the passengers and driver, but still render it safe for both by having strong half partitions. This allows the equines to look out of the windscreen forwards, and the humans to attend immediately to any problem or worry that the horses might have. We can also travel a mare and a stallion, or two stallions together in this arrangement, and we can stop and camp wherever we want.

(vi) The effect of the **roads, speed and the driver** when horses travel.

Monitoring the heart rates with fitted pulse monitors during journeys allows us to find out the degree to which different types of road, drivers and speeds cause the heart rate to rise (a sign of increased emotional response) and to monitor fatigue. It is interesting to note that despite the amount of traffic, sights and noises of vehicles coming close to the side, motorways are characteristically less worrying for the equines (that is the heart rate goes up less) than small country roads. Motorways have less steep hills and gentler bends than small country roads. It is the braking and lurching of the vehicles which seems to be most difficult for them to cope with. The heart rates of four horses we have measured on motorways remained at around their resting rates, even for journeys as long as 10 hours(38-48bpm). Heart rates when driving on minor bendy and hilly roads, were very much higher (50s-60s bpm), showing how much more stressful they were, even if the vehicle was driven slowly and carefully. It is likely that the EU maximum requirement for travel time for equines in a vehicle (8 hours) can cause more stress by increased loading and unloading in strange environments. However, much of this depends on the individual equine's experience and the roads.

> On a trip back to UK from La Drome in France, after five hours or so, Shemal started pawing and head shaking. We had started very early in the morning, and we noticed that she had not urinated, and only mucked once. We found a lay-by with a little space, and unloaded her and Oberlix. Both almost immediately urinated and mucked, and then we loaded them again and were on our way! Now we regularly stop for 'pee stops' when travelling long distances, and they also are asked to muck before they enter the van in order to cut down smells on the journey. Oberlix is very good at this, Shemal a little slack!

With experience, equines become very adaptable travellers in transporters; some only need to be told to get in the box or trailer and they will walk in unaided.

Crystal, Omeya and Aisha watch as their container is towed onto the ferry from Oban to Mull.

We had an old friend Deborah Howell who was around 68 when I first met her, had been a vet all her life, and liked to hunt at least 3 days a week. She had a rather delightful mare who carried her safely until her 78th year out hunting, but Deborah had bad hips and could not walk well. She simply led the mare up to the trailer and told her to get in, and she walked in unaided to a narrow single horse trailer.

Many people have found that when the horses see their own vehicle at a ride or a competition, they perk up, go straight to it, and relax quickly, apparently associating it with 'home'.

When we were travelling in France Shemal cut a hind leg very severely, so we had to have the vehicle with us to transport her to the next stop. After a couple of weeks, not only did both of them call and approach the vehicle if they saw it coming, but they were unlikely to leave it and wander off (unless of course they were chased or frightened by something), so it was sometimes possible to leave them for short periods, at least, unenclosed with the vehicle.

Train travel is little used, alas, nowadays for horses. In Kenya when we were children, the roads were so bad or non-existent that we used to travel all over the country in the train with our ponies. They either travelled loose in a livestock wagon, or more usually in boxes either side of a groom's passage. Racehorses used to be transported all over Europe in this way. Again, equines become relaxed travellers after a few experiences when they have not been frightened, and are easy to load. One of the delights of train travel is that one has many hours with the horses, even overnight sometimes as the train rattles on. It can be a relaxing and enjoyable period of companionship for both equine and human. When I went as a working student to Fulmer in Buckinghamshire to Robert Hall's centre to learn about classical riding as a school girl in the 1950s, my horse, Kathiawar (the grandmother of Baksheesh, great great grandmother of many others from our stud see page 264) and I travelled from Lewes in Sussex, to Slough by train. I remember sitting for hours being shunted about, but relaxing on the hay with a good book, and a good horse companion, I didn't care! If you ever get an opportunity to travel with your horse by rail, take it.

Air travel is now common but unfortunately the airline companies often do not allow the owner/groom to travel with the horse. This is a pity as it is often the presence of a familiar person that can help the equine not to worry or panic unduly. Panic and hysteria is a particular risk when transporting equines by air, as, by damaging the aircraft, they can put the whole plane and its occupants in danger, so it is usual to carry drugs to prevent this happening. It is vital that before travelling the equine by air, he has travelling experience. New experiences will have to be coped with so some previous experience without fear is important to stop panic. For example they may be lifted in a container into the aircraft: the engine noises, pressurising, and restricted space all have to be coped with without panic.

Boat travel is usually done now by loading a motor vehicle onto the boat in Europe, although in Africa many donkeys may travel on ferries. Horses that have had sufficient experience in the vehicle in which they are travelling generally do not become disturbed by this, although no one has looked very carefully at the effect of very rough seas. Travelling to France, for example, our horses were quite relaxed out on the deck in their vehicle (see previous page). Long sea journeys for equines are now made in containers which often sit on the deck, although the horses are able to walk around in an enclosed area on the ship for short periods when the weather is good. It is often possible to go with the horses on such journeys as their groom, but nowadays unfortunately sea journeys are often more expensive than going by air and are gradually being phased out.

Boats and ferries in some countries allow the equines to travel on the boat rather than in a vehicle. They can stand on the deck or in the hold, or be secured into livestock caging on the decks. It is again remarkable how equines that are confident with their handlers will adapt easily to this.

I once took Cariff, a three-year-old Arab stallion at the time, from the Isle of Mull (in the Hebrides) to the Isle of Tiree (where I was to teach) on the small inter-island ferry boat. He had to walk onto a particular part of the deck, and then it was cranked down with a lot of noise. He then had to walk off it into the small hold about 3metres lower. We had a four-hour very rough journey to Tiree followed by the same type of disembarkation. Much to my surprise he was relaxed at all time, presumably partly because he had been handled well and was with his familiar handler, he was young and had never had a fright with humans.

Another time we decided to take three horses from Oban to Mull on the ferry without a vehicle, They had to be loaded into wiremesh containers which were then rolled onto the boat. Again they were quite relaxed about this! (picture page 224).

Equines in other parts of the world become extremely adept boat travellers: donkeys pull wagons onto small boats and then keep still as they tip around in a rough sea. Indeed, they have often been used to supply the energy for ferry crossings by being harnessed to pulley ropes. The cavalry transported equines all over the world on sailing boats, so we must not underestimate their ability to adapt to extraordinary conditions. Over-protecting our animals, or not going places because of the worry of a strange journey for the equine, is a loss for us and our horses; they can adapt given half a chance, even if the humans can't!

Route planning
Neither equine nor human movements around the world are random. Wild equines (like all who travel with equines) have some overall plan of where they are going, where to stay at different times of the year or meet up with different groups. The nomadic movements of the Mongolian horsemen (until recently) were largely controlled by the need to find food for their horses. This meant that they covered considerable areas of the steppes, visiting different types of area at specific times of the year. The modern full-time traveller with his/her horse-drawn wagon will have some similar overall long term plan, although daily movements may be controlled by who one meets, where the grass is to be found, how often the police move one on, where friendly sympathetic folk are to be found or where jobs are.

In Britain, because there are bridle rights of way, planning with good maps allows for nicer routes. Some of the best riding can be found in the South East around very large cities where there have traditionally been big farms and consequently, through history, well established bridle paths.

In the US, Australia and New Zealand there is no tradition of rights of way, so, although there may be fewer people and roads, it is often necessary to do a great deal of research and apply for permission to cross land.

Other countries without the same idea of enclosure and land ownership, such as Kenya, Zimbabwe, South Africa, many other African countries, France, Spain and Portugal, often have better access and less planning is needed. In France, the government finances a network of 'randonnees', marked tracks for walking, cycling or riding all over the country. The result is some of the best riding in the world.

The first thing of course is to learn to read a map well!

Securing equines overnight
There are several ways of doing this :
(i) **Stabling** or hiring field **grazing**. Finding bed and breakfast accommodation for

both horse and rider is becoming more common in the UK but extremely expensive. Hiring grazing for the horses while the humans go off to a bed and breakfast is slightly less expensive but can destroy the 'togetherness'.

Having to stop where stabling, grazing or human accommodation can be hired dramatically cuts down options. In order to stop where the fancy takes, we need to discuss the various methods that are used for overnight securing of the equines.

(ii) **Tying.** The usual way of ensuring horses do not wander off or get into trouble on roads and so on is to tie them up (picture below). This means that overnight they need to be supplied with food and fodder since they will be able to reach very little grass. This was the way the cavalry kept their horses overnight. They had rope lines where 50 horses might be tied up and would be supplied with food and fodder. It can be a satisfactory way of securing them, particularly when there are supply wagons bringing the food. This method is used much by the West Australians who trek off with their horses for several days, and have supply wagons, but it needs a great deal of organising.

(iii) **Tethering.** Another way of securing the equines is to tether them with something securely fixed into the ground so they can, by moving around, eat all the grass within the circle described by their tethering rope. After they have finished this, the tether is moved to another place where they can graze again. This is the preferred way of securing horses by many travelling folk, and allows the horses, ponies or donkeys to acquire their food. A tether of up to around 10 metres can be used for the experienced animal. Many equines become extremely skilled with coping with the rope on the ground, and it is not unusual to see equines disentangle

Shemal tethered with a corkscrew tether.

Gaynor, an experienced traveller, using her tether to scratch herself. Note the big metal tether, her collar and a short chain to begin with. She is not tangled, she is using her tether.

themselves carefully. All equines, including thoroughbreds and Arabs, can learn to be tethered, but it must be practised when they are being supervised, and gradually the tether period lengthened. Pure-bred Arab horses of both genders are often tethered by the Bedouins in the desert.

It is vital to have the tethering stake well into the ground or the equine may pull it out. If the tether is too large and heavy, and the horse pulls it out, he can get a fright as it leaps about and this may well cause the horse to gallop off; the more he gallops, the more the tether follows, a good recipe for disaster. It is sensible to ensure the horse has some months of practise with any tether before tethering overnight.

When travelling with a wagon, carrying the tether is no problem but when riding, it can be a nuisance and heavy. Recently we have used some light corkscrew type tethers developed for keeping dogs tied up. These work reasonably well with experienced horses for short periods, like the lunch break. I would be cautious of using them overnight.

Another tip that a traveller told me was to use a chain for the first part of the tether for the experienced horse at least. The chain should be the length of the horse, and heavy enough to fall down off his foot should it get wrapped around. When riding, even a short piece of chain adds to the weight.

(iv) **Hobbling**. Another way of securing equines so they do not go too far away overnight is to shackle their front legs with a pair of hobbles. Here they can only take small steps but can have access over a larger area to forage, moving slowly. Obviously, hobbling is not a good idea if you are stopping near roads or cities, but in open areas where they do not have to search too far for grass, it can work well. Practise at home with the hobbles, first with a relatively long chain between the bracelets (make sure these are well padded so the horse does not rub himself), and gradually shorten the chain so that he becomes accustomed to taking very short strides. We have used hobbles for short breaks only. But, be warned, they can learn to gallop off at a great rate with them on.

One lazy sunny day in France when we had stripped off and were bathing in a river for the lunch break, Shemal was hobbled and grazing nearby, Oberlix (who will not leave her) was loose. Suddenly someone started a chainsaw some 300 yards off, and at the same time Shemal saw a woman on a bicycle with a dog 500m away. Maybe she thought this was another horse, but she suddenly took off at a fast dog-like gallop, closely followed by Oberlix. Rushing off in our knickers and no shoes to catch them was amusing for the onlookers. Luckily, after 500m they stopped and we caught up with them.

(v) **Corralling.** This is the most common way of securing horses overnight nowadays. An electric fence unit, batteries, insulated poles that can be quickly stuck in the ground, and white tape which can be seen from a distance is the usual arrangement. The fence encloses a small area, anything from around 10 to 50 square metres. The horses can either be put together or in separate corrals and if there is enough grass they can graze, if not they are given fodder for the overnight stop. If there are individuals who do not know each other, or stallions and mares or geldings, a double fence between the corrals so they cannot touch each other over the boundaries may be necessary.

It is now possible to get a small light unit powered by torch batteries (see picture page 212, 6). When travelling without a vehicle, we dispense with the insulated poles but carry insulators which carry the tape and are attached to trees or bushes.

When using an electric fence, it is essential to teach the equines about the shock before they discover it by galloping through. We do this by taking them up to the single strand fence and touching their noses on it when it is on. Be careful, they may jump back. Once they have had a shock, they are wary and disinclined to touch it again or barge through it. This learning is important otherwise when they do get a shock, they may barge though the tape in panic, and then learn to barge through rather than stay within. They also learn quickly that when the fence is ticking, it will shock, when it is not, it will not, and walk through the tape when it is not on. Consequently we are careful to pretend the fence is on, and to instruct any humans clambering over it to pretend to get a shock. The equines see this and are then not keen to try it out.

(vi) **Loose.** The best way of all of keeping your equines overnight with you is to have them want to stay with you, so, like many dogs, they can be loose. Here the humans are considered part of the group and, provided they have enough to eat and drink, and are not frightened by some untoward occurrence or other horses turning up, they will stick around. Be warned that it is not wise in crowded

Shanti and Sioban are relaxed and all ready to depart on a two-day trip carrying everything they need even for the weather in the UK. Four saddle bags, two in front, two behind, sleeping bag under the saddle, tent in left hind bag, map and camera in left front bag, easy to get at.

places, but when in wild places without roads and people, it can be very useful and pleasant. However, if you are far from home (that is further than around 100km) this works better. If they know the area and the way to even a temporary home, they are inclined to go back there, and are gone in the morning. Well into the expedition, though, they will, usually be found within a one kilometre circle of the camp. Equines have a different idea of space (*Equine Lore* chapter 9) therefore even though you think they have departed, they may still consider themselves nearby. When there is no food, fodder or water available anywhere but at the camp (such as in deserts or in very cold conditions) they may take a wander around, but they will be there at breakfast time. The Bedouins and others travelling with equines and camels in the deserts often rely on this.

We have found, like the Bedouin, it is better not to have them all loose. Mares will tend to go off together leaving the secured geldings or stallions behind, but if you secure a couple of the older mares, the others, as well as the geldings or stallions, will usually stay around; but don't have both the geldings and stallions loose together or the stallion may see to it that the geldings depart!

'Helpful' humans may make matters worse! They usually try and catch loose horses, often getting excited, and as a result the equines become excited and charge off, ensuring you have a few kilometres' walk to find them again.

Having equines that come when you call is definitely conducive to laziness. They can be easily taught by always giving them a tit bit when they do come towards you; start from a short distance and then, using the same call, increase the distance. Eventually practise when you are out of sight. The longer you travel with them, the more likely they are to remain with you without restriction ... provided of course they have not had a bad time with you, and their own social structure is right.

Veterinary controls when abroad

Apart from the cost, the biggest obstacle to taking your equines on travels with you in different countries is veterinary controls. The best thing is to talk to a local vet as soon as you arrive in the new country and obtain any inoculations or drugs that may be necessary for the local diseases. Here is a sample of our very basic multi-species red cross kit. Be careful do not over load yourselves.

BASIC MULTI SPECIES RED CROSS KIT
(with prescriptions drugs from your vet if travelling away from possible vet care, and where there are endemic diseases)

 A couple of sterile large dressings, 2 stretch bandages. Elastoplast roll, small roll cotton wool.
Some antibiotic eye ointment, and an antibiotic injection course. Needles and hypodermics.
Paracetemol or even a stronger pain killer in case of severe wounds or breaks.
Castor oil, paraffin oil or Epsom salts for colic treatment and or indigestion.
Surgical spirit or methylated spirit for disinfecting and hardening skin.
A silver anti-hypothermia rug.
Chocolate bars and electrolytes for exhaustion.
Citronella oil, against flies and biting bugs (has a nice smell, and works).
Any recommended treatments for local diseases (including anti tick treatment or anti malarial drugs etc.).
A stethoscope.

The route, and route finding

The first and most important thing is to get hold of a large scale map of the area which marks rights of way.

Reasonably fit equines should be able to cover around 25 miles (40km) a day in around 4-5 hours. Some people prefer to cover 50 miles(80km) for a day or two, and then stop for a couple of days, or some to ride or drive for only around three hours a day (10 miles). The only control on this is (a) how fit the equines are and (b) that they have enough time to forage for food when they arrive, and therefore have sufficient energy to cover the distances required at the preferred speed. They also need time to rest and sleep.

Many people doing long treks carrying equipment will only walk. Personally,

I find this very exhausting, and prefer rather to go reasonably fast (around 7.5-9 mph) for two to three hours some days, have some days staying in the same place, and may be sometimes do a longer ride of around 5-6 hours a day (43-50 miles/70-80km per day).

Equipment for the equines.

Carrying equine food when riding is bulky and heavy. We generally only carry around one to two days' **cereal supply** (2-5 kg/horse). We have never carried **water** for the horses, but it is important to ensure that there will be a source of water at least at the night stop, that the water will be drinkable, and that the horse can get to it.

> Riding around in the Margaret forests in Western Australia we found that water was available, but too low down for the horses to reach it, so we carried a canvas bucket.

A **skeleton grooming kit** can be carried, but more important is **skeletal farriers equipment** if the equines are shod.

MINIMAL FARRIERY EQUIPMENT

Spare front shoes (if the equines have more or less the same size feet, then one set of shoes may be sufficient as an emergency).
Hammer
Nails
Rasp
Pincers

There are many different approaches to farriery, so it is very important to have a serious understanding of shoeing and be able to at least put on a previously fitted shoe, in case of emergency where there are no farriers available.

Different people decide on different priorities, but the important thing is to think long and hard about every item you are taking, particularly if you are riding, extra unnecessary equipment is a veritable nuisance for both horse and rider.

Working on the land and driving

Whatever history has to say, now we *can* enjoy the time we voluntarily spend working our equines on the land and in harness. It can be important 'quality time', spent not only learning about each other, but doing a useful job which has another important modern attraction – it can save money!

It is widely believed that thoroughbreds, Arabs, warmbloods, and so on, are not fit to work on the land or in harness. But, it seems to have been forgotten that most of the northern European 'warmbloods' were in the first place bred to be ridden and to work in harness and on the land (such as the Frieslands, Hanoverians,

Trakheners). The idea was that they would look more splendid, go faster and do as much work as the less aristocratic heavy barbs or cob-like horses. The performance tests for some of the German breeds reflect this, although they rarely, if ever, are driven or worked on the land these days. Arab horses have been driven and ridden for centuries and still are throughout the Middle East. Lady Blunt, one of the first Arab horse breeders in 19th century Europe, bought some of her Arabs off the Cairo streets where they were pulling carts. The thoroughbred, bred for racing by the rich, is probably one of the only breeds which, through history, has not often been harness trained, although they have been crossed with every breed to produce working horses of many types.

The adage 'Jack of all trades, master of none' is largely untrue. There are more indications that the way forward to understanding and studying the mind, and being able to educate better, is a multi-disciplinary approach. Everyone has to learn much about each others' specializations in order to advance in this field.

Equines are also trained to 'specialise'. They are rarely given the opportunity of pursuing different activities. They are taken out of their isolation in an individual stable once or maybe twice a day and practise the same activity every day. Occasionally some are let out in a field for a few hours, rarely with other horses, and it is news if, for example, a dressage horse is even taken out for a ride! (e.g. *Horse and Rider*, January 2001). No wonder there are large numbers of horses with behavioural problems, and many become 'stale' and give up performing well, or even at all. Whoever heard of a Badminton eventer harrowing his field before leaving for the competition, or, harnessed up to a light vehicle, going shopping with his rider/driver?

Equines first associated with humans in order to help to lift, transport and pull things. In addition, equines, like humans, need land to live on and to grow the crops they eat – so why can they not help produce them? The advantages of doing this are:

(a) The equine has new and different things to learn which will help provide his cognitive or intellectual needs and consequently will be likely to improve his performance in any discipline.

(b) He is doing something useful for the human, and gives her a new skill and interest.

(c) It is a more environmentally sound and acceptable way of both keeping your equine and looking after the land he occupies.

(d) It saves money (and time). The alternative is to buy or hire machines and other people to do the work both of which cost a great deal more than the equine they support!

(e) As we have mentioned, it can help get him fit without putting mechanical stress on his legs (chapter 10).

The work of competitive horses such as eventers or endurance horses may be restricted to looking after their own pastures, or harrowing their own maneges, but even this will be a benefit. Harrowing with competitive horses once they have been educated to do this is simple, quiet, easy and very pleasant. It brings the horse and the handler closer together in joint slow work, is excellent exercise for

Oberlix weeding with me up, and Chris on the cultivator going between the rows.

both, essential to have a productive pasture, and requires as much skill and learning as to ride well.

Donkeys are the most numerous working animal in the world today. There are some countries where, far from being replaced by mechanical transport, they have been shown to be more efficient, easier to keep, less expensive, more reliable and can reproduce themselves. Consequently, they are being reintroduced in some developing countries in order to help the poor people farm, transport material and trade .

Thus, there are many arguments for keeping equines working in both the less developed and 'developed' world.

Efficient use of horse power on the farm in the 'developed' world, or in the stable
On a commercial farm in the Western world, some jobs are more efficiently done with a tractor, some with a horse, some using both.

Recently, one of our students did some experiments with three different horses to test their efficiency for pulling different weights. It would appear that lighter horses, who are fit, are more efficient, and sometimes faster for agricultural/ horticultural work than large heavy animals that are not used for other tasks.

The main reasons why people do not use their horses, at least to help maintain their grassland, are because:
(i) They are ignorant, and do not know how to set about it,
(ii) They are scared. They are frightened that the horse will be damaged (and themselves may be).
(iii) They are lazy – and do not have the equipment.

The bridle. For driving on roads horses usually have blinkers over the eyes to obscure their peripheral vision. This is to stop them getting a fright when they see shadowy things (not clearly) coming up behind.

Long reins to enable the human to drive.

Blinkers are very disturbing for equines when they are first put on. The equine cannot make the normal judgements since his visual field is suddenly restricted, and he cannot see sideways or behind. **So take great care when leading the horse through any sort of gateway or narrow place** when he has the blinkers on, at least to start with.

We start our equines working without blinkers, and only put them on later when we are progressing to light vehicles. This is partly because he can then see the person behind, albeit rather vaguely. Since he knows and trusts the handlers, this can give him confidence as he does not feel all alone in this new world attached to a wheeled vehicle that follows him very closely.

LIST OF WORK ON THE LAND WE HAVE FOUND APPROPRIATE TO DO WITH OUR LIGHT HORSES

1. Carting muck out to the fields in a small cart, and dumping it in piles to be spread by hand or with harrows.
2. Harrowing grass (with a flexible grass harrow) to spread the faeces so that the field does not develop latrine areas and over-grazed areas.
3. Not mowing hay (difficult to find a light mower and also rather dangerous) but turning and tedding the hay to help it dry, then racking it up ready for baling (difficult to get light equipment though).
4. Helping to bring in the hay in small bales with a pair in a four-wheel trailer or, if you have only a little, loose stacked in the small cart with one horse.
5. Bringing in firewood with a home-made sleigh that is light and can be pulled over grass.
6. Carrying hay to the stock on the farm (picture page 245).
7. Not ploughing (unless you have a very small area and a single furrow small plough, when it can be helpful) but spring tyne harrowing after ploughing to break up the sods and furrows. This we often do with two horses.
8. Spike harrowing after this to make a good tilth for planting.
9. Seeding vegetables with a small drill that can seed two rows at once (can be adapted from the hand drills that you can buy).
10. Weeding with a small cultivator between the rows (see picture opposite).
11. Making the furrows for potato plating, then splitting the furrows over the potatoes and finally digging them when they are ready with the potato plough.
12. Delivering organic vegetable boxes to customers within a five-mile radius.
13. With a good dog, gathering sheep over large areas such as the Highlands.
14. Carrying fencing materials to outlying places where difficulty of getting a tractor.
15. Spot felling trees and dragging them out of difficult, wet or steep areas through other trees.
16. Acting as shelter against snow or hail in mountains in seriously bad weather!
17. Transport to and from the pub, when, if in a vehicle, one would be unable to drink alcohol.

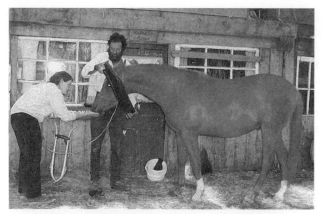

The first harness lesson for Shanti (aged three). Stretching the neck forward to some grain, so that the collar can easily be placed over his head.

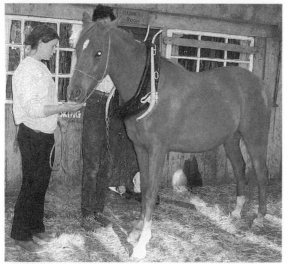

After the haymes have been placed on the collar, he is rewarded.

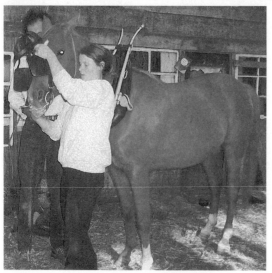

Putting on the bridle with blinkers.

When driving, it is important to understand that just the weight of the relaxed rein is sufficient to stop many a draught horse. It is also important to realise that since the driver is more remote from the horse and cannot use weight and leg aids, it is more crucial to use the voice.

The reins must be non slip, we prefer to make ours out of baler twine which are cheap, can look smart and are certainly very serviceable.

If the equine is going to be working quite hard on the land pulling a harrow or plough, then he should have a **collar** as he can pull better in a collar and it is less likely to rub. It is put on upside down, that is, with the widest part at the top to go over the ears. Once on, it is turned around so the narrow part is at the top. We teach our horses to put their noses through the collar and then to push it over their heads with the word, 'push' (picture opposite).

If you do not have a collar or anything to make it out of, then a breast plate will do as long as the work is not going to be too hard. A breast plate can be made out of any well padded piece of broad leather, or even a few ropes together, padded with felt or foam rubber or covered with sheepskin.

The traces (ropes/ straps that do the pulling) are attached onto the haymes on the collar. The other end to the **whipple pole** which is a piece of wood or 2/3 cm wide metal pipe which is just longer than the equine's width behind. The implement

Long reining Shanti down the drive, being led by Chris, who is relaxed and chatting to him. Look at how he is touching and listening to him with his right ear. Vicki drives him and Fats accompanies them all.

A trip up the drive being long reined by Vicki (with Fats) alone, and quite happy with this.

is attached to the centre clip.

The length of the traces is important: too long and, as the horse turns, he will be able to put his hind leg over one and so when he moves forward the trace is between his hind legs which will give him a fright. If they are too short, the implement will be too close behind and the whipple pole may clip his heels. If the implement has no wheels or is not round and able to roll downhill (such as a grass or arable roller) then this is all that is required.

If **shafts** are going to be used (which is necessary for any implement on wheels to prevent it running into the back of the horse), then a full harness will be necessary (picture on page 240). The **crupper** is attached to the pad and breeching

*Gaynor and Sioban bringing in some sheaves of wheat for our flour.
Gaynor is an old experienced traveller's horse and can be safely left to stand
until asked to move again. The collar is halfway down her neck because she
has been grazing, and does not mind it falling down her neck at all.*

and goes under the tail. Its function is to stop everything slipping forwards or
sideways. It needs to be put on with care and thoughtfulness the first few times.

Have the harness ready and then perform these exercises.

Exercise 1 Put on, turn around and take off the collar five times, praising the
equine and giving him a food reward every time after the collar passes over his
ears and he does not put his head up or draw back. Then hold the collar up and
when he voluntarily begins to put his nose and then his head through, praise him
and give him a reward. By the end of a few days of this, he will be putting his
head in the collar and pushing it on himself, all you have to do is hold the collar
for him to put it on!

Exercise 2. Many horses put their heads up or their noses out when the person
tries to put on the bridle. Hold some food in your hand and the bridle in position
to slip over his ears when he voluntarily opens his mouth to take the food. Repeat
several times, and you will eventually have a horse who opens his mouth as soon
as the bit is in place.

Exercise 3. Put on and take off the pad and the crupper around his tail, and the
breeching around his hind legs. Flap all the pieces of leather, canvas or rope and
continue while talking to him quietly, until he stands still whatever piece you are
flapping. Take it all off, and do this again,

Exercise 4. Repeat harnessing him up, making sure that you ask him to stand
still; reward him when he does, and tick him off when he moves. Repeat this

again and again until he does. Then harness him up; without him being tied up, and continue until he will stand wherever you ask him and not move until you ask him to. This is very important when driving so that you know you can fix a broken or wrongly adjusted piece of harness without him moving off.

Now the equine is ready for his first long reining lesson. He is driven forwards with the voice. It is easier to start this on a drive, or lane with enclosed sides as he may try and turn around to see the driver. If the driver is inexperienced, it can be tricky to stop quick enough to stop the horse turning around to you and both of you becoming tangled in the reins. Also it is helpful, if you have no experience, to have someone lead him until both of you have understood what it is all about. One thing that is very important is **not to flap the reins on the rump to get the horse to move forward.** If he is not going forward properly, then the driver must carry a short stick and tap him with it. If you get into the habit of flapping the reins on his rump, you may get into very difficult situations later when for example, putting the horse in and out of the cart, the reins flap by mistake, he takes off, you fall out and you lose horse and cart in a crash!

The intellectual challenge: do not tread on the ridges where the potatoes are growing.

GOLDEN RULES FOR TEACHING DRIVING OR WORKING IN CHAINS

(1) Ensure that the horse responds to the voice at all times.

(2) Ensure that the horse has been taught to stop and stand still until he is asked to move again.

(3) Never flap the reins on the rump to drive him forwards, use the voice and a stick if necessary.

(4) Never walk between the horse and the implement or vehicle when you are putting him to (attaching the vehicle).

(5) Ensure that, if you are inexperienced, you have a reliable helper who is not frightened.

(6) Never progress to the next stage without having a quiet horse at the previous stage for at least three sessions.

(7) If you are frightened yourself, return to performing the stages that do not frighten you and go on with these until you are confident to going onto the next, even if it takes you months!

(8) Never shout, allow others to shout or run about or have any frightening distractions while you are harness training.

Exercises. These should be practised several times, and as he grasps what is required, he is praised with a 'yes', 'well done', 'good' and so on.

(1) Long reining can be started while lunging or free schooling with the outside rein gently keeping the horse out. He will be familiar with this, but start without blinkers so he can see you, and then if you have decided to use blinkers, repeat with them so that he knows the arrangement and so do you, before he has his visual field dramatically restricted.

When he is quiet at the walk with the full harness, then try a trot; it may be necessary to have someone at his head to start with to reassure him with the flapping pieces all around.

(2) Have someone walking beside him, not leading him if he is quiet, and long rein him at a walk all the way around a field, or down a quiet road. Gradually increase the difficulty of where you go – through narrow places, under trees, stopping and waiting at gates and so on.

(3) Make an obstacle course around a field, or the manege with ropes, or rails, and make sure you can guide him around and through the course which can gradually be made more difficult. Have your friend do this with her horse too, and make it a fun exercise for you all.

(4) Go into a large open field and make circles, squares, figures of eight and any other movements you can make up, go though narrow places, over logs.

These exercises are as much to develop your skills as the horse's. You will find that it is easier with short reins to start with, so stay close behind, or even walk slightly to the side by his quarters until you and he get the hang of how to give and receive very slight changes of tension on the rein meaning different things backed up by your voice.

Teaching the equine to pull in harness

It is very important to realise that each of these lessons may have to be repeated for some days until the equine is quiet and relaxed. But in the hands of someone with experience, who is very relaxed, some equines go through at least the first 6 stages in one lesson. Lessons should always be at least half an hour, even if things are going well, as the horse must become familiar with the process. If he is worried, then the lesson may have to go on for several hours, perhaps even going back a stage or two; the goal is to have a quiet equine, so failing this the lesson must be repeated until he is.

Be very careful with your body language throughout, and use of the voice, be consistent and clear at all times.

Do not have anyone helping who is frightened or even anxious; the equine will cue into this and gradually he will become more wary. Think very carefully also about personal safety: avoid treading or tripping on ropes, getting reins tangled around your hand or standing in a stupid place, otherwise the next time you will be wary and this will make matters much worse. You, and the helper, need to exude confidence.

The voice is crucial The person leading also uses her voice, particularly to reassure if necessary. We find a quiet sing-songy voice, chatting all the time to the equine often helps them to relax.

It is very important that he learns at this stage to stand still when told to. If the horse learns to stop and stand still when asked and always obeys, then whenever

Weeding potatoes: the physical challenge for Oryx and Vicki behind.

The social challenge: Aisha, in season, harrows in front of Oryx (stallion).

something goes wrong one can ask him to stop and gradually he learns that if things go wrong, he stops and stands still. If he becomes worried when asked to stand still, move on again and then stop, and do this again and again and again, gradually trying to lengthen the standing time. There is no point in insisting on him learning to stand still when he is very worried to start with, he will jig about and probably get worse if you prevent him moving, so choose your moment and the place, and gradually make it more difficult.

The next stage is to put on the traces and whipple pole. It is a good idea to have a short chain at the end of the traces and a clip onto the ring on the whipple pole.

Have someone carrying this on a string to begin with while the other person long reins so that it does not drag on the ground. If this goes well, allow it to fall on the ground and let it jump about a little, and make a jangling noise behind him. If he is too worried, it is pulled up again, then dropped again when he relaxes until in the end he will be confident with it and its noise and jangle. Be sensible about this, it will make much more noise and be more disturbing on tarmac or gravel than on grass, so if you are having trouble, do half an hour on the grass before going onto a noisier surface. Either way, ensure that before you stop he is relaxed and familiar with this; it may take 10 minutes or 3 hours. Stopping when he is not relaxed will mean he has learnt it is rather scary and next time it will take longer still to get him to be quiet, and he may start worrying as soon as he sees the equipment.

Introduce the concept of 'pull'. He has learnt to go forward to the voice, stop, go backwards perhaps, change gaits forwards, and so on. Now he has to learn that when pressure is put on the collar (or breast plate) it is different from pressure on the bit or headcollar, and does *not* mean give and stop. A helper holds up the whipple pole and gradually puts her weight on it so she is pulled along. To start only a little pressure is put on the pole; if the horse stops, he is encouraged to continue forward with the voice, and then when he is going forward, the weight is put on the whipple pole again gradually until he understands the difference in the required response: weight on the rein means give and stop, and weight on the collar or breast plate means pull.

Getting used to things moving, and noise behind. We usually use a wheelbarrow full of metal objects and stones with someone wheeling the wheel barrow. Every time he moves forward, the wheelbarrow moves and makes a racket. Go up and down an enclosed lane or drive, or a jumping lane or gallop; or you can make up a lane around the manege with a temporary single non-electrified electric fence. Continue until he has come to grips with this noise associated with his movement.

Putting to. In this stage, the pulling and the noise are put together, and the object of both is attached behind him to the traces. The easiest thing to use here is a tyre, or a small set of harrows. But before this is attached, it is vital that the horse is confident enough not to back into them, or panic, if things get difficult. Always have a person who is not nervous holding his head. The best idea is to stand straight in front of him so he cannot go forward, and have him on a leading rein attached to the bit; the helper must not hold the driving reins or it interferes with the action of the rein. If the person is nervous of standing in front, then they can stand to the side but hold both sides of the bit by having the lead rein attached through the rings on the bit.

The driver puts the horse to while holding the reins, or if there is another person they clip the traces onto the object or implement, and are careful not to step between the horse and the implement.

He is asked to go forwards, by the driver but with the leader also going forwards. He walks a few paces, then is asked to stop. I prefer with our reactive horses to do this stage initially in some enclosed space. If he is worried, he takes a few steps and is allowed to stop and this is repeated again and again, but the number of steps gradually lengthens before he stops, always with someone leading him and chatting to him.

After a few times, as he gains confidence, it is important to keep him going so he does not learn to stop whenever he likes. Here again the use of the voice is vital to keep him going, but at the same time reassure him that all is well and that nothing could be simpler. A constant quiet repetition of praise and calm in the voice does wonders, provided of course he has already learnt about the voice and

The physical challenge. Shemal carrying bales of hay to feed the sheep through the autumn woods.

about the handler's positive emotional state with regard to himself.

Beginning to do some work. Start initially where the tyre or harrows will not jump about too much and make a noise, such as on grass or in a manege. When you progress to the field, make sure there is a well defined boundary to it, a hedge or post and rails, and that it is small; harrow or pull the tyre round and around without making tight turns at the corners.

Keep going until he has really settled and, if harrowing, you are both doing a good job. This means that you slightly overlap the previous line which you have harrowed, not leaving pieces out, going in crooked lines or doing each piece of the field twice.

Once you can go around and around, ensure that he does not step over the inside trace, which becomes slack on the turn, so take the turns wider before trying to make them tight. Then make tighter turns which will make the trace touch the hind leg on the outside of the turn, to which he should have already have become accustomed. If he does step over the trace, make sure that the person at his head holds onto him, as the driver quickly releases the trace and re-attaches it, or lifts his hind leg over it. It is wise to practise this frequently before putting to, because it frequently happens if one is not very careful,

As usual, it is very important to continue long enough for the equine to come to grips with what he is doing and be relaxed in it, even to the point where he is familiar enough to find it boring and wants to stop. We like to start off making the horse work hard. Hard work will relax him much quicker than pulling a light vehicle for example.

We never start our Arabs and part breds in a vehicle for this reason; first they must do draught work on the land, and as they become familiar, and realise that draught work is hard work not just rushing around, we progress to a light vehicle.

Forty-five minutes' actual work will probably be necessary for both horse and human to start with, and the same each day for the next five days or so. The driver must be aware all the time of what is happening around, and be able to choose where to go to avoid problems, but at the same time gradually accustom the equine to a variety of conditions and difficult things as he works.

Things to avoid to start with are bumpy land where the harrow jumps about, major roads nearby (unless he is very used to traffic), busy farm buildings with tractors and implements coming and going, a fence next to a bunch of young horses who will gallop about and excite the student. Make progress daily coping with these more difficult situations. Harrowing the manege is not a bad place to start. We often volunteer to harrow the manege before our demonstrations, and you would be surprised how many people turn up just to watch this!

Gradually the time can be built up to two hours and a bigger set of chain harrows used. The more you do it and the more regular it is, the better. Short rests may be necessary every now and then, but be sure to stop at different places, otherwise he will soon form the habit of stopping always at that place and it will become increasingly difficult to get him to keep moving. Plenty of puffing and sweating is a good way of beginning to get a horse fit (chapter 10), build up the muscles, particularly on their quarters, and put no strains on the legs.

Many people believe that such work, pulling with the shoulders, encourages the horse to put more weight on his fore hand and consequently it is more difficult to get him to use his hind legs and pull himself together, raise his head to do more collected work. I have found in our versatile horses, who have to do everything, including dressage up to at least advanced medium standard (and some now Grand Prix) that this has never been a problem; the problem, as always, is whether the rider knows what she is doing to ask the horse to get himself together. It is not that the horse cannot do it, particularly as he has to develop serious muscles in his quarters after some draught work, and consequently should find using them to carry a little more of his weight, and bending his hocks easier.

One note of caution: keep a careful eye that the collar or breast plate does not rub. Even without the skin breaking, it can be sore and discourage the horse from draught work. We usually start the youngsters rather carefully on heavy work for this reason. A useful tip is to rub the skin under the collar or breast plate with methylated or surgical spirit for a week or two before starting work, to harden up the skin. With constant work, though, the skin quickly adapts, even on the thinnest skinned Arab. It is worth remembering that if your horse is being uncharacteristically difficult or unrelaxed when working, it may be because the collar or breast plate is rubbing: sore skin can usually be identified by being slightly hotter than the surrounding part.

If you have a second horse, pony or donkey, you might like to progress to working them as a pair, because much of the work may need more pulling power, or at least can be done faster with two.

Personally, I don't like walking behind much, so I tend to ride on one of the harrowing horses. The grand thing here is that one can trot when harrowing, and what good exercise it is for the horse/s; an hour pulling a decent set of harrows, and they have had a good physiological workout, with no mechanical damage to their feet as they are on soft ground and going slowly, and on top of all this there is a necessary job done. A fine way of practising one's singing too without anyone hearing, except for the critical ears of the horses!

Omeya learnt to do simple work by herself. She was hitched up in the field and sent off around it, while the person relaxed sitting in the middle. Some bits were done more than others and some bits missed, but the general principle of covering the field she understood, and could be directed by hand signs and voice if she had left out a piece. There is little doubt this teaching could be developed much further for both equine and human.

There is now a small revival of using heavy horses at least in forestry.

Safety

Throughout this chapter we have emphasised safety, and it must be repeated that teaching an equine to be driven or work in draught is dangerous, like most other things with horses, but provided the elementary teaching has been well done, and various golden rules for safety are observed, there is no need to worry any more than when backing a young equine.

THE GOLDEN RULES OF SAFETY

(1) Make sure the harness is minimal, appropriately designed, and comfortable, strong and safe, and he is accustomed to all of it before you put the equine to an implement or vehicle. If you use a bridle with blinkers, make sure that the equine is very used to them.

(2) Ensure the horse has been well co-operatively handled and has a strong trusting relationship with humans, and particularly the teacher.

3) Take the teaching in stages, and ensure that he is relaxed with each one in different situations, before going onto the next.

(4) Teach the equine to stop and stand still if things go wrong, and make sure he will remain still while you sort it out.

(5) Ensure that you have a helper who can act fast but not be flustered or nervous.

(6) Never walk between the implement and the equine as you are attaching it.

(7) Always have a breeching, or a brake with a wheeled implement to ensure it cannot run into the equine's heels.

(8) Make sure when working the horse that he does not step over the traces; if he does he must have learnt to stand still.

(9) Make sure that you can stop the horse in an emergency, but be very careful not to hang onto the reins as this will make him nervous and excited.

(10) Make sure you have thought about the location and what is going on there before you start driving or working the horse so that you have a plan and schedule for his improvement.

(11) Start him working with a reasonably heavy implement or object so that he tires relatively quickly and does not want to rush off, and continue to work him until he is relaxed. When equines are attached to the implement, never let go of the long reins. Have some help from someone who goes to the equine's head or unhitches the implement, don't do it yourself as you hold the reins.

(12) Being to the side of the implement or behind is a lot less dangerous than in front. Consequently, always have at least one person to help you put to and unhitch, even with experienced horses. Two helpers with an inexperienced horse: one to take his head, one to unhitch while you hold the reins.
(13) Never leave a horse (unless it has worked for years in harness and is quiet and reliable in any situation) standing by himself in an agricultural implement, unless he is held or tied up.

It is essential to work together with your horse on these sorts of jobs, particularly if he is a reactive, energetic soul. It is necessary to cue into his intentions and next likely actions. Often the job goes on for some time; all the time one has to be aware of him, his reactions and the whole environment around in order to predict his next actions. In the process one really gets to know the personality of one's work mate, and begins to appreciate the world around in a way which concentrates more on how the horse may be doing this. The difference from the human workplace is one can often choose one's work mates.

There are few better moments than stopping for lunch under a tree after harrowing half the field, absorbing the thin spring sun, with a lump of bread and cheese and a large mug of coffee, observing one's work mate tucking in to some flowering dandelions. It does not have to be just romantic stuff, 'the stuff that dreams are made on'; it can be a reality, anywhere any time. These experiences with your horse are not worth missing out on because you must rush off to a competition with him in a human dominated environment.

Rendle, C. 1996. 'Appropriate harness and implements for working equines. Symposium on Working Equines'. Rabat. *Eco Research Centre. Paper 15b.*

12

Problems

Throughout this book, I have tried to point out how to use the information that we have about equine mentality and behaviour (see *Equine Lore & Horse Behaviour* for more details) in order to improve how we educate them. However, in the nature of things, this will not always have been done as well as it can be. Both you and I, as well as the present and past handlers of each equine, may have made mistakes. There is no let out by blaming 'others'. The task of the good educator is, whatever the problem, to find a way of overcoming it, and improving the life of the horse and his general education. However much 'others' are blamed, the problem does not go away. It is like being a parent. Those who have no children are for ever giving advice to those who have. The vast majority of parents want to get it as right as they can for their children, but we often get it wrong. The one way in which the problem of a horse or a child can improve is by thinking carefully about it, how it may have been caused, whether the present environment is as good as it can be, how to improve it, and then how to set about reducing or curing the problem. To escape by blaming someone else, whether this is a human or a horse, or his genes, for his unpleasant or undesired behaviour only ensures that the problem grows. So, first, consider how he lives and is kept and whether the environment fulfils all that particular individual's needs (see pages 18-20); then, think about how he is being taught and what type of contact he has with humans. This must of course include an analysis of your own behaviour as well as that of anyone else involved. It is a difficult thing to do, particularly when you are older and a professional, to admit to yourself, and to others, that you have, and continue to make mistakes; perhaps you have changed your mind, but it is only people who are able to do this who can be respected in any field.

We know that the vast majority of behavioural problems in equines are not genetic or the result of some physiological problem. Only a very small percentage of behavioural peculiarities in equines are related to abnormality or damage to the brain, because those that are likely to have such problems have been heavily selected against (they died *in utero* or when very young); we do not know as much about equine neuro-anatomy and physiology as we do about human neuro-medicine and do not try and keep them alive. In addition, equines are considered more disposable so mentally or physically handicapped animals die or are culled.

But there are some behavioural problems that may have a physical basis, head shaking for example. This may be the result of irritation by parasites in the ears, or it may be a behavioural problem, the result of frequent frustration of the horse which has then become a habit and is performed at all sorts of times. If you have any suspicion that a problem may have some physical basis, then the first thing is to have the equine checked for physical problems by a vet who specialises in these.

> A young woman bought an Arab mare, but found that she was bad tempered and then she fell when she rode her out once. She discussed the problem with her friends who suggested she should consult an alternative therapist about it. The alternative therapist (actually I think there were about four of them) declared that the mare had a bad back, and this was giving her real pain. The last one, a 'horse communicator', told her that the mare was in such pain, it was very unlikely she would ever be able to ride her, and in fact perhaps 'for her own good' she should be put down! This the young inexperienced woman found very upsetting, but she believed it. She told me about it. After some questioning, it turned out that the mare was athletic in the field, that she galloped about, was sound, and even leaped around. I asked her if she had consulted a vet and had the horse thoroughly inspected and x-rayed if necessary to find out exactly what the back problem was(if there was one, which I rather suspected from her account that there was not). She said she had not consulted a veterinary surgeon at all. The next week I heard that she had had a vet inspect the horse, and he could find nothing physically wrong which even warranted an x-ray. The problem, as I had expected, was behavioural: the mare had learnt, or been taught, that by wincing, moving away when touched, and being very bad tempered, the humans went away and left her alone, a much more pleasant arrangement, from her point of view .... Little did she know that such behaviour was balancing her on the edge of being killed. The cure was to teach her – by reversal learning - that being handled and ridden by humans was *fun* not unpleasant.

There are many examples of this type that I could quote, this is just the latest in a long series. This is not to say that all alternative therapists are not knowledgeable or able to do their job, the problem is to sort out the one who does, from the one who does not. The easiest way is to go *first to the vets to have the horse physically inspected*. Thereafter you can take your choice. I am biased of course, and would suggest that the person most likely to be able to help you with a behavioural problem is an equine behaviour consultant who is properly qualified and with experience (not true of all of them either, just because they have helped Lord X or the Queen does not mean they know their job all that well!).

There is also a problem with vets, I am only too aware. Far too many of them believe that they know a great deal about handling, teaching, how to keep the equine, and all aspects of behaviour, and they will pontificate about it rarely with a basis of specialised knowledge (vets generally have around 3 lectures, if they are lucky, on the behaviour of horses, and one afternoon learning how to handle, usually taught by another vet who may not be very good at it!). Many a time a vet will recommend euthanasia for an animal with a behavioural problem when it is really quite simple to cure or at least reduce the problem. So consult vets on their expertise – the physical problems – and consult equine behaviour consultants about behaviour problems (if s/he is any good, and knows her job, she will recommend that if the problem could be a physical one; you go and consult the vet first and if there is not one, come back to her). There is a move now in the English speaking world at least to allow only the animal behaviour consultants who take cases recommended by the vets to be registered as fully 'qualified'. This means that a vet must be consulted first (and earns a considerable sum). He then recommends the client to take the horse to a behavioural consultant if it is not a physical problem. This may be alright in the above example (although people are loth to have to pay twice without sometimes having much improvement) but the problem is that there are many behavioural problems that are nothing to do with a physical problem; so it would be a waste of time and money consulting a vet about, unless he is also a qualified animal behaviour consultant.

> Mrs J. had a horse that would not enter a trailer. She took the horse to the vet, hoping that he would give her a drug to fix it. The vet told her that there was not a drug that was likely to work, and that she must consult an equine behavioural consultant.

In this case, the vet behaved appropriately, but, alas, many of them do not in such cases, and do give drugs for 'mis-behaviour' which will not cure the problem. Vets should stick to physical problems, behavioural consultants to behavioural ones, and respect each other's areas of expertise. The same should apply to all the other various alternative therapists.

When thinking about behavioural problems of equines, it is very important not to get stuck in a rut, a dogma of one's own, or to adopt someone else's without very careful evaluation. This is difficult, as humans can develop a 'habit of mind' to accept the way things happen without question. The habit of mind to encourage is one where questions are always being asked and answers pondered, much harder work than just assuming what you are told without question.

When confronted by a behavioural, and sometimes a physical problem of a horse, it is important first of all to try and understand the fundamental cause and then, by removing the cause, work on achieving a cure. This may seem common sense, but an in depth assessment of the cause for that individual by looking at their total environment is necessary. This approach when treating humans' mental disorders was first publicised by R. D. Laing (1960), and has been, at least in part, adopted by psychiatrists and psychotherapists. For the treatment of equines it is invaluable.

The truth is that *we do know* how the vast majority of 'misbehaviours' of equines are caused, and we definitely can design environments and educational strategies where they do not occur in the next generation, if we really want to. We do not need further money spent on research in order to try and excuse particular husbandry practises because they are traditional or convenient.

In the last two decades, there has been considerable amount of research money spent on stereotypies in stabled horses – in the region of £500,000. Stereotypies are repeated actions that are apparently purposeless, and include things like wind sucking, crib biting and weaving. In the late 60s and early 70s there was some research already published on stereotypies in equines and in other animals and humans in similar restricted conditions, and the causes were outlined. Little if anything more has been discovered since even though almost every equine research scientist has published a paper on stereotypies, and many degree students as well. The truth is, as we all know deep down, that keeping an equine shut up in a stable, isolated from others, with little to do for long periods, and often nothing to eat for many hours means that, although the equine may be physically healthy, he is not mentally. Like humans, rhinos, elephants or foxes in similar situations, he invents something to do to give himself some stimulus. We need never have another animal develop a stereotypie if we change the way we keep them, but we do not want to, so the research is performed to try and excuse our practices, rather than trying to improve them. Inventing 'horse balls' or giving them special drugs to stop them doing it, or even, cutting the muscles in the neck (a practice used much in the US) to prevent them, is not what science should be about. We know why horses perform them; no more research is needed.

What we do need is to change the way we keep our horses. This would solve many behavioural problems, inconvenient though it may be. There are many many examples: another that springs to mind is in the breeding of equines: infertility in mares and loss of libido in stallions who are never allowed to court or have natural sex as a matter of choice. The mare is raped and the stallion has been taught to copulate the twitched, tied up and hobbled mare ... Any normal male of many species, including humans, might find this a little unrewarding after a few hundred times, and give up sex, if they could.

We now know quite a lot about how equines learn, and something about what they can learn – which is a great deal more than we thought. We have some idea of their mental life and their emotions, although many questions still remain. But if we give the benefit of any doubt to equines, we can design their education so that we do not have problems, or if we have them we can put them right by changing our teaching or handling.

One thing is clear: if we are to progress and learn more about our equines and how to educate them better, we need individuals who analyse their own behaviour, think about how they keep and teach their equines. We could redesign equine environments and teaching tomorrow so they have no behavioural problems, or very few. The real problem is whether we want to.

We can do this if we use a **conditional anthropomorphic approach,** that is recognise our mammalian similarities, then mould this by an awareness of what we know of the species differences and the slightly different worlds we live in. In this way, we can ensure the horse has a happy, healthy life and is an educated, delightful companion.

Many people on visiting our stud, or seeing the horses perform somewhere will shrug their shoulders and either believe that we are sort of magicians, that we are so talented that it would be impossible for them to have horses who can do all these things, or that we are just lucky and have horses that 'behave perfectly' because of their genes. None of these is true: it is not luck, magic, talent or genes. It is the result of persistence, motivation and hard work to find a way of doing everything we want with our horses . Learning from our own mistakes, that is 'experience', has also been very important. We have had problems and made mistakes. (I have pointed out some of these in the text.) By thinking about mistakes, it is easier to put them right, nip them in the bud, correct one's own behaviour or the type of life that animal is leading which may be contributing to the problem.

Everyone wants an instant recipe: 'my pony knocks my son with his head when he is just talking nicely to him, what do I do?' Think about it, think about what you know about equines, about his life, about how your son is behaving, about how the equine learns, and then **change things** to ensure that the pony does not want to do this. This approach is about solving it for yourself, thinking about it trying things, and not just listening to someone else who may or may not have the solution.

Clues towards understanding the fundamental cause of the problem can be gained by asking the following questions:-
(i) What is wrong in his environment from his point of view? Are all his needs being fulfilled? The answers are dealt with in more detail in *Equine Lore*.
(ii) What has he learnt from past experience?
(iii) Consequently, how do we re-teach him?
To summarise:
Ensure that the way he is kept fulfils his various needs: physical, social., emotional, cognitive/ intellectual. If they do not, work out practical ways within your circumstances and his situations that will more closely fulfil them. Observe, self-analyse and put effort and time into changing things. If we understand why he is not doing what is required, we can make sure this does not happen again. But it may require time and, certainly, motivation before there is improvement.

We all make mistakes, but we can learn from them. Here is another of mine:

Some 25 years ago, I loaded my young Anglo-Arab stallion Baksheesh (three years old) into a trailer for the first time. He was kept with mares, and easy to handle, confident and relaxed with humans. He walked in quietly and well. The trailer did not have a canvas over the roof, and he was able to stick his head up through the roof trusses, he hit his head, and was hurt and scared. I was young and inexperienced, but nevertheless, the reason for problems loading thereafter was quite obvious. It did not need an 'expert' to tell me, nor did it need an 'expert' to tell me how to put it right. All I had to do was to convince him this would not happen again. It took me a while to do this, largely because I was lazy and did not do enough loading and short journeys in a trailer with a roof. It was a stupid mistake and I was slack about correcting it, although it was obvious what I had to do.

The first step is to admit the mistake, and then try and put it right.

Equines do not come from Mars, it is not a complete mystery how they think, what they know, how they learn, what they need. They are very like us, which is why we like them. But in some ways they are different. If we critically assess what we observe and review what is generally known about equines, we can learn more about their 'world view' which will help us solve their behavioural problems, help us teach them better and quicker and in addition, enrich our own lives and appreciation of the world.

The equine, or human being, is the result of a fusion of both the body and the mind. There are problems which have their origin in 'mind problems', psychological problems which show themselves physically. There are also problems which have their origin in the body (physical ones) but show themselves in behavioural problems ('mind' problems). Thus, if the equine is constantly frustrated, frightened, worried or anxious he is likely to become physically ill, as well as behave in undesirable ways. If he is frequently physically ill, it is not helpful just to treat the disease with the appropriate medicines, it is crucial that the entire environment is looked at and assessed for its appropriateness (or lack of it) for the equine's body and mind needs.

A typical series of developments of a serious behavioural problem.
The first thing is to look at the animal's environment and the degree to which his needs are or are not fulfilled. Individuals vary in how closely these needs need to be fulfilled. What might cause no problem for one animal may well be a source of continual distress to another. But we do have a way of monitoring if we have things right for that particular equine; if it is not right, he will show **distress** (see page 23). If he is distressed, for whatever reason, he will not learn fast, will be more likely to be physically ill as well as have behavioural problems.

Having said this, however, there always have to be caveats, and well known reasons why things cannot be rendered 'perfect'. These are usually:-
(1) It may not be possible to fulfil all of his needs completely in the situation in which the equine lives, but this is not the point. It is nevertheless, **always** possible to make improvements ... if the owner or trainer really wants to. This is where the trouble lies.
(2) If improvements are made, but the problem remains, then consider whether it is related to **fear,** particularly fear of the unfamiliar, whether this is a process, a place, another individual, a human, or all of these. If he is allowed time to investigate and get used to the situation without negative reinforcement (which will enhance his fear or anxiety), the problem will usually disappear, although this will take time and commitment from the handlers.
(3) Equines, like humans, prefers a straightforward, problem-free, easy life. If when he stops, bites, kicks or does what ever else is undesirable, he is frequently hit, shouted at, or his head pulled about, the second phase of his learning begins as a result of the handlers inappropriate teaching. **The equine's fear of the situation is confirmed:** it is frightening and dangerous. As a result, he is less likely to do what is that is required, and more likely to do something that is not, including

being aggressive, over reactive, leaping about and so on. Eventually if this treatment continues, he may panic hysterically, make greater efforts to escape such as rearing, bucking, kicking, biting, persistent heading throwing and shaking or bolting.

(4) Once the horse has done one of these undesired things, and the problem has gone away (for example, he has been taken away or the rider has fallen or got off) then the next phase is entered into: **the handler/ rider has begun to teach him/her to do the wrong thing.** The equine learns quickly that by behaving in this undesired way, he achieves his goal which is not to have to do whatever has been asked. This is *not* because he is 'trying to get away with it', or 'dominate you' but because the original cause of fear and anxiety has been confirmed. When his solution works, he will repeat it again in similar circumstances, even with greater vigour, so it may become increasingly undesirable (from the human's point of view), sometimes dangerous. This undesired behaviour has then become a habit.

(5) Finally **he will begin to generalise this behaviour** and do it in a wide range of situations when he does not want to do this or that. He may not be unduly frightened at this stage, but he will have learnt, by associative learning, that the behaviour achieves the goal he requires. Hitting and shouting at him is unlikely to stop the behaviour, indeed it may frighten him further and cause him to renew it even more. A better solution is to work out why he does not want to do whatever is asked, remove this cause, and substitute an enjoyable pleasant outcome immediately he begins to do it, so that he is rewarded for *not* doing the undesired behaviour, rather than punished for *not* doing the desired thing.

This will have to be repeated and repeated as, of course, he has developed a 'habit of mind' by this time and it will be difficult to undermine, but it is always possible. Use your own common sense, understanding and judgement and work at it. If you begin to believe he is just being 'silly', or 'trying it on' and start punishing him, you will probably end up having to have the horse put down as being 'dangerous'.

It takes commitment and hard work to correct something the equine has learnt to do wrong. It is much easier to avoid him learning the wrong thing in the first place. This book has been how to do this. The main points are:

(a) Making sure that all his needs are fulfilled.

(b) His behavioural restriction is minimum for the majority of the day, every day.

(c) Recognise that mental stimulation is very important and cater for it by giving him intellectual/cognitive challenges and problems. One simple way of doing this is to give him many different types of work to do and things to learn. Many examples are given in this book

(d) Show him that learning and education with humans is exciting and fun, rather than frightening, boring and repetitious. By understanding how equines (and humans) learn and using reward rather than negative reinforcement and punishment and other ideas that originated when improving the teaching of children, co-operative teaching can be achieved.

(e) It helps to divide the teaching into the 'what' it is you want, the ' that' and when they have understood the basic concept, the 'how' to do it.

(f) The equine is capable of learning to comprehend much language, and performs many of the mental tasks that humans do. He has a some what different, but nevertheless complex mental life, and can learn very fast if well taught.

(g) Training equines with violence, trying to dominate, or be 'the leader' is not in line with their comprehension of the world, and likely to lead to fear not co-operative 'doing it because I want to' performance.

(h) Equines can learn many more things than is usually thought they can, and their behaviour, like ours, is the result of a mix of their instinctive tendencies and past experiences. We know they are conscious at some levels, make decisions and choices, and acquire a great deal of knowledge during their lives. The result of this is that we can enrich our own lives greatly when we teach them or have much to do with them by glimpsing their equally complex, but different, world view.

In this way one can avoid behavioural problems and work towards preventative equine psychology by practising co-operative equine education!

There are many ways of making life more enjoyable for a horse, particularly when you remember that his joys and fun will not only come from associating with other horses, or running around loose, but also from association with humans who like him and he likes and trusts. He likes to learn new things and attract praise from people, particularly those he knows and likes.

One of the most common sources of what are considered 'behavioural problems' in the horse have their origin in the handler or rider's fear. The human is frightened of the horse, of what might happen, of thinking about how to progress, and inadvertently, this is conveyed to the horse through body language, he becomes anxious. The first thing to understand is to recognise your own fear, admit it and then only do what gives you confidence with him. In the process you will get to know him better, and gradually your confidence will grow until you can do other things. The first thing is to build up one's confidence with older, smaller, confident equines who have already been educated. Be open to learn from them, rather than considering you must 'be in control' and organise them.

There are undesirable behaviours the equine may perform which are **the result of bad riding,** such as bolting, head in the air, hollow backed, or leaping and bucking around excitedly. A good riding teacher will be able to put those right by encouraging the rider's balance, communication and rhythm. But it is very difficult for humans as well as horses to change their habits so ensure if you are beginning to learn to ride that you are being taught to ride co-operatively, it is so much easier to learn correctly from the beginning than have to put problems right later. Another important thing is to find a teacher whom you like and whose method you respect, and stick with her/him. It is not at all helpful, even at an advanced level, to swap from teacher to teacher as there are many different roads that will lead to the same goal. Mixing up the methods just causes confusion for rider, and horse.

One thing that, in the great majority of cases, is not appropriate, is the use of drugs to try and overcome equine behavioural problems. There are very occasionally some helpful results of using a tranquilliser, but the equine still has to learn not to behave in the way he generally does in that situation without the tranquilliser. It is just taking time and being careful not to put anyone at risk that will begin to make progress in the desired direction, whether this is trying to handle a wild zebra, load a thoroughbred who has had a car crash before, teach an Arab to pull a set of harrows that he ran away with last time, or a horse to stand still and wait while one gets on.

Young horses learn to do the right thing remarkably quickly, if they are given the appropriate education. Even the youngster being ridden out for the first time need not be frightened and jump or tense up at all. He may even be able to take the lead of the bunch at some stage, and rapidly learns to balance the rider up and down hills and follow others through difficult places. But if the equine's needs and desires are not well understood, he will learn equally fast to do the wrong thing.

The bottom line, however, is it is not difficult to keep him in appropriate conditions and educate him well so he does not have behavioural problems.

Equine educational psychology. How to improve the teaching of equines for the thinking horse-person.
Through the ages there have been good teachers who have taught equines many extraordinary things. What we have attempted to do is to articulate how they have done this by a careful consideration of 'what it might be like' to be an equine; how they learn; and apply this to how we teach them, as well as how we keep them. There is no doubt that this new science can and will develop further, the aim here is to launch it and to have empirical studies as well as people from all backgrounds and levels of experience directed towards this aim. For a start, we have drawn up some general rules to help with teaching, but it must be emphasised that progress will be made by a willingness to self analyse as well as by trying out different approaches within the general rules of how we know that equines (and humans) learn and how to teach them (chapter 3, page 67). We will list these rules once more:

GENERAL RULES FOR EQUINE EDUCATION, AND A WAY OF REMEMBERING THEM

'More Pleasure Attending Accurately to Very Consistent Clear Instructions for Horses'

That is:

(1) **M**otivate the equine to want to do what you are asking because he will receive some reward.

(2) **P**ositive reinforcement is the best way to learn. Food, the voice, pats and strokes and all of these used at the appropriate time are very effective.

(3) **A**ttention of both the teacher and the equine is crucial.

(4) **A**ssociative learning is one of the easiest ways for equines to learn.

(5) **V**oice is very useful, and can be used to express emotion and for words with particular meanings.

(6) **C**onsistent cues are essential.

(7) **C**larity, and creativity in teaching is important.

(8) **I**nnovation in what and how you teach is very helpful.

(9) **F**amiliarity of the equine with the situation will reduce fear.

(10) **H**abits form fast in equines.

Equines, just like humans are, as we all know, individuals, the result of both their nature and their nurture. This makes it particularly interesting for the teacher, because, although there are some general rules (as above) that apply to all equines, superimposed on these are ways of teaching that may work well for one, but not for another, so one has to adapt, invent, try out, and rethink when teaching. My students, equines and non equines, never cease to teach, amuse, delight and surprise me, as well of course as trying my patience and frustrating me ... the latter are my problems. Let us not be over romantic; as with humans, there are some horse individuals that one likes more than others, in fact some one may not like much at all, not all are saints, but equally not all are 'stupid beasts'.

A problem that emerges for many, is that people are not consistent and clear enough concerning both what they would like and what they expect from an equine. Either they are slightly frightened of the equine, or they indulge him one day and then not the next. Soon the equine may learn that he can call the tune; if he does not like to have one area of his body touched, and the handler, instead of continuing slowly and quietly to do this, avoids it, soon the equine learns that if he moves away or puts his ears back or even bites her, she does not try again. The horse has taught the person. In this case the horse needs to be told in one way or another that this will not do, and that the human has needs and desires too, one of which is not to be hurt, which the equine must respect, and equally the human teacher will not hurt the horse. The easiest way to do this is to talk crossly to him when he looks as if he will bite and then continue, quietly and with thoughtfulness, do whatever it is you are trying to do. However, if he continues to bite or kick, then a redirection of his attention, and a swift and surprising response from you may be necessary for him to understand that you also have needs and desires, and one of them is not to be hurt by him. Hitting something to make a noise may help here, or pressing a clock alarm to make a loud and sudden noise when he lunges at you will help. Afterwards, it is necessary to give plenty of praise and reward when he does *not* do it when you approach again, and think he might. If all else fails, because the horse has developed such a habit of doing this, then a rapid cuff at him when he lunges at the person together with a furious angry shout (one motivated by anger) will certainly take him by surprise. If he fails to repeat it, then praise him and reward him.

Hitting an equine is by no means something that should be advised, but the cause of a problem of biting or kicking humans is often that this bad behaviour has been taught; one quick negative reinforcement may help the horse rethink, but before doing this, be sure that the behaviour is not the result of fear. It must also not be repeated, one short hard clack can be followed by a growl or serious 'no' when the equine looks as if he might attack. When he does not, plenty of praise and even a tit bit will help. In the long run the correction will be in the horse's interest, as well as the humans. But, the important point is that your relationship should never have got to this point.

Studying and applying what we know about 'what it might be to be an equine' can lead us to designing husbandry conditions and teaching so that there are no behavioural problems with equines, but the really fun thing is that it leads us to an appreciation of other's world views. It is fashionable to say how much equines have taught one about 'oneself'. If this means to think about one's own behaviour in relation to them, then indeed they certainly do this, and consequently help to educate humans. But, they can teach us other new things and enrich our lives greatly. They have taught me an enormous amount about many things in the world and to view them in new ways.

Equine thinking is not controlled, like ours, by language which is linear, that is it progresses through a sentence and you cannot understand what is being said until the end of the sentence. By contrast, equines are acutely aware of the whole world around them at any one time, and pick up a whole series of messages from another, including a human, instantly. They are very good observers, and one of the things they have taught me is to observe better, and not just concentrate on what is being said by who, but pay attention to this and the whole world around at the same time. They have taught me in this way to be very much more aware of the world around.

By their sheer physical beauty, energy, strength, athleticism, and particularly their mental attributes, they have enormously enriched my life, and will continue to do this every new day, as many other people also find.

The more one learns about them and 'what it might be' to be an equine, the more options of 'world views' one has, and the more delight in being alive. Even after 35 years of studying our group of the Druimghigha Stud, almost every day there is something surprising that happens in the equine soap opera, a similar yet different one from the human one I live in, that takes me by surprise. One thing is clear: they have taught me (through experiences living with them, teaching them and studying them empirically) not to be so sure that the belief that humans are cognitively/mentally superior to other mammals can be assumed. More and more questions about the world and its interpretation are posed as a result of our association with equines, as well as the emotional delight many of us have from our association with them, or the fun of galloping, jumping, or doing anything with them, riding, driving or just having them as companions and friends. We have much more we need to learn about how to educate them better, but the most important point of this book is to make you question the way you have been taught, think about it and try and see if you cannot improve it. You will be surprised as the results, I can guarantee.

REFERENCES
Bortof, H. 1996. *The wholeness of Nature. Goethe's way of science*. Floris books. Edinburgh.
Braddon-Mitchell, B. D. , & F. Jackson. 1996. *Philosophy of mind and cognition*. Blackwells. Oxford. British Horse Society. 1982. *Horse Management*. BHS. Stoneleigh.
Burghardt, J. M. 1991. 'Cognitive ethology and critical anthropomorphism. A snake with

two heads and hog-nosed snakes that plays dead', in: *Cognitive Ethology.* ed: C. A. Ristau. Erlbaum. Hillsdale.

Fisher, J. A. 1991. 'Disambiguating anthropomorphism: an inter-disciplinary review', *Perspectives in Ethology.* 9. p124-35

Griffin, D. R. 1992. *Animal Minds.* Univ. Chicago Press.

Hickman, J. 1984. *Horse Management.* Academic Press. London.

Bortof, H. 1996. *The wholeness of Nature. Goethe's way of science.* Floris books. Edinburgh.

Braddon-Mitchell, B. D. , & F. Jackson. 1996. *Philosophy of mind and cognition.* Blackwells. Oxford. British Horse Society. 1982. *Horse Management.* BHS. Stoneleigh.

Burghardt, J. M. 1991. 'Cognitive ethology and critical anthropomorphism. A snake with two heads and hog-nosed snakes that plays dead', in: *Cognitive Ethology.* ed: C.A. Ristau. Erlbaum. Hillsdale.

Fisher, J. A. 1991. 'Disambiguating anthropomorphism: an inter-disciplinary review', *Perspectives in Ethology.* 9. p124-35

Griffin, D. R. 1992. *Animal Minds.* Univ. Chicago Press.

Hickman, J. 1984. *Horse Management.* Academic Press. London.

THE INDIVIDUALS IN THE EXPERIMENTAL EQUINE HERD

It all began in 1959 when I was 16. We had recently returned from East Africa, where I was bought up, and bought a farm in East Sussex. I bought a crib biting, 8 year old, 16. 2hh beautiful chestnut thoroughbred mare from a friend of my father's with my £40 post office savings. Her registered name with Wetherby's was 'Stirrup Cup', I later found out, but I called her 'Kathiawar'. She was an ex-racehorse who had been kept in an isolated box all her life from weaning through training, and had become a crib biter and unmanageable. I later discovered she had been sold on as dangerous and unpredictable. She had reared over backwards with various people, and, as is often the way, had ended up, before I had her, in the hands of some unsuspecting novices who had a horse to convince their shooting friends they were really 'of the countryside'. They never rode her, and were relieved to have her off their hands. I had had Somali ponies and Arab horses in Kenya where we had adventured with them in what would now be considered wild ways.

A large thoroughbred was a new beginning. I did not know much, but I had no fear, and could stay on almost whatever happened. Kathiawar and I got to know Sussex quite well, and then started forays out to shows to jump, which I discovered she could do well. I had no money, but managed to borrow a single horse trailer from an aunt, and my mother's small car to pull it, and between school and university, I spent a year helping on the farm, reading the classics and riding Kathiawar. We went to many shows, always putting in a great effort and with clean equipment, but it was not the right type! I could not afford the right coloured beeches and all the rest of it, but nevertheless, we won in gymkhana races and jumping, qualifying for national championships, and so on. Kathiawar was not keen on getting into the trailer, particularly coming home. As a rather shy teenager, I did not like to ask people to help, particularly since they had always been so rude to me during the day (with that very particular sneering sniff that the 'horsey people' in the UK sometimes, even now, have). This took me by surprise, since in Kenya we did not go in for that sort of behaviour. No one ever offered to help me, few ever talked to me ... but we continued to win, or lead the field over fences the huntsmans' horses would not jump in our few forays out hunting. At the end of that summer, I vowed I would never have to do with any of these 'horsey people' again, at least until I would be old enough to give as good as I got. The next 25 years were spent in learning about equines in practice, breeding and studying them through academic channels (it was 25 years later when I next went to a horse competition in the UK; by then I could give as good as I got, and still did not have the right equipment or money). When I left for a University in Scotland, Kathiawar visited a local Crabbet Arab stallion. The following year, when the Syringa was out in May, she produced

(Above)Omeya, one of the
foundation pure-bred Arab mares
(Genzi x Zumana). Mother of
Oberlix and Oryx, placed in 100
m solstice (7th), marathon (twice),
dressage, flat racing, worked the
land, driving, a great companion
and friend with superb paces,
beauty and personality.
(Above right) Cariff, son of
Crystal and Cherif. Muddy but
definitely Arab. He performed
dance, long reining, driving, long
distance, jumping cross country,
taught and was a real gentleman
of the highest order.
(Right) Shella (Shereen x Oberlix),
at one year. A large boned lovely
filly, born in 1997 and still
growing up.

(Above) *Agean in front (a filly, Aisha x Oberlix), now grown and doing well in endurance, and Shukrune (1994, Shiraz x Oberlix) who has so far not competed, but is ridden over Dartmoor.*
(Below) *Crystannah Royal (Crystal King X Hannah of Fairfield), a pure-bred Arab we bought at an auction , the mother of Cariff. Here she is at 6, now 26. She competed in the AHS marathon, 50 mile races, dressage, jumping, cross country and taught many people, worked the land, and featured in many pictures. The chestnut is Shiraz (aged 6 here)(Baksheesh X Sheba; 3/8th Arab, 1/8th thoroughbred, 50% Irish draught, older sister to Shereen. She won in ride and tie, long distance, placed in the marathon, dressage, jumping, taught, worked the land, driving classes, and so on. She was the first of our horses who we could put in a plough one day and win a race the next.*

Syringa. By then I was back in Africa researching wild animals, and my long-suffering dairy-farming mother was looking after the two of them. Eventually, she rightly announced that I must sell one. I sold Kathiawar to the New Forest, and when eventually I returned to the UK to further studies, babies intervened and Syringa visited another Arab stallion: Harwood Asif from the Harwood stud. The result was Baksheesh, an Anglo-Arab stallion (3/4 Arab 1/4 thoroughbred), one of my most important mentors.

We moved to the Cuckmere valley in Sussex, and started an ecological farm and there was room for a small herd of horses: Sheba, a white Irish draught 18-year-old mare (who was said to have leukaemia) was bought for a song, and came to stay. I bought six Welsh mountain pony weanlings at an auction in Wales while my friends were in the pub. All but one we sold on, but Aderin, a section A registered wild Welsh mountain pony weanling joined us.

Sheba and Baksheesh produced a series of foals; we kept Shiraz and Shereen who became the important performing and breeding mares of the next generation. Baksheesh and Aderin produced a string too, Achmed, a gelding we retained for 5 years, Alia and Aisha Evans among others. Aisha Evans we retained for her long life.

The first letter of the horse's name refers to their mother's family, so relationships are evident. All the S's relate back to Sheba, the A's to Aderin.

After a few years of saving, my partner and I decided to go to the Arab Horse Society auction and try and buy a pure-bred Arab filly, something I had wanted for many years. We went and bought Crystal (Crysthannah Royal), a sensible pretty two-year-old. But, then Omeya, all slimness and bones, floating action, staring eyes and blowing nose, came in to the ring. We had no more money, Chris turned to me and said he would buy her, so we bought her for £700 as a three-year-old. It was only afterwards that I realised that Chris had no money either, but who cared, we had Omeya!

Crystal had four foals, and then my arm was twisted and she was sold on at the age of 20 to one of my ex-research students in Devon, but we see her still, and, aged 28, she is still competing in 25 mile(40km) endurance rides – and obtaining Grade 1s.. Omeya stayed with us until her death aged 24. Both Crystal and Omeya produced foals that we kept. Crystal x Cherif (a pure-bred Arab to whom we were given a reduced covering because of our performance successes) produced Cariff, the next generation of our pure-bred Arab stallions who stayed with us until his death (aged 15). The C and the O families were established. Crystal produced foals with Baksheesh (e.g Cara, Carma), but, unfortunately, we did not retain either, selling them on as performing horses aged three. Baksheesh and Omeya produced a string: Osnan, Omen and Oscar. Oberlix was by Aboud, a pure-bred Arab exported to Oman, now in Bahrein National Stud. We were given a free service to him because of our performance record. Oryx was Omeya's last foal (by a Friesland stallion).

Baksheesh died in 1987, very sadly at the age of 18, on the Isle of Mull where we and all the livestock had moved in 1983. So then Cariff became our main stallion, and the next generation was founded. In 1989 we moved to Devon and there Cariff and Shiraz, Shereen, Aisha and Omeya produced a string of particularly able and enchanting youngsters, all of whom have been sold on aged three and are performing in many disciplines, some internationally. These included Shere Khan, Shiera, Shirak, Shergar, Omen, Oscar, Amanita, Acolyte and Aroha while Oberlix grew up and then, with Crystal, produced Christmas Time, with Shiraz: Shemal (the princess who features a great deal in this book), Shukrune and Shanti. Shereen produced Shella with Oberlix, and then Shindi and finally Socrates. Young Oryx and Shereen produced Shezam. We bought Lilka from the Lindsays' famous Polish Arab Stud in 2000 as a frightened weanling and future wife for Oberlix to breed some more pure-bred Arabs. They have now produced Luxor, a strapping 2-year-old, and Lilka had a brief affair with Oryx, without our knowing, and produced Liloni, a big sturdy filly. At around the same time, Shindi also had a flirtation with Oryx, while I was away in Cambridge, and to our surprise produced Shenandoah, the 7th generation starting from Kathiawar around Christmas 2004.

In total the stud has bred around 60 youngsters. The horses run out all year around, but have some form of shelter in the winter. From time to time they are shut in yards for short periods when the weather is particularly wet or they are wrecking the fields. They all learn to stay the odd night in a single stable, the mares run with a stallion, and if we have too many males, they form a bachelor herd which is kept separately. We often have two adult stallions at a time, and, consequently, two small herds. We have been studying the behaviour of this group since 1976 (see list of publications), but also competing on them, and educating the youngsters to secondary level (be ridden quietly and do three track work) before we sell them. We have specialised in long distance, dressage and dance, but the horses can turn their hoofs to racing, jumping, cross country, competitive driving, western, and almost any other sport we have tried.

The main thrust of the stud has been to experiment with improved living and teaching conditions, from the equine's point of view. We have studied the economics, monitored closely distress and behavioural problems, assessed fertility, longevity and soundness. The competitions we take part in are partly for fun, but mainly to test whether or not our horses kept and raised in this way can compete with others successfully, internationally if possible. Only by winning competitions will the changes to husbandry and teaching be applied more widely.

Having started as an experiment to learn more about equine behaviour, we have learnt a great deal about their view of the world in this 35-year project, and demonstrated that improvement of equine lives is necessary, practical and of benefit to humans too. Now we are going to continue with the research particularly focusing on advanced learning and teaching: trying to find where the limits might be to what equines can learn, and answering some of the open questions in this book with at least Oberlix, Shemal, Shindi and Oryx. We also are establishing an educational centre and wildlife park in Africa to continue our research and educate local people about animals, working with traditionally wild animals, including zebras and donkeys, elephants, buffalo and eland.

Apart from meeting many delightful people and making the majority of our friends through our equines, the most valuable thing that the horses have done for me is enrich my life by opening my eyes to different world views, something that has no end. If nothing else I hope they will start this process for the reader through this book.

BIBLIOGRAPHY

Anon. *L'equitation, le cheval et l'ethologie. Colloque du 18 Sept 1999 a l'ecole National d'Equitation*. Belin. Paris.

Adam, C. & M. Bekoff. 1997. *Species of Mind*. MIT. Cambs USA.

Barney, E. B. , B. Landjerit & R. Wolter. 1991. 'Shock vibration during the hoof impact on different track survaces'. p97-106 in *Equine Exercise Physiology* 3. ed S. G. B. Persson, A. Lindholm & L. B. Jeffcott. ICEEP publ Davis.

Bateson, P. P. G. 1966. 'The characteristics and context of imprinting', *Biol. Rev.* 41. 177-220. ch8,p2.

Bavidge, T. & G. Ground. 1994. *Can we understand animal minds?* Routledge. London.

Bentham,J. 1789. *Introduction to the principles of morals and legislation*.

Bernstein, I. S. 1981. 'Dominance: the baby and the bathwater', *Behav. Br. Sci.* 4. 419-29. *The Bible*.

Blake, H. 1977. *Thinking with horses*. Souvenir Press. London.

Bonner, J. T. 1980. *The Evolution of Culture in Animals*. Princeton Univ Press. Princeton.

Bortof, H. 1996. *The wholeness of Nature. Goethe's way of science*. Floris books. Edinburgh.

Braddon-Mitchell, B. D. , & F. Jackson. 1996. *Philosophy of mind and cognition*. Blackwells. Oxford.

Brady, E. 1999. 'Sniffing and savoring: the aesthetics of smell and taste', *Philosophy & Geography*. 4.

British Horse Society. 1982. *Horse Management*. BHS. Stoneleigh.

Broom, D. M. & K. G. Johnson 1993. *Stress and Animal Welfare*. Chapman & Hall. London.

Bryne R. & A. Whiten. 1988. *Machiavallian Intelligence. Social Expertise and the Evolution of Intelligence in Monkeys, Apes and Humans*. Oxford Uniersity Press. Oxford.

Buckingham, S. H. W. & L. B. Jeffcott. 1991. 'Skeletal effects of long term submaximal exercise programme on standard-bred yearlings', in *Equine Exercise Physiology* 3. p411-418. ed. S. G. B. Persson, A. Lindholm & L. B. Jeffcott. ICEEP publ. Davis.

Budiansky, S. 1996. 'Don't bet on faster horses', *New Scientist*. 10th August. p 29-31

Burger, U. 1959. *The way to perfect horsemanship*. J. A. Allen. London.

Burghardt, J. M. 1991. 'Cognitive ethology and critical anthropomorphism. A snake with two heads and hog-nosed snakes that plays dead', in: *Cognitive Ethology*. ed: C. A. Ristau. Erlbaum. Hillsdale.

Butler, P. J. ,A. J. Woakes, L. S. Anderson, K. Smale,C. A. Roberts &D. H. Snow. 1991. 'The effect of cessation of trining on caridorespiratory variables during exercise', in *Equine Exercise Physiology* 3. p71-76. ed. S. G. B. Persson. A. Lindholm & L. B. Jeffcott. ICEEP publ Davis.

Candland, D. K. 1993. *Feral Children and Clever animals*. Oxford Univ Press. Oxford.

Chambers, T. 1993. 'Recognition of pain ad distress in horses'. Brit. Vet Ass. Roadshow. *Pain in Practise*. BVA. Plymouth.

Cheney, D. L. & R. M. Seyfarthe 1990. *How Monkeys see the World*. Univ of Chicago Press. Chicago.

Dantzer, R. 1986. 'Behavioural, physiological and functional aspects of stereotyped behaviour: a review and a re-interpretation', *J. Anim. Sci* 62. 1776-1786.

Darwin, C. 1868. *The Expression of the Emotions in Man and Animals*. John Murray. London.

Dawson, F. L. M. S. 1984. 'Equine Reproduction' in *Horse Management*. ed: Hickman. J. p 1-54. Acedemic Press. London.

Declaration of Human Rights. 1948. United Nations. Geneva.

DeGrazia, D. 1996. *Taking Animals Seriously*. CUP. Cambridge.

Dickinson, A. 1994. 'Instrumental conditioning', *in Animal learning and cognition. ed*: N. J.

MacIntosh. Academic Press. San Diego. p 45-79.

Feist,. J. D. & D. R. McCullogh. 1976. 'Behaviour patterns and communication in feral horses', *Tierpsychol.* 2. 41. 337-371.

Fillis,J. 1969 *Breaking and Riding.* trans M. H. Heyes. J. A. Allen London

Fisher, J. A. 1986. 'Taking Sympathy Seriously: A Defense of Our Moral Psychology Towards Animals',*Environ. Ethics.* 198 p197-215.

Fisher, J. A. 1991. 'Disambiguating anthropomorphism: an inter-disciplinary review', *Perspectives in Ethology.* 9. p124-35

Fowler, W. 1990. 'Early stimulation and the development of verbal talents', in *Encouraging the Development of Exceptional Skills and Talents.* ed. M. J. A. Howe. 179-210.

Fox, M. W. 1968. (editor) *Abnormal Behaviour of Animals.* W. B. saunders. N. Y.

Galef, B. J. Jr. 1986. 'Tradition and Social Learning in Animals', *in Animal Intelligence. Insights into the Animal Mind.* ed: R. J. Hoage & L. Goldman. Smithsonian Institution Press. Washington. p149-163.

Gallistel, C. R. 'Representations in Animal Cognition: An Introduction', in *Animal Cognition.* ed: C. R. Gallistel. MIT. Cambridge. Mass.

Griffin, D. R. 1992. *Animal Minds.* Univ. Chicago Press.

Gueriniere, F. R. de la. (1733) 1994. *The School of Horsemanship.* trans T. Boucher. J. A. Allen London.

Haangi, E. B. 1994. 'Serial reversal discrimination learning using shape cues in horses' (*Equus caballus*). *Equine Research Foundation,* California.

Haangi, E. B. 1996. 'Conditional discrimination learning in the horse (*Equus caballus*)', *Equine Research Foundation.* California.

Harris, R. C. ,D. J Marlin & D. H. Snow. 'Lactate kinetics, plasma ammonia and performance following repeated bouts of maximal exercise' p173-178 in *Equine Exercise Physiology 3.* ed. S. G. P. Persson, A. Lindholm & L. B. Jeffcott. ICEEP publ. Davis.

Hauser, M. 1996. *The evolution of communication.* Cambridge. MIT Press.

Hearne, V. 1987. *Adams Task Calling Animals by Name.* Heinemann. London.

Hermann, L. M. 1987. 'Receptive competencies of language trained animals', *Advances in the study of behaviour.* 7. Academic Press. New York.

Hickman, J. 1984. *Horse Management.* Academic Press. London.

Hockett, C. F. 1960. 'Logical considerations in the study of animal communication' in *Animals Sounds and communication.* (ed) W. E. Lanyon & W. N. Tavolga. American Inst. Biological Sci. Washington. DC. (p392- 430).

Horak, V. P. Draber, J. Hanak & S. Matolin. 'Fibre composition and tubulin localisation in muscle of Thoroughbred srinters and stayers', p 262-268. in *Equine Exercise Physiology 3.* ed. S. G. B. Persson, A. Lindholm & L. B. Jeffcott ICEEP press. Davis.

Houpt, K. A. 1979 'The intelligence of the horse', *Equine Practise.* 1. 20-26.

Howe, J. 1997. *IQ in question. The truth about intelligence.* Sage. London.

Hughes, B. O. & I. J. N. Duncan. 1988. 'The notion of ethological "need". Models of motivation and animal welfare', *Anim. Behav.* 36. 1696-1707.

Hutt C. & Hutt S. J. 1965. 'The effect of environmental complexity on stereotyped behaviour of children', *Anim. Behav.* 13. 1-4.

Imam, S. A. H. A. A. 1983. *Mis-en-Main without a bit.* Imam Hazaribagh.

Imam, S. A. H. A. A. 1987. *The Centaur. A critical analysis of horsemanship plus relevant equitant history.* Indian Heritage. Hazaribagh.

Iwanowski, G. 1987. *You and Your Horse.* Shutter and Shooter. Jo'burg.

Jackson, J. 1992. *The Natural Horse. Lessons from the wild for domestic horse care.* Northland. Flagstaff. Arizona.

James, W. 1890. *The principles of psychology.* Henry Holt. New York.

Jerison, M. 1973. *Evolution of brain size and intelligence.* Academic Press. London.

Johnson, B. 1995. *The skilful mind of the guide dog.* G. D. B. Herts.

Kasselle, M. & R. Hanway 1995. *Touching horses. Communication, health, healing through*

Shiatzu. J. A. Allen.

Kennedy, J. 1992. *The New Anthropomorphism.* Cambridge University Press.

Kiley-Worthington, M. 1977. *The behavioural problems of farm animals.* Oriel Press. Stockton.

Kiley-Worthington, M. 1987. *The behaviour of horses in relation to management and training.* J. A. Allen. London.

Kiley-Worthington, M. 1990. *Animals in Circuses and Zoos. Chiron's World?* Little Eco-Farm Publishing. Basildon.

Kiley-Worthington, M. 1998. 'Competition and Cooperation. A detailed study of communication and social organisation in a small group of horses' (*Equus caballus*)'*Eco Research Centre.* ISBN 367-2045, paper 024.

Kiley-Worthington, M. 1998. *Equine Welfare.* J. A. Allen. London.

Kiley-Worthington, M. 2000. *Right in Front of Your Mind, Equine and Elephant Epistemology.* M. Phil thesis in Philosophy. University of Lancaster.

Kiley-Worhington, M. 2004. *Equine Lore. What is it to be an equine?* J. A. Allen. London

Kiley-Worthington, M. & H. Randle. 1997. 'Animal educational psychology. A comparative study of teaching 4 mammals of different species' *Eco Research Centre.* 013.

Kiley-Worthington, M. & H. D. Randle. 1997. 'Animals handling and Animal Educational Psychology. Symposium Comparative Psychology'. Montreal. & *Eco Research Centre* 012a

Kiley-Worthington, M. & H. D. Randle. 1997. 'An investigation into the effectiveness of improved handling and teaching techiques in five large herbivores'. *Eco Research Centre.* 012b.

Kiley-Worthington, M. & D. Wood-Gush. 1987. 'Stereotypies in Horses', in *Current therapy in equine medicine.* ed N. E. Robinson Saunders. London.

Koehler, O. 1951. 'The ability of birds to count', *Bul Anim. Behav.* 9. 41-45.

Kummer, H. 1982. ' Social knowledge in free ranging primates', in *Animal Mind- Human Mind* ed: D. Griffin. p 113-130. Springer. Berlin.

Laing, R. D. 1960. *The Divided Self.* Penguin. London

Lawrence, M. 1980. *Flyers and Stayers. The book of the greatest rides.* Harrap. London.

Lea,S. & M. Kiley-Worthington. 1996. 'Do Animals Think?' in *Unsolved Myseries of the Mind.* ed. V. Bruce.

Lijsen, H. J. 1993. *Classical Circus Equitation.* J. A. Allen. London.

Lieberman, P. 1976. 'Comments on Mounin's paper', *Current Anthropology.* 17. p14 (quoted by Desmond).

Lilly, J. C. 1961. *Man and Dolphin.* Gollanz London.

Linden, E. 1986. *Silent partners. The legacy of the ape language experiments.* N. Y Times Books.

Masson, J. & S. MaCarthy. 1994. *When Elephants Weep. The Emotional Lives of Animals.* Jonathan Cape. London.

Merkens, H. W, H. C. Schamhardt, G. J. V van Osch & J. van Bogert. 1990. 'Ground reaction force analysis of Dutch Warmblood Horses at canter and jumping', p 128-135. in *Equine Exercise Physiology.* ed. S. G. B. Persson, A. Lindhom & L. B. Jeffcott. ICEEP Publ, Davis California.

Meyer-Holzapfel, M. 1968. 'Abnormal behaviour of zoo animals' *in Abnormal Behaviour of Animals.* ed: M. W. Fox. W. B. Saunders. London.

Midgley, M. 1978. *Beast and Man: The Roots of Human Nature.* Cornell Press. Ithaca. N. Y.

Midgley, M. 1992. *Science as Salvation. A modern myth and its meaning.* Routledge. New York.

Miller, R.1999. L'impregnation comportementale du poulain nouveau-ne', p13-21. in *L'equitation, le cheval et l'ethologie.* Colloque du 18 Sept 1999 a l'ecole National d'Equitation. Belin. Paris.

Miller-Graber, P., L. Lawrence,J. Foremen, K. Bump, M. Fisher & E. Kurz. 'Effect of dietary protein level on nirtogen metabolites in exercised Quarter horses', p 305-314. in *Equine Exercise Physiology*. edit. Persson. S. G. B, A. Lindholm & L. B. Jeffcott. ICEEP publ Davis California.

Mohr, E. 1971. *The Asiatic Wild Horse*. J. A. Allen. London.

Nagel, T. 1974. 'What is it like to be a Bat?', *Philosophical Review* 83. 435-50

Noske, B. 1989. *Humans and Other Animals*. Pluto Press. London.

Oliveira, N. 1976. *Reflections on Equestrian Art*. J. A. Allen.

Oxford English Dictionary 1986. Oxford University Press.

Parelli, P. 1999. 'Natural Horsemanship' in *l'Equitation, le cheval et l'ethologie*. Colloque du 18 Sept 1999 a l'ecole Nationa d'Equitation. 23-34. Belin. Paris, and Demonstration.

Pearce, D. 1987. *Introduction to Animal Cognition*. Harvester. Hove. UK.

Pearce, P. , Lindholm & Jefscott 1991. *Equine exercise physiology 3*. ICEEP. Davis Cal.

Pepperburg, I. M. 1993. 'Cognition and communiation in an African Grey parrot (*Psittacus erithacus*) Studies on a non-human, non-primate, non-mammal subject', in *Language and Communication, A Comparative Perspective*. ed: H. L. Roitblat, L. M. Herman & P. E. Nachtigall. Lawrence Erlbaum Assoc.

Piaget, J. & B. Inhelder 1969. *The psychology of the child*. Basic Books. NewYork.

Pojansky, 1997. *My horses, My Teachers*. J.A. Allen. London.

Randle, H. & M. Kiley-Worthington 1997. Social relations in a small group of African elephants. (*Loxondonta africana*). *Eco Research Centre*. occas paper 008.

Rees, L. 1991. *Riding: The True Techniques*. Stanley Paul.

Rendle, C. 1996. 'Appropriate harness and implements for working equines. Symposium on Working Equines'. Rabat. *Eco Research Centre. Paper 15b*.

Roberts, M. 1992. *The man who listens to horses*. Hutchinson. London.

Rollin, B. 1989 *The Unheaded Cry. Animal Consciousness, Animal Pain and Scientific Change*. Oxford University Press.

Romanes, G. 1883. *Animal Intelligence*. Kegan Paul & Co. London.

Rubenstein, D. I. 1986. 'Ecology and sociality in horses and zebras', in *Ecological Aspects of Social Evolution*. ed: Rubenstein D. I. and R. W. Wrangham. Princeton Univ Press. p282-302.

Ryle, G. 1949. *The concept of mind*. ch8, Penguin. London.

Salt. ,H. 1980. *Animal Rights*. Cetaur. London.

Sainsbury, D. W. B. 1984. 'Housing the Horse', in *Horse Management*. ed: J. Hickman p63-91. Academic Press. London.

Schott, H. C, D. R. Hodgson, W. M. Bayly & P. D. Gollnick. 'Renal responses to high intensity exercise' p 361-367, in *Equine Exercise Physiology 3*. ed. S. G. B. Persson, A. Lindholm & L. B. Jeffcott. ICEEP publ. Davis.

Schmidt. , J. 1991. *Animal Welfare Science*. Academic Press. London.

Schjelderup-Ebbe, T. 1922 'Beitrage zur Social psychologie des Huashuhns',*Z. Psychol.* 88. 225-252.

Selye, H. 1950. *The Physiology and Pathology of Stress*. Acta Inc. N. Y.

Sherpell, J. A. 1986. *In the company of animals*. Blackwell. Oxford.

Shettleworth, S. J. 1998. *Cognition, Evolution and Behavior*. Oxford Univ Press.

Skinner, B. F. 1938. *The Behavior of Organisms; an Experimental Analysis*. Appleton-Century-Crots. New York.

Svendsen, E. 1994. *The Professional Handbook of the Donkey*. Whittet Books. Stowmarket.

Swift, S. 1996. *Centred Riding*. J. A. Allen. London.

Syme, G. T. & C. A. Syme. 1979. *Social Structure in farm animals*. Elsevier. Amsterdam.

Tellington-Jones, L & S. Taylor. 1992. *The Tellington - Touch*. Cloudcraft Books. Berks.

Tinbergen, N. 1951. *The study of instinct*. Oxford University Press.

Thorpe, W. H. 1963. *Learning and Instinct in Animals*. Methuen. London.

Toates, F. 1995. 'Animal motivation and cognition', *in Comparative Approaches to Cognitive Science. ed*: H. Roitblat & J-A Meyer. MIT Press.

Toates, 1994. Motivation. CAEC meeting. Provence. France.

Tolman, E. C. 1932. *Purposive Behavior in Animals and Men*. Century. New York.

Tschiffely, A. F. 1933. *Tschiffely's Ride. 10,000miles on horseback through South and North America*. Heinemann. N. Y.

Wanlass, M. 1987. *Ride with your mind. A right brain approach to riding*. Methuen. London.

Waring, G. 1983. *Horse Behaviour*. Noyes Press. N. Y.

Watson, J. B. 1919. *Psychology from the Standpoint of a Behaviorist*. Lipincott, Philadelphia.

Watson, L. 1999. *The Organ of Jacobson*. Allen Lane. Penguin. London.

Welsh, B. L. 1964. 'Psychological response to the mean level of environmental stimulation - a theory of environmental integration', *in Medical Aspects of Stress in a Military Climate*. US Gov. Washington.

Welsh, D. A. 1973. *The life of Sable Island wild horses*. Ph. D. thesis. Dalousie. Canada.

Wemelsfelder, F. 1993. *Animal Boredom towards an empirical approach to animal subjectivity*. Proefschrift Leiden.

Wickler, S. J. & W. Troy. 1991. 'Blood volume, lactate and cortisol in exercising Arabian equitation horses'p 397-401. in *Equine Exercise Physiology*. 3. ed. S. G. B. Persson, A. Lindhol & L.B. Jeffcott. ICEEP publ. Davis.

Williams, M 1960. *Adventures unbridled*. Methuen. London.

Wright, M. 1975. *The Jeffery Method of Horse Handling*. Williams. South Australia.

Wright, M. 1983. *The thinking horseman*. Edwards printing. Tamworth. N. S. W.

Xenophon, 350BC. (1972) *The art of horsemanship*. J. A. Allen. London.

Zeuner, F. E. 1963. *A history of domestic animals*. Hutchinson London.

INDEX